Sound Beginnings

The Early Record Industry in Australia

Ray Tellier's San Francisco Orchestra recording at the World Record studios, Melbourne 1925.

SOUND BEGINNINGS

The early record industry in Australia

ROSS LAIRD

Illustrated

CURRENCY PRESS • SYDNEY

First published in 1999
by Currency Press Pty Ltd
PO Box 2287
Strawberry Hills NSW 2012 Australia
Email: currency@magna.com.au
Website:www.currency.com.au

Copyright © Ross Laird 1999

This book is copyright. Apart from any fair dealing for the purpose of private study, research or review, as permitted under the Copyright Act, no part may be reproduced by any process without written permission. Inquiries concerning publication, translation or recording rights should be addressed to the publishers.

NATIONAL LIBRARY OF AUSTRALIA CIP DATA

Laird, Ross
Sound beginnings: the early record industry in Australia.
Bibliography.
Includes index.
ISBN 0 86819 579 0

1. Music trade–Australia–History. 2. Sound recording industry–Australia–History. I. Title.

338.47781490994

Designed by Robyn Latimer, Eye Visuals
Set by Dean Nottle
Printed by Robert Burton Printers, Sefton, NSW

Cover picture: Ray Tellier's San Francisco Orchestra at the World Record recording studio, Brighton, Victoria, 1925. From the author's collection.

CONTENTS

Foreword, *Warren Fahey*		vii
Introduction		xi
1	Prehistory	1
2	The Distressing Effects of Syncopation	31
3	Pemberton Billing and World Record	53
4	Brunswick	73
5	His Master's Voice (HMV)	89
6	Columbia	143
7	Parlophone	175
8	Vocalion	187
9	Unbreakable Records	215
10	'Dumping': The 1927 Tariff Board Inquiry	229
11	Phonograph v. Wireless	277
12	Clifford Industries	297
13	The Depression and the Formation of EMI	307
14	The End of the Beginning	313
Appendices		
Statistical Appendices		319
Record labels available in Australia before 1934		323
Bibliography		346
Index		357

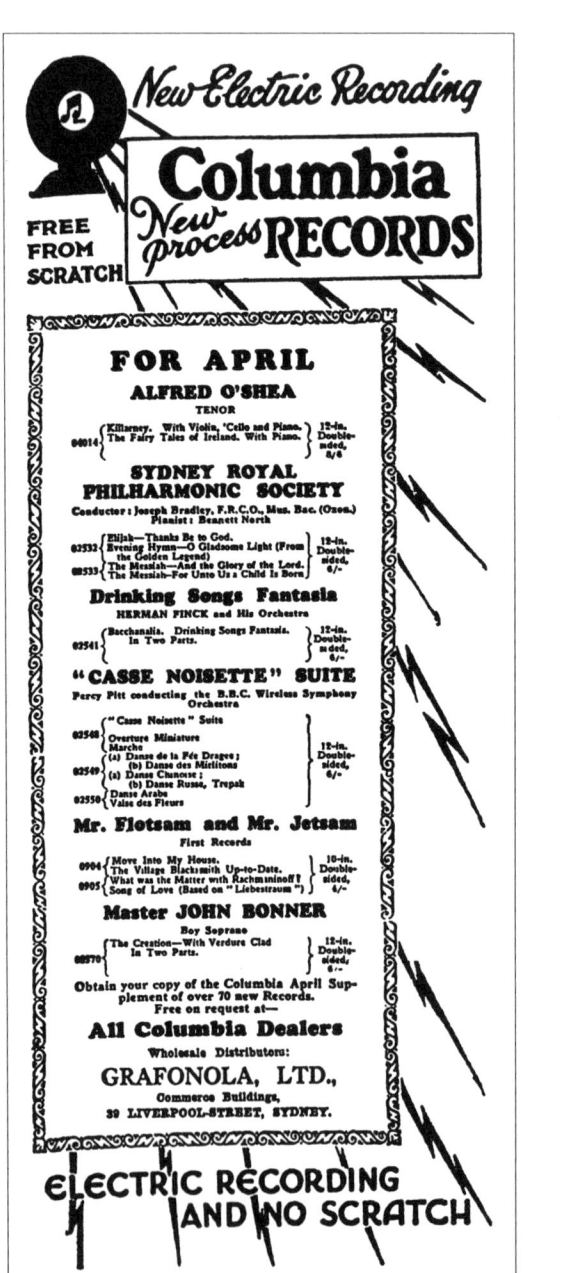

Columbia advertisement circa 1926. From the author's collection.

Foreword

When I first recorded for EMI, way back in the mid-1960s, the Australian record industry was a mysterious entity and very much under the thumb of foreign management. Managing directors were imported as readily as repertoire and when I established my own label, Larrikin Records, in 1974, neither WEA nor Polygram had a single Australian artist in their extensive catalogues. In the 1970s I witnessed the changing of the guard with local management coming to the fore, the birth of several independent lables and domestic repertoire assuming a boisterous stance. In the 80s Australian music successfully rocketed around the world and the local retail sector stumbled from success to financial disaster with Australia's dominant retailer, Brash, liquidating. The 90s presented other challenges including pirating, censorship and a series of government inquiries that led to the introduction of legal parallel importation. The industry now faces the next century and the two most important challenges of its life: technological change and cultural protection.

One cannot face the future unless armed by the experience of the past. Ross Laird's *Sound Beginnings* is the first book to document the early years of the Australian record industry and what a fascinating study this is. Laird takes us behind the lines in what was obviously a cultural war as British, American and, later, Australian record companies fought to establish their music, technology and rights. There is a definite feeling of *déjà vu* as the youthful industry comes to grips with the 'fashion' aspect of an ever-fickle market; with copyright licensing partnerships, independent distribution, confusion caused by new technology, retail price fixing, the machinations of overseas management and the seemingly never-ending negotiation with government over tariff protection and cultural boundaries.

This is also a useful guide for anyone fascinated by popular music and cultural imperialism. Readers will discover all the drama of a good television 'soapie' as Laird's assiduous research takes us into the boardrooms and factories; and, in particular, company correspondence files. Here is real detective work as the pieces slowly come together taking us from cylinders to records and into the offices of legendary record lables like Columbia, Parlophone, Vocalion, Gramophone Company, Brunswick, His Master's Voice and, my favourite, the Unbreakable Gramophone Record Company of Melbourne.

Above all this book provides us an opportunity to study the progression of Australian music in its important and formative years. There is also proof that the British and American companies had little interest in local repertoire, regarding us as simply a market to be exploited. In a letter (1926) to His Master's Voice head office, local general manager, William Manson, writes: 'We, personally, do not think there is a great deal of talent in Australia – talent that would interest the public – but it is just the publicity which the Columbia Company would gain by recording here that we would like.' In a further letter to the company he elucidates: 'One has to consider the general policy of Australia, namely, to declaim loudly the necessity of buying everything Australian but in their private life to buy imported articles and to "swank" amongst their friends that these are the only ones good enough for them. This attitude obtains even with the working classes. In fact, I believe it is very strong with them.' Music publisheres also came in for criticism in a letter to the Victor Talking Machine Co. later that same year: 'In this country, the publishers, like a good many other peole here, are imbrued with the idea of getting rich quickly, and if they have a chance, they will threaten and squeeze for all they are worth.'

Ross Laird has done the study of popular music a massive favour with this two-decade chunk. Hopefully this is a work-in-progress and we will see further histories of the Australian music industry. For my part the book has sent me scurrying off to locate the recording of 'West Australian Beryl Mills, who won the first Miss Australia contest in 1926, and recorded a double-sided 'Miss Australia speaks to Australians', on Columbia 0601, in which she describes in wide-eyed terms her trip to America. In this she strikingly captures the degree to which Australia in the mid-1920s was still relatively unaffected by direct contact with American culture.'

Beryl – we're not in Kansas anymore!

Warren Fahey A.M.

INTRODUCTION

This volume is the first publication to document in detail the early history of the Australian record industry. It is not a comprehensive history. Rather, it focuses on a single decade out of the more than a hundred years since Edison invented the phonograph: the period from 1924 through to 1934. This is without question the most significant decade in the history of the Australian record industry; seventy years later the events of those years are still echoing in our musical culture.

The first chapter ('Prehistory') briefly documents the initial reception in Australia of Edison's phonograph during the late 1870s and the eventual commercialisation of his invention during the last decade of the nineteenth century. The first decade of the twentieth century saw the pioneering of small-scale efforts to begin a cylinder record industry in Australia, although these fledgling attempts were undercut by the importation of superior products at cheaper prices within a few years. At the start of the 1920s all records sold in Australia were imported, and no commercial recordings were being made here. Within a few years, however, several disc record factories had been established in Melbourne and Sydney, and the first locally-recorded discs had been made and marketed.

The bulk of this book is concerned with the events of this tumultuous decade which saw a new industry rise, flourish and decline. It traces how it was threatened by a

SOUND BEGINNINGS

flood of cheap imports; how the relatively new Federal Government responded to pleas for protection (which led to the first Tariff Board Inquiry in 1927); the first struggles to establish Australian-owned record companies in 1927-28. It shows how the independent record companies (as well as several of the larger foreign-owned companies) were mortally wounded by the Great Depression; and how its effects on the record industry worldwide forced the two biggest, most bitter rivals to amalgamate and form the giant corporation EMI. By 1933, the once vibrant local record industry had been reduced to a single corporation and for the next decade this company had a virtual monopoly on the record business in Australia. These circumstances formed the basis for all future developments in the Australian record industry and today we are still dealing with the results.

Much of this story is told in the words of the pioneering record company executives directly involved in these events. Most of the rest is in the form of press reports or other contemporary sources that not only describe what took place, but also retain the outlook and attitudes of the period. One of my major concerns has been to retain the integrity of the documents, letters, articles and transcripts of evidence which form a major part of the source material for this book, and I have generally refrained from adding analysis of the issues raised by the sources quoted. The exception is where a claim made by the original sources is factually incorrect. Where a claim was questionable but expressed as personal opinion or interpretation, I have let the statement stand. Essentially, my commentary has been restricted to maintaining a flow between the various sources quoted, or to filling in details where no suitable contemporary source could be located.

In order to preserve the style of the original sources, great care has been taken to retain the original form of the material used in this study. Only obvious spelling mistakes have been corrected. Punctuation has been standardised to allow for easier reading, and minor changes have been made in the interests of clarity, such as the addition or deletion of some capitalisation. No attempt has been made to extract the 'history' from the source materials used and to discard the other elements present – whether gossip, speculation, self-justification, or any other material which might have been considered extraneous. To have done so would, in my view, seriously detract from the value of the unique contemporary sources used in this book. I strongly believe that it is as important to preserve the style, tone and 'flavour' of the original, as it is to record the essential names and dates.

Another important facet of this study is the use of previously unpublished primary sources. Prior to my obtaining copies of the transcripts and other documents associated with the various Tariff Board Inquiries of 1927-31, these files had lain undisturbed and unread since they were last part of the working papers of the Department of Trade and Customs in the 1930s. As they include a large quantity of first-person commentary by most of the senior record company officials directly involved in the establishment of the record manufacturing industry in Australia during the mid-1920s, these papers are an extremely valuable first-hand account of events so important in Australian cultural and business history. The first Tariff Board Inquiry of 1927 was held little more than a year after the major players had established themselves here, so these documents also provide invaluable background information on an Australian industry still in its infancy.

Another major source of material was some unusually frank and informal company correspondence between the managers of local record company branches and their London head offices, which were obtained through the courtesy of Ruth Edge of EMI Archives in London.

Without the very considerable quantity and outstanding quality of material from these sources, this study would not have been possible. While public sources in the trade press and other periodicals provide the basic outlines of the history of the Australian record industry, their accounts are limited and lack the immediacy and wealth of detail that emerges from the documentation drawn on here. The company files and business correspondence of the Australian record companies active during the 1920s and 1930s have been largely discarded or destroyed and this is a great loss.

The Australian record industry itself seems amazingly ignorant of its own origins. In *Profile of the Australian Record Industry* produced only a few years ago by ARIA (Australian Record Industry Association) the pre-1950s history of the Australian record industry rates three lines. The next paragraph begins: 'Prior to the 1950s there was little Australian recording activity of Australian compositions or performers...' [127] In fact, over 5,000 commercially issued recordings had been made in Australia by 1950, and this does not include an even larger number of recordings made for private use, for radio broadcast, or for other specialist purposes (like sound-on-disc films).

So this study of the establishment of a record industry in Australia is an attempt to view the early development as far as possible through the eyes of those who were involved in these events or who lived through them. It also aims to reflect the opinions and attitudes of the times. Rather than impose a more conventional retrospective and purely historical view, the unique sources used for this volume allow us to hear the participants' own account of these events. In my opinion, such a direct form of commentary is superior to third-hand and non-authentic reconstructions that inevitably incorporate views and attitudes not current at the time of the events.

INTRODUCTION

Even when these sources represent narrow tastes, musical intolerance, business practices of dubious ethical standards, or attempts to manipulate the truth in the pursuit of commercial advantage, they are enunciated in terms familiar to their peers and free of concepts evolved decades later. We are privileged to witness at least some measure of the debate as it was propounded at the time.

As the social background in which these events took place is as vital as the purely historical analysis, I have retained a considerable amount of 'peripheral' material. Although not strictly related to the history of the record industry, it adds that social dimension so important in understanding the attitudes expressed. I have tried to convey some sense of the period and of the individuals who made the decisions that determined the success or failure of the many business ventures which make up this story. Even where their views are obviously biased by the promotion of their own interests (or those of their companies), I have not imposed my own perceptions unnecessarily.

I sincerely hope that this study of an important and influential part of our cultural and business history will be viewed in the light of the above comments. It is a story which has not been adequately told before, and which is in many ways unique. I would be pleased if any insights gained from reading this volume are put to use in further research and analysis.

The record industry during the period covered by this volume was, and often still is, an unusual combination of purely commercial endeavour, motivated by the same profit-making incentives as any other business; and, at the same time, a culture-enriching enterprise which has preserved some fascinating, amusing and instructive fragments of our history and cultural heritage. No other medium from this period allows us to hear the voices of a

SOUND BEGINNINGS

wide variety of Australians 'fixed' in time, and able to be replayed at will. Edison's invention has been developed in ways he could not have imagined, but it still retains that magical element of preserving the voices of those who can no longer speak to us, a fact which so amazed and excited our Victorian ancestors.

The contemporary sources used in this book are listed in the Bibliography and numbered for reference in the text. I suggest that anyone interested in reading further on this subject consult the more recent publications also listed.

Finally, I would like to thank Mike Sutcliffe and John Whiteoak for their assistance during my research for this book. While they provided some additional source materials, or clues to where these might be found, I am of course solely responsible for the selection and interpretation presented here.

Ross Laird
CANBERRA

A NOTE ON CURRENCY AND MEASUREMENTS

The prices quoted throughout are in imperial currency: sterling pounds (£) shillings (s) and pence (d).
$1 = 20s = 240d.
When decimal currency was introduced in 1966:
£1 = 2 dollars ($2) = 200 cents. Therefore:
£1/2/6 = $2.25
2/6 or 2s 6d = 25c.

Imperial measurements are also mentioned occasionally.
1 lb or one pound = 454 grams
1 cwt or one hundredweight = 50.8 kilograms
1 gallon = 4.55 litres.

78 rpm means 78 revolutions per minute of a disc recording.

Chapter 1

PREHISTORY

On 24 December 1877 Thomas Edison filed a patent application for 'Improvement in Phonograph or Speaking Machines'. The patent was granted on 19 February 1878. The earliest Australian report on Edison's invention of which I am aware was published in the *Telegraphic Electrical Society Journal* of February 1878. This report was a reprint of an item which appeared in *The Times* of 18 January 1878.

It begins by recalling that 'not many weeks have passed since we were startled by the announcement that we could converse audibly with each other, although hundreds of miles apart, by means of so many miles of wire with a little electro-magnet at each end, yet we are on the point of realising some of the many advantages promised by the telephone.' It then continues:

> Another wonder is now promised us – an invention, purely mechanical in its nature, by means of which words spoken by the human voice can be, so to speak, stored up and reproduced at will over and over again, hundreds, it may be thousands, of times... The highly ingenious apparatus by which this wonder is effected is the invention of Mr Thomas

SOUND BEGINNINGS

> A. Edison... To the present invention Mr Edison has given the name of the phonograph, and it depends for its action upon certain well-known laws in acoustics...

After a brief description of the technical aspects of the apparatus, the report concludes: 'The invention has been so recently and so quickly developed into existence by Mr Edison that he himself can hardly say what its practical value is or will prove to be.' [156]

Although the article quoted above claims that 'numerous applications suggest themselves...', the only ones mentioned are related to recording the human voice, such as 'it might be of the highest importance to have oral evidence mechanically reproduced in a court' or 'authors... may perhaps be saved the trouble of writing their compositions'. There seems to have been little comprehension at this time of the variety of recordings which further development of Edison's 'phonograph' would make possible.

One interesting aspect of the reports is the speed with which this latest advance in technology was received in Australia. In fact, it seems there were plans to exhibit the phonograph in Australia during the second half of 1878, but these plans did not eventuate. However, the first phonograph reached Australia in early 1879, according to the following report:

> A genuine Edison's phonograph, that is, an instrument made in America under Mr Edison's directions, was exhibited here for the first time at a *conversazione* held in the lecture hall of the Collins Street Independent Church, and its performance was such as to create considerable amazement and amusement. [186]

Further confirmation was an advertisement in the *Sydney Morning Herald* of 7 June of that year which lists among

PREHISTORY

the attractions to be seen at the School of Arts exhibition 'Edison's world-renowned phonograph, or "talking machine"'. [185]

Dr W.H. Lane was active in promoting an early form of the phonograph in Australia during 1879 and 1880. He exhibited the tin-foil machine at the 1879 Sydney Exhibition, and at the International Exhibition held at Melbourne in October 1880 and a gold medal was awarded to Edison's invention at each of these Exhibitions. But by 1880 the primitive tin-foil phonograph had been around for several years and it seems that public interest had dwindled, as reports of additional exhibits or promotions of the apparatus in Australia fade out completely during the remainder of the 1880s.

Edison himself seems to have shown little interest in further developing the phonograph during this period. It was not until Alexander Graham Bell and Charles Sumner Tainter were granted a patent for 'Reproducing Sounds from Phonograph Records' on 4 May 1886 that Edison was motivated to return to his earlier invention. By June 1888 he was able to market the Perfected Phonograph, and it was also in 1888 that the first attempts at utilising the potential of the phonograph for recording and playing music were made. These developments resulted in renewed public interest.

One of the first to take advantage of the opportunity presented by these developments was Professor Douglas Archibald (MA Oxon) who began a series of public lectures and demonstrations of Edison's Perfected Phonograph in Britain early in 1889. In April 1890 Archibald visited Edison at his Menlo Park laboratory in New Jersey, where he acquired the latest model phonograph, spare parts, and a quantity of cylinder records, including one by Edison himself. A short time later he sailed for Australia, and arrived in Sydney on 28 May 1890.

*Leaflet from Professor Archibald's tour, 1890.
From the author's collection.*

PREHISTORY

Archibald's intention was to tour Australia giving lectures and demonstrations of the phonograph. In an article for the London *Phonogram* published in June 1893, after his return to Britain, Archibald wrote: 'As I was bound for such an outlandish place as Australia, where a phonograph of this civilised and highly organised type had never been heard...'. The implication was that he was the first to bring the improved phonograph to Australia and this statement is probably true, though other entrepreneurs were also quick to see the potential for similar types of promotion. Mr C.L. Garland exhibited an Edison Perfected Phonograph to a 'representative audience' in Sydney during August 1890; contemporary press reports described the machine as 'similar in construction to that now exhibited in Melbourne by Professor Archibald'.

In any case, Archibald was certainly the most theatrical, best received and most influential promoter of the phonograph in Australia at this time. He toured widely under the management of Messrs Charles and James MacMahon, and appeared in almost every town or city of any size in all of the six colonies and New Zealand during an 18-month period. A typical Archibald performance included a lecture illustrated by lantern slides, followed by a demonstration of the phonograph. He had taken the trouble to acquire a wide range of cylinder records including popular vocals and instrumental performances, plus some speeches by prominent persons of the time such as William Gladstone and Thomas Edison. He also recorded some Australian performers (including Nellie Stewart), as well as various colonial dignitaries. Few if any of his competitors could offer their audiences such a wide range of entertainments.

Archibald particularly featured a cylinder of a speech by Prime Minister Gladstone, which he had recorded in Britain prior to his visit to Edison. Titled 'A message to the Governor of New South Wales' it went as follows:

SOUND BEGINNINGS

My dear Lord Carrington,
I gladly avail myself of this opportunity to assure you with how much pleasure I hear of you and your career as Governor of New South Wales. I am also alike honoured and gratified in being the first person to make a communication through the phonograph to Australasia, as worthily represented by the great colony at whose head you have been placed. In the phonograph is a new bond of amity between Australasia and the United Kingdom, and I regard each addition of these free and friendly ties as an inspired benefit and a fresh guarantee for the endurance of a connection alike honourable and beneficial on that side of the water and this.
I am, my dear Lord Carrington, very faithfully yours, W.E. Gladstone.

While in the United States visiting Edison, Archibald also asked the world-famous inventor to record a message to the people of Australia. Edison said: 'What shall I say? I can't talk to them people, I don't know anyone in Australia.' Archibald suggested that he recite the poem 'Mary had a little lamb', as these were the first words reproduced by a phonograph. Edison replied: 'I won't put that in, but I will give you another.' [69] In the event, Edison recorded:

> Mr Archibald, who is going to Australia, wants me to say something, so I will repeat a bit of poetry:
>
>   A soldier of the Legion lay dying in Algiers,
>   there was a lack of woman's nursing,
>   and a dearth of woman's tears,
>   but a comrade stood beside him,
>   as his life-blood ebbed away,
>   and bent a pitying glance to hear what he might say.
>
> That's all I know of that, Edison.

PREHISTORY

*Professor Archibald demonstrating the phonograph, Launceston, 1891.
From the ScreenSound Australia collection.*

 SOUND BEGINNINGS

Among the dignitaries who made recordings for Archibald in Australia was Sir Robert Hamilton, Governor of Tasmania. According to a report in the Launceston *Daily Telegraph*, Sir Robert was given 'a private exhibition' by Archibald on 19 June 1891 where he 'spoke a neat little "Dream of Federation" into the machine...' saying:

> My dream as regards the future of the colony of Tasmania, where I have the honour of being the Queen's representative, is that she will be rich beyond our wildest conceptions of material wealth, and rich also in the arts and sciences, and that she is destined to be an important educational centre, and the health and pleasure resort of the great Commonwealth of Australia, of which she will form a part. As regards the Commonwealth, my dream is that it will ever remain united with the grand old Mother Country and that in process of time all English speaking peoples will be linked in one federation, which will secure the peace and progress of the world.

This recording was evidently played at subsequent public lectures held in the Hobart Town Hall, as the report describes 'the articulation being distinctly heard and generally appreciated' by the 2,000 people who attended the lectures over four nights. Archibald was clearly able to attract considerable attention and useful publicity with his recordings of the famous.

Archibald's lectures were sufficiently lucrative to encourage James MacMahon to travel to Edison's phonograph factory in New Jersey in late 1890 and arrange the purchase of some coin-operated machines. These arrived in Australia at the beginning of 1891. By the end of that year, the extensive tours of Archibald and other lecturers, together with the coin-operated machines, had saturated the market for this form of entertainment.

PREHISTORY

Archibald sailed back to Britain from Perth early in 1892, giving demonstrations on the way in Batavia, Burma, Ceylon and India.

Douglas Archibald's legacy deserves recognition for creating at the outset a high level of awareness of the perfected phonograph throughout Australasia. There is no doubt he played a large part in Australia becoming in due course a small but significant market for recordings and gramophones. An intriguing postscript to Archibald's visit is provided by a classified advertisement in the *Sydney Morning Herald* of 27 February 1892:

> PHONOGRAPH —The only one for SALE in the colony. Edison's very latest perfected and electrically actuated Phonograph, with magnificent selection of record from America, including Mr. Gladstone's speech, &c., &c., complete set of views and all details for exhibition. magnificent investment, for Sale on terms Apply
> CHAS. HUENERBEIN, 818 George street.

It is not known if anyone replied to this notice, or what became of the 'magnificent collection of records'. Parts of Archibald's prototype phonograph are believed to exist in the Museum of Victoria, but none of the cylinders are known to have survived.

C.L. Garland was also actively exhibiting the phonograph during early 1891, and a notice [see page 10] appeared in the 'Amusements' column of the *Illawarra Mercury*. A few days later the same newspaper published an article, 'The phonograph', describing the exhibitions:

> This wonderful mechanical invention was on view at the Town Hall on Wednesday and Thursday evenings, but the patronage accorded the proprietors was not so liberal as it might have been. As we previously pointed out, the phonograph is the latest and greatest achievement of the mechanical inventive genius, Mr Edison, and it is very

SOUND BEGINNINGS

TOWN HALL, WOLLONGONG.

WEDNESDAY AND THURSDAY,
MAY 6TH AND 7TH.

FOR TWO NIGHTS ONLY!

When will be shown to the public of Wollongong the most marvellous and ingenious instrument of the modern scientific world yet perfected—

PHONOGRAPH.

By special arrangements with Mr. C. L. Garland, M.L.A., this wonderful machine will give true and original performances by the Greatest Celebrities and Artistes in the world, including Her Majesty the Queen, Madame Patti, and Lord Carrington; also, all the leading Colonial and English Stars in the Theatrical Firmament. Full instrumentation by the celebrated Coldstream Guards. Cornet and other solos by the best instrumentalists in the world, including Levey, Remenyi, Wellielmj, and Hallé, also others too numerous to mention.

For further particulars see Day Bills and Hand Bills.

ADMISSION—3s., 2s., and 1s. Box plan at Mr. Tynan's, Crown-street.

JOHN O'DONNELL,
Business Agent.

C.L. Garland was actively exhibiting the phonograph during early 1891; this notice is from the 'Amusements' column of the Illawarra Mercury.

PREHISTORY

properly regarded as the marvel of the century. The first part of the recital consists of an interesting lecture on the apparatus, the lecturer being quite *au fait* with his subject. He explained fully the wave theory of sound, illustrating his remarks by lantern views, by which means also the various parts of the instrument were depicted and made understandable to the audience. The phonograph, which is only a small instrument, was said to consist of 337 parts, each part being made by machinery also invented by Edison, who was now employing in his manufactory 250 men, women and children, none of whom, however, were engaged in any manual labor beyond attending to their respective machines. The instrument, it was explained, had got beyond the toy or exhibition stage in America, and was now extensively used in telegraph offices, in newspaper offices, and in counting houses. The manner in which the machine can be made to repeat messages to the type-writer or the compositor was shown by the lantern views.

A brief history of the career of Mr Edison was given, and how he was led to make the experiments that ended in his perfecting the phonograph, which there can be no doubt is destined to play an important part in the affairs of the world in future. The *modus operandi* was fully explained; how the wave sounds, passing into a tube, were carried, as in the human ear, to a kind of tympanum in the mechanical contrivance, leaving indentations or impressions upon a wax cylinder placed for the purpose. This wax cylinder, or in orthodox parlance, gram, as it is called, is sufficiently soft to receive the impressions, and hard enough to retain them when made. All that was necessary afterwards was to place the gram in position, supply the motive power (electricity) to work the apparatus, and the sound was reproduced. On Wednesday, Mr P. Ryan sang a comic song into the machine, and on Thursday Mr T. Rogerson gave his parody on Eileen Alannah – 'A Lean Banana'. In each instance the songs were

SOUND BEGINNINGS

reproduced with wonderful distinctness; but to get them at their best it was necessary to use the ear-tubes on the stage. When given out for the delectation of the audience (through a large funnel) they necessarily had a metallic or ventriloquial sound – as indeed had all the pieces so reproduced. By means of ear-tubes, however, as used with the telephone, almost a *fac simile* of the sound thrown into the apparatus was evolved herefrom, though even here there was a fizzing kind of sound. In this respect there is room for improvement in the apparatus, but doubtless the gifted Edison will speedily remedy this defect. Several cornet solos and full band selections were given, and these were heard in the hall to the best advantage. Some of the masterpieces were encored and repeated, and instances were given of how the machine could be manipulated to dwell on a word or note, to repeat it, or to go either fast or slow at the will of the operator. Those who had the pleasure of attending the recitals were not only highly edified, but much instructed by what they saw and heard, and the general verdict was that the talking machine was a veritable wonder. [155]

This report gives us a graphic impression of how these early demonstrations of the phonograph were conducted, and we can well imagine how this 'veritable wonder' must have impressed audiences at that time.

During the early 1890s phonographs were very expensive. They were run by electric motors that required banks of Grenet primary batteries and were difficult to maintain in good running condition. As a result their use was largely restricted to professional exhibitors and penny arcades. Home use was not really practical until cheaper and more manageable clockwork motors were developed after 1895. However, by the late 1890s phonographs for home entertainment purposes began to become more widespread, but according to a history of one of the families which ran a large music business in Melbourne at this time:

PREHISTORY

> ... cylinder records were very scarce in the early days of the phonograph so Charlie [Tait] decided Allans would make their own. If a popular song was required, an assistant, Frank Plummer who had a nice tenor voice, sang the number, with piano accompaniment into the funnel of the phonograph and within minutes it was recorded on wax. If a comic song was requested, Charlie willingly obliged... [191]

It should be understood that all Edison cylinder phonographs sold from 1888 until the early 1900s were provided with recording heads. This meant that the machine could be set up for recording as easily as for playback. Almost all recordings made in Australia up until the 1920s utilised this type of equipment. An Allan and Company advertisement [222] published on the back page of the Melbourne *Argus* of 9 July 1898 confirms this (see page following).

Apart from mentioning that Allan & Co. 'are able to supply records of any popular song at a few hours' notice', this advertisement provides many interesting details, including statements that the graph-o-phone 'is not a toy' and that 'no ear tubes are necessary'. These references indicate that the phonograph was still emerging from its early public perception as a novelty similar to the 'toy gramophones' which did require ear tubes and had extremely limited volume.

Other local record distributors such as W.J.N. Oldershaw's Edison Electric Parlour in Sydney which opened in early 1896, or E.J. Thwaite's Edison Phonograph Company in Melbourne which opened in mid-1898 are also known to have made cylinders 'on request'. However, sales must have been small as a premium price was required for this service, and few, if any, of these pioneering recordings have survived.

Cheaper and less cumbersome spring motor-driven phonographs became available for domestic use in 1896

SOUND BEGINNINGS

An Allan and Company advertisement published on the back page of the Melbourne Argus *of 9 July 1898.*

PREHISTORY

and they soon became common in more well-to-do households. 'Home' recordings began to be made. Few have survived to the present day and this is probably no great cultural loss, but it is unfortunate that so few examples of early Australian cylinder recordings are known to exist. An exception is the collection of home-recorded cylinders found amongst Thomas Rome's record collection in 1984. A few of the cylinder recordings in this collection (eight out of about 60 records) were made in Warrnambool in 1896-97.[226] The collection represents the earliest known Australian recordings extant and is held in the Victorian Arts Centre's Performing Arts Museum.

Other early Australian recordings which still exist include anthropological field recordings of native songs from the Torres Strait taken by Alfred Haddon in 1898, and some songs recorded in August 1899 by Fanny Smith, a Tasmanian Aborigine, for the Royal Society of Tasmania in Hobart. Further anthropological items were collected on cylinders by Sir Walter Baldwin Spencer during expeditions to Central Australia between 1901 and 1912.

A report in the American Edison trade publication the *Phonogram* during 1913 comments on some of the recordings made by Spencer:

> The value of the Edison phonograph for recording the voices of our far-away black races has recently been vividly demonstrated. A lecture was delivered on August 25th in the Great Hall of Sydney University by Professor Baldwin Spencer entitled 'Aborigines of the northern Territory'.
>
> It proved intensely interesting, and was made all the more attractive by a fine series of Kinetoscope views of the country passed through, and also by phonograph records of quaint native songs. These latter were recorded on Edison blanks with the aid of an Edison phonograph. They were taken by the professor himself on a 'Standard'. The reproduction of

SOUND BEGINNINGS

some of the Aborigines' chants by means of the Edison won great applause. [177]

And some of the earliest known 'oral history' recordings were made in Adelaide between 1903 and 1908 by a local Edison agent named J.H.M. Davidson, which included a cylinder by Lord Hallam Tennyson (son of the famous poet) entitled 'A Federal message'. This last item, containing the following text, is still held by the South Australian State Library:

> May I repeat what I have said before, that it is my fortune to inherit a strong and passionate desire to endeavour to the utmost to share in helping the British Empire to realise her mighty and manifest destiny. My belief is that this destiny will find its accomplishment through a yet closer union which, while preserving, strengthening and developing every individual part, will so bind the whole together with a common loyalty and a common patriotism that we shall be able fearlessly to lead the nations in the path of truth and justice, righteousness and freedom, peace and progress. In the same manner, the more real the union of Australian states is, the stronger the individuality of each separate State remains, within the limits of the constitution, and the more keenly and the more deeply every Australian feels a personal sense of responsibility in the heritage of citizenship, the greater will be your Commonwealth and the more potent will be your influence for good throughout the world.
>
> Record made by me for the Public Library of South Australia, Tennyson, January, Nineteen Hundred and Four.

While similar items exist, there are relatively few surviving cylinders recorded in Australia before 1903 and even fewer are of any real historical or musical value.

After the early attempts by various record outlets during the late 1890s, commercial recording was actively discouraged. In 1899 the Edison-Bell Company's barrister, S.L. Latham, was dispatched to Australia with instructions to ensure the enforcement of British patents, which required a 15% royalty payment on all cylinder recordings made here. It was not until Edison-Bell's rights expired in 1903 that any significant quantity of local recording was again attempted.

While the cylinder phonograph had become widespread by the end of the 1890s, the disc record gramophone was not generally available in Australia before 1900. The earliest known advertisement for disc record reproducers appeared in early 1899. This was for a spring motor gramophone, and was priced at £7. [190] Advertisements for cylinder phonographs were much more numerous that year and they were also much cheaper – from as little as 50/-. [118] By mid-1899 disc reproducer advertisements were appearing with increasing frequency, suggesting increasing market acceptance. A typical notice advises:

> Winter evenings are long and cold, and residents of the interior of Australia can beguile the weary hours by entertaining themselves and their friends with the Gram-O-Phone. This instrument has now reached a high state of perfection, and is widely known and appreciated. It fascinates the listener by its marvellous reproduction of sounds originating many thousands of miles away... It makes the weary and tired man or woman bright and cheerful, gives the children endless amusement, and is at the same time a money maker. If you desire to hear Sousa's military band, you can do so in your own home in the interior of Australia, by putting a record on the Gram-O-Phone just as easily as any of the residents of New York city. Albert Chevalier will sing to you on demand, and gives you encores *ad lib* without getting tired, and he will do this in any part of Australia, and save you going to London, provided you buy a Gram-O-Phone. [116]

SOUND BEGINNINGS

The earliest attempts to set up a local record industry were in fact in the manufacture of cylinder records. And the most significant of several such undertakings was that of Edwin C. Henderson who established his Federal Phonograph Record and Supply Co. at 375 George Street, Sydney in 1903. He initially began by selling copies of about 20 operatic recordings of the Italian tenor Carlo Dani, who had visited Australia the previous year. Henderson must have had some success with this initial offering as he gradually built up a range of local recordings on his *Federal* label. Artists mentioned in advertisements published between January and October 1904 include concert singers such as W.A. Peterkin (basso of the Ada Crossley Company), Ernest Fitts (basso) and Wallace Brownlow (baritone). Comic vocals were supplied by Will Whitburn, Edward Ford, and George Bentley; and marches by the Naval Brigade Band. Many of these vocalists appeared on the Tivoli Theatres circuit. There were also unspecified 'instrumental solos'.

The *Federal* cylinders would have either been individually recorded or, more likely, 'pantographed' onto soft brown wax blanks. The survival rate for wax cylinders is very low, and none of the *Federal* records are known to still exist. The process for manufacturing moulded cylinders was developed in 1900, but was not widely used until 1902. Edison moulded cylinders of superior volume and durability began to reach Australia around 1903 and their competition brought about the demise of *Federal.*

A new company called the Australia Phono Record Company was set up on 10 October 1904 with capital of £2,000, but business disagreements between Henderson and his financial backer (a Mr Binnie) saw it wound up on 28 April 1905. [228] Undeterred, Edwin Henderson moved to an address in Glebe Street, Glebe (an inner Sydney suburb) and continued development of his own process for manufacturing moulded cylinders. By late 1906 he had apparently succeeded: production under the previously registered *Australia* label of 'gold moulded records' had begun by early 1907. A February 1907 advertisement gives the price for these as 1/6d. [153]

The *Australia* repertoire was mainly confined to comic songs by Leonard Nelson, Tom Dawson and others; standard concert songs like 'Rocked in the Cradle of the Deep' by Percy Herford; marches played by the Naval Brigade Band or the Australia Military Band; and assorted instrumentals on the banjo, piccolo or cornet. A few Australian compositions were evident, including some with local references such as 'City of the Plains' (about Bathurst), 'Goodbye Melbourne Town' and 'Manly Pier' (also recorded as 'Brighton Pier').

Further developments in cylinder manufacture, such as the fine-grooved four-minute record, and increased competition from imports, reduced the price of the Australia cylinder by early 1908 to 1/3d and by December 1908 they were selling for 6d each. It is probable that a fire at the Glebe Road premises around 1909 was the final nail in the coffin for Edwin Henderson's pioneering endeavour.

In Melbourne a similar attempt was made to establish local cylinder production but on an even smaller scale. Records on the *Empire* and *Entertainer* labels were produced around 1908, but little is known of this operation. The recorded repertoire seems to have been even more limited than that on *Federal* or *Australia*, consisting mainly of instrumentals by mouth organ, piccolo or bagpipes. Competition from fully imported brands of superior quality was fierce. All those labels mentioned above had ceased production by 1910.

In the period before 1907, a large part of the Australian record market was still being supplied by cylinder recordings. It was the large-scale import of relatively cheap high-quality cylinders which undermined the first attempts to establish a local record industry. The imported cylinders were sold through local distributors, known as 'jobbers', who were supplied directly by the manufacturer. The Edison trade publication *Edison Phonograph Monthly* of 1907 published an article 'How I became an Edison jobber' by one C.D. Westbrook of Melbourne, Australia:

> I had worked for many years at the iron industry, when the depression owing to the land boom troubles caused me to look for something with better prospects. I tried the leather business, and manufactured, first of all, shoes and boots in a small way, finally acquiring an extensive trade in the sale of leather goods, both wholesale and retail. It was during this time that Dr McCarthy, of Footscray, Melbourne, drew my attention to an Edison phonograph, which he had brought back from the United States on one of his world tours. I became so much interested in it and its possibilities that I wrote to the Dealer from whom the Doctor had purchased his machine and received full particulars as to terms. After studying these I at once placed what seemed to me then to be a large order [for 4] phonographs and 140 wax records.
>
> In due time they were delivered to Melbourne, and this 'huge shipment' became a center of attraction, for at that time Edison goods were poorly represented in Melbourne. The goods were soon disposed of and several further small shipments on Dealers' terms were landed. Later on negotiations were entered into with the National Phonograph Co. for a Jobber's order of 100 phonographs and 5,000 records. Once started as an Edison Jobber business soon assumed such proportions that the once highly prized leather goods business received less and less attention, and was pushed out by Edison products, and I moved from the suburbs to suitable premises in the center of Melbourne. The business increased wonderfully and for two years

PREHISTORY

shipments of all types of Edison phonographs and records were arriving weekly, and it soon became evident that these spacious premises were all too small for the fast increasing trade. Whilst at this address I had opened two retail stores – one in the city, and the other in Ballarat, the garden city of Australia. With these two stores to look after and my fast increasing Dealer's business to attend to, new and commodious premises were taken and moved into during April, 1906. At times we carry over 1,000 phonographs and 50,000 records in stock, which shows to what an extent my Edison Phonograph business has grown in the four years that have elapsed since my first order was sent. The Australian public buys well and knows good things when it sees them; cheap and nasty goods find no market... [216]

Cylinder records continued to be available as fully imported products until 1929, but the disc format became more and more dominant from the early 1900s onward. Even Edison introduced his *Diamond Disc* in 1912, after years of refusing to abandon the cylinder. A short-lived series of Edison cylinders made specifically for the Australian market were first released in 1917, featuring American artists performing Australian compositions. By 1920, Edison was virtually the only significant American manufacturer still producing cylinders and most of these selections were also released as discs. The British market had few companies which still produced cylinders after 1920; most were no longer in existence or had completely gone over to the production of disc records.

The most significant Australian recording artists during this period – Frances Saville, Nellie Melba, Ada Crossley, Peter Dawson, Billy Williams, Florrie Forde, Percy Grainger and Evelyn Scotney among others – were mainly active far from Australian shores in centres such as London, Paris, Vienna and New York. Even had they chosen to do so, there was really no way for them to be adequately recorded in Australia before the 1920s. The deficiency was articulated in an item in the *Star* newspaper in 1909:

> Why are there no Australian made records of importance? is a question to which there is no satisfactory answer... Sydney sees the arrival of the world's best singers and instrumentalists and also the pick of variety artists. Nothing would advertise their stay here like a set of records made on their first arrival. It would pay them directly and indirectly. There is plenty and increasing room in Australia for the imported record. There is also room here and the world over for a distinctive Australian article. The land of the beautiful voices with the 'velvet' tone should be the home of specially beautiful records. Perhaps the big companies with branches here may consider the matter and so give United States yet another Australian industry. [71]

The sentiments expressed in this article were certainly ahead of their time as it was to be over 15 years before an Australian record industry was established.

Although no disc records were manufactured in Australia before the 1920s, this is not to say that no efforts were made to supply records specifically for the local market. As early as 1910 the Homophone Company in Berlin produced several disc record labels especially for export to Australia. These included *Rexophone* (made for Jos. Jackson & Macdonald, Sydney), *Rondophone* (made for the British Record Prop. of 732 Harris Street, Sydney), and *Universal Double-Disc* (made for an unknown outlet). Only *Rexophone* continued, as a British-made disc, after 1914. Other labels were produced in Britain for export to Australia such as *Possum* (for Allan & Co. in 1917), *Kalophone Grand* (for Beale & Co.), and *Excelophone* which was made for John G. Murdoch & Co. of London who marketed this label in Australia. *Excelophone* and *Rexophone*

PREHISTORY

records were priced at 2/6 each, *Rondophone* sold for 3/-, and the other labels probably sold at similar prices.

Australian musical criticism of the pre-1920 period (and for quite some time after) was generally conservative and Eurocentric. The 'great composers' were endlessly discussed, and the public taste which, as ever, preferred less elevating fare, was endlessly bemoaned. A typical example from the *Australian Music and Dramatic News* of 1913 attempts to adopt a more tolerant approach, but lapses into a characteristically condescending tone:

> Popular music is one stage in the musical development of the race, and the fact that a larger number than ever before are singing and playing it must not be considered as a retrogression or in the nature of a calamity. We must not overlook the obvious fact that more people than ever before are studying the classics. We should do all in our power to see that this popular stage is not unnecessarily prolonged, but that most of its devotees will outgrow ragtime and two-steps is certain, for progress is an eternal law, and cannot be suspended. [166]

The public's response was to ignore the critic's pleas to 'outgrow' their regrettable tastes; dance music and popular vocals quickly came to dominate the Australian market and have done so ever since.

Another form of marketing was to record Australian compositions in Britain and to release these recordings to Australia on the company's regular label. Such companies included *Aco, Actuelle, Regal, Vocalion* and *Winner*. In some cases – such as *Vocalion* and *Aco* – selected issues were not available in Britain, although there is nothing on the record labels to indicate this. Such advice was not considered necessary at the time – Australia was seen as an extension of the British market and there were British Preferential Tariffs which provided for lower duties, or none at all, on

British-manufactured goods imported into Australia. All the same, one wonders what the typical Britisher of 1924 might have made of a *Regal* record by the American-born music-hall 'artiste' Ella Shields singing 'I'm Going Back Again To Yarrawonga'.

In the absence of an Australian record industry, overseas record manufacturers increasingly took the opportunity to meet the growing demand for Australian compositions or for labels produced specially for local outlets. During the period 1922-26 a number of Australian composers, including Jack O'Hagan, Reg Stoneham, Jack Lumsdaine and Russ Johnstone had the first recordings of their compositions produced in Britain, usually played or sung by British artists. There were also many Australian artists working in Britain during the early and mid-1920s. The most notable of these were John Amadio, Florence Austral, Una Bourne, Lionel Cecil, Frederick Collier, Peter Dawson, Florrie Forde, Gertrude Johnson, Godfrey Ludlow, Malcolm McEachern, Jean Melville, Gladys Moncrieff, Browning Mummery, W.S. Percy, Max Pirani, Stella Power, Kitty Reidy, Clara Serena, Horace Stevens, Elsa Stralia, Albert Whelan and Harold Williams. However, very few of these artists elected to – or were asked to – record Australian compositions other than their own. One of the few exceptions was Malcolm McEachern who recorded Jack Lumsdaine's 'Somewhere South of Shanghai' for *Vocalion* in 1925.

There is no doubt that all the artists named above thought of themselves as Australian, but at that time this was not seen to exclude strong feelings for the 'home' country or even a sense of 'Britishness'. Recording specifically Australian compositions would probably not have been considered; the record companies determined the repertoire, and they were mainly interested in well-tried pieces by British or American composers.

There were exceptions of course, such as the work of the Australian-born composer May Brahe, best

PREHISTORY

remembered for her songs 'I Passed By Your Window' (1916) and 'Bless This House' (1927). She had her first composition published by Allan & Co. (Melbourne) in 1910 and two years later she travelled to London to further her career. By 1914 she had relocated there permanently. Her first major success was 'Down Here' which was recorded by the noted British contralto, Dame Clara Butt, in 1915. Following this Brahe became well known as a composer in the ballad genre which was popular until the early 1920s. 'She was undoubtedly the most successful Australian songwriter of her generation'. [224] She wrote about 600 songs of which almost 300 were published. May Brahe eventually returned to Australia at the outbreak of the World War II, and died in Sydney in 1956.

Other Australian-born contemporaries of Brahe were George H. Clutsam (whose best-known composition is 'Ma Curly-headed Baby') and A. Emmett Adams (composer of 'The Bells of St Mary's'). What is most noticeable about all three is that their work fits seamlessly into the longstanding British ballad tradition and contributes no specifically Australian character to this genre at all.

While an Australian identity was certainly evolving during the first three decades of the twentieth century (partly as a response to Federation), there was also a deeply-rooted attachment to British tradition. A strongly developed awareness of American popular culture and at some levels of society a degree of exaggerated reverence for the 'great masters' of Europe also existed. All these cultural forces were strongly present in Australian musical life during the 1920s, and an emerging interest in, and acceptance of, the work of Australian composers had to compete with these dominant British and American influences.

Before turning to the beginnings of the disc record industry in Australia one additional and little known aspect of the industry's pre-history deserves mention: the work of

Stuart Booty in Sydney. Booty was an electrical engineer who dabbled as an inventor during the early 1920s in an effort to combine his early attempts at recording with his previous work on designing equipment for reproducing records. His are the best known, and were probably the most highly developed, of several small-scale localised attempts to begin production of disc records in Australia. Very little is known about most of these fairly amateurish undertakings, and none is believed to have produced any records which were actually placed on sale. However Stuart Booty developed a number of products in his Leichhardt home which were promoted under the Vitavox name, and his most successful invention was the Vitavox 'lenticular horn gramophone', which received extensive praise including a testimonial from Dame Clara Butt. However it was expensive compared to imported machines of similar quality and few were sold. But, as Booty was on friendly terms with several classical and vocal artists, he began making experimental recordings. By the early 1920s, he had built his own cutting machine and within a few years some of these recordings were being successfully demonstrated, according to contemporary press reports.

An article in the *Daily Telegraph* of 29 April 1925 headed 'Australian record' informs us that:

> An interesting feature of the recital by Mr S.B. Booty, inventor of the 'Vitavox' at the last meeting of the Phonograph and Gramophone Society of New South Wales, was his demonstration of the first disc 'master' record to be made in Australia. The production of this record by Mr Booty is the outcome of a long period of research and much expense. The disc has a twelve-inch diameter, and is made of a special soft wax. The pieces recorded were 'Comfort ye my people' from Handel's *Messiah* sung by Mr W.H. Roberts (tenor) and 'My task' sung by Mrs Rogers (soprano). It was

interesting that the two vocalists were present at the recital. Mr Booty's success in disc recording signifies boundless possibilities for the manufacture of records in this country by local artists. Mr Booty said that from information supplied by the Customs officials it was evident that dance and other light forms of music constituted 75 per cent of the music contained in imported records, and could be recorded in Australia. [74]

Booty had obviously conducted some research on the feasibility of manufacturing records in this country utilising the processes he had developed, and it is believed he was actively seeking financial backing for such an undertaking. It also seems quite likely that the selections mentioned were the first disc masters to be recorded in Australia. However, his process does not seem to have developed beyond the production of masters at this time, and there is no evidence that any commercial pressings resulted.

About a year later, a further report appeared in the *Daily Telegraph* headed 'New industry – Australian-made records':

> These records are the result of 20 years' close study, and are the first to be manufactured in Australia. Mr George Portus, who addressed the audience at a recital in the Beale [piano manufacturers] Salon last night, was referring to the invention of Mr S.B. Booty – Vitavox Australian-made records. It was explained that the records reproduced at the recital were in the first stage of manufacture – soft wax. Mr Portus said that it was intended to erect a plant in Australia, and the records would be 'equal to the world's best'. Last night, as each record was played, the artist who made the record performed the same item. The artists included Signora Aida Bulmas, Miss Alice Prowse, Mr Paul Vinogradoff, Mr Ernest Abeshouse, Signor Ubaldo Russo, Signor Marini, Mischa Dobrinski, and Mr Percy Nicholls. [141]

From this it seems that little progress had been made since the previous demonstration of 'wax masters' in April 1925. By March 1926, when the second report appeared, it was no longer true to claim that these were 'the first to be manufactured in Australia'. Noel Pemberton Billing had established World Record (Australia) in Melbourne during 1924-25 [see Chapter 3] and had marketed almost 150 Australian recordings by this time. Booty's inability to process his wax masters, and his apparent failure to attract sufficient capital to effectively market his technological achievements, fatally restricted the development of Vitavox. By early 1926 the major companies had already established their own factories in Australia or were actively involved in doing so and Booty's hopes for producing commercial recordings faded.

However, Stuart Booty does have one further achievement to his credit, as reported in the *Daily Telegraph* of 4 March 1927 (coincidentally in the same newspaper as the previous reports, and once again almost exactly a year later). The item was headed 'Unique test – At radio exhibition':

> Visitors to the Radio Exhibition last night saw and heard a unique experiment, in which figured the two wonders of modern times – wireless and the phonograph. In the course of the concert programme, which was broadcast from the stage of the Town Hall by Station 2BE (Burgin Electric), a baritone solo was sung by Mr Charles Mills. This was conveyed by land line to the station and thence broadcast. Simultaneously the song was received by radio at the recording studio of Mr S.B. Booty, and electrically recorded on a master disc. This disc was rushed to the Town Hall by car, and reproduced on a phonograph, shortly after the original solo, again being broadcast. The reproduction of the song was notably clear and faithful to the original. [203]

This seems to be the first reported instance of an 'off-air' recording being made in Australia.

There are no further reports of the activities of Vitavox or Stuart Booty after 1926, although he made a brief attempt to revive Vitavox in the early 1950s, apparently with support from Peter Dawson and others, but once again his plans came to nothing. Booty died at Leichhardt around 1974. He was a pioneer of limited achievement who attracted some attention at a time when no other Australian entrepreneur was doing so; but ultimately he remains an interesting but unfulfilled figure now all but forgotten.

SOUND BEGINNINGS

From Musical Australia, *January 1921*

Chapter 2

THE DISTRESSING EFFECTS OF SYNCOPATION

The early 1920s in Australia was a period of relative prosperity and optimism. There was a feeling that in the aftermath of the Great War the world had entered a 'modern' era, and that new and developing technology meant that progress was inevitable. This chapter will examine how this outlook affected music in general and the newly established record industry in particular.

In reading contemporary sources, which essentially means the daily newspapers and those few periodicals that paid attention to musical matters, it quickly becomes apparent that little analytical commentary about music was published. Apart from those magazines which concentrated on the classical end of the music spectrum, such as the *Australian Musical News*, there were no magazines catering to those interested in contemporary music. A few periodicals functioned as trade magazines for the record industry, but their discussion was confined to sales. There were several magazines aimed at radio listeners, but despite the large proportion of recorded music in radio programming there was little musical comment: most articles were of a technical nature, such as 'How to build your own radio receiver'. A number of general interest periodicals had a column or page devoted to music, but the content of these pages is superficial at best. There were certainly no books written in Australia during the 1920s which attempted to examine the significant social changes which are now so obvious and yet seem to have been almost taken for granted at the time.

After the Great War the mass production of gramophones, and the availability of portable gramophones at very low prices, put such items within the reach of working people for the first time. By the early 1920s the gramophone was generally considered an essential item in any home, offering self-improvement through an interest in music, home entertainment and an increasing awareness of the latest 'hits' from musicals and operetta. A contemporary report announced that 'it has been estimated that there are about one million phonographs... in Australia.' [127] That is almost one gramophone for every six members of the population.

'How can we keep our children at home?' asks an advertisement from 1921:

> In these days when the cost of living is an item to be reckoned with seriously, the problem of giving one's children the entertainment and enjoyment they naturally require is difficult. Difficult, because when one has a moderate income and the necessities of life have been paid for, there is precious little left for theatres, jazz parties, and expensive city entertainments. Young people desire entertainment – and while the joys of frequenting public places in a city is quite natural – yet, from a parent's point of view, it should not be allowed to become a habit. Parents should make the home

THE DISTRESSING EFFECTS OF SYNCOPATION

the centre of attraction... Examine your home carefully – what actually have you done to provide your family with amusement? [123]

This advertisement is clearly aimed at the lower middle class with 'a moderate income', and reflects typical middle-class concerns about how to keep growing children at home more of the time. The advertisement continues that for 2/6 deposit and 2/6 a week, the answer was to purchase

> ... the Salonola, which has been highly commended by M. Henri Verbrugghen [then head of the Sydney Conservatorium of Music] as a musical instrument of inestimable value, is an investment showing handsome dividends in family happiness. If you have a Salonola installed you can encourage young folk to hold jazz parties at home...

While making claims that the advertised gramophone is both 'an investment' and has the approval of those concerned with 'good' music, there is also a recognition that the 'young folk' will want to have jazz parties. The dual concerns with acquiring a taste for a 'better class' of music while enjoying popular musical theatre and dance music effectively characterise the main elements which dominated the musical debate in the 1920s.

Most of the published material on this subject, even that found in the more popular journals, tends to fulminate on the enduring values of 'good' music. The high moral tone suggests a reluctance to accept that attitudes and tastes, along with general lifestyle, had dramatically changed since the beginning of the twentieth century. An article published in the *Graphic of Australia* in 1924 headed 'Music and life' is typical, and seeks to analyse this topic:

> The exact relationship existing between music and life is not easy to define. The poet and the psychologist might

conceivably come to blows in arriving at a definition. But that such a relationship exists is beyond question, past challenge. Just as some really great authorities insist that poetry preceded prose, so might it be argued that sound as a medium of expression went before articulated speech. Probably it is because our emotional nature is easily aroused by sound, and because our emotions are the doorway to our reasoning faculty, that even the most savage and primitive peoples utilise music to gain dynamic effects in life that could not be obtained in any other way.

The savage booming of the war drums, the wailing of pipes and other wind instruments, have roused men to a fury – equally of patriotism or destruction. Music in warfare is vital. Some poet has said that a kingdom can be founded on one song, and that with three ballads an empire might be tumbled to the dust. As a centre, an emotional rallying point in whatever nation there is found its national anthem. Yet music has a much more important part to play than merely arousing and stimulating the emotions – it should also rest and refresh them...

The need for emotional rest is being constantly stressed by all modern psychologists as an offset to the increasing strain of modern life. The sensible business man provides for himself a specimen glass and perhaps one exquisite blossom for his desk; every time his eyes are lifted from his papers unconsciously he is being rested by the contemplation of the perfection before him... but at the end of the day he is less mentally weary than he would otherwise have been. Rightly understood, music can be used in the same way. But it must be music of the right type. The atrocity known as the saxophone, the horrible atavism that sees beauty in a jazz band, the distressing effects of syncopation (in the hands of anyone less than Tschaikowsky) will be of little benefit, and may do incalculable harm. Modern music itself too often reflects the very causes and conditions from which we are

THE DISTRESSING EFFECTS OF SYNCOPATION

seeking a way of escape. It is from the finer music that the best results may be expected. The great compositions belonging to an age less bitten with sordid commercialism will sooth and bless... [137]

This piece is representative of many which attempt to attribute the more highly developed human instincts solely to music of the writer's choice (which is unfailingly the 'classics' or the music of the 'great masters'). Even those who try to be more objective reveal their predisposition. An article entitled 'Musical culture' begins by suggesting that '... each one knows within himself what he means by the term "music", even what he feels to be good music, though he may not be able to find adequate words to express his thoughts, but is soon claiming that only by living in the company of good music and by becoming intimate with the best works of great composers, can correct musical taste be attained...' [138]

There are numerous similar articles suggesting that anyone given an adequate opportunity to hear 'good' music will lose interest in what the writer considers to be inferior forms. There are diatribes along these lines from almost every newspaper music critic, and many other types of publications contain similar articles at regular intervals. While less frequent, there are also articles which offer more informed comment and, more commonly, short items which indicate that the declamations of musical bigotry were not representative of all those with a musical background. For example, a 1926 issue of the *Graphic of Australia* claimed:

> Percy Grainger, the world famous pianist now at the Auditorium, Melbourne, has nothing to say against jazz. 'Why should I?' he queried, when his opinion was asked. 'Anything that adds to the popularity of music should be encouraged. Jazz, after all, is another form of music that is

SOUND BEGINNINGS

intended to make it intelligible, or give it more appeal, to certain people. And, after all,' he added, 'there are many jazz melodies, or ragtime, that are based on music of the great composers. I certainly do not join with those who declare that jazz is a debasement of music. My views are quite to the contrary. [151]

Support by now was coming from other quarters. An article from 1924 'In defence of jazz' declared:

Much has been written from time to time, in condemnation of popular music, particularly that type known as 'jazz music.' To be sure, not a little of that turned out by the prolific song writers has little or no musical value, but there is no question but that some of the better class... are far from devoid of musical qualities. Furthermore – and this is the most important argument in favour – there is a decided public demand for such music. Thousands of copies of popular music and thousands of records and rolls featuring popular music are sold each year, and there is no easing up in the demand.

In view of these facts, the music world has to give some recognition to popular music. Concerning this subject it is worthy of note that the tendency of the day is to get away from the noisy 'jazz' effect. The great demand of today is for popular music of a better type, played in a more harmonious way than a few years back.

In this respect it is interesting to note the change that has come over the popular orchestras during the past few years in getting away from the 'jazz' tendency. Only a few years ago 'noise' was the big essential in the dance orchestra. Not today. The most popular combinations of the present day, such as Carl Mehden's Band at Carlyon's, and George Arnold's at the Palais, etc., are anything but 'jazz bands.' The musicians engaged are highly skilled, since the excellent wages being paid today by the better class of dance orchestras

THE DISTRESSING EFFECTS OF SYNCOPATION

attract musicians of the finest type. This has naturally had its effect on the development of the public's taste in popular music.

If a singer can put a negro spiritual like 'Banjo Song' on a Town Hall programme without being mobbed by the audience, if an operatic singer can sing an Italian [opera] tune like 'Donna e Mobile' at the theatres and be solemnly appraised by the critics, why shouldn't someone sing 'Carolina in the Morning', 'Wodonga,' or 'I Wish I Knew,' music that is just as sincere, just as good, and just as profound as the other two? [200]

One of the most popular styles of popular music during the 1920s was what became known as 'symphonic jazz' because it combined elements of jazz with a more conventional style of highly-arranged dance music. In this way it managed to sound more modern and exciting than 'serious music', while simultaneously giving to those who liked their 'jazz' heavily diluted by elaborate arrangements and string sections – a style of music that was not too close to real jazz. It is well described in 'The place of jazz in music' published in the *Graphic of Australia* in 1925:

> Hamilton Webber, the debonair musical director of 'Little Jessie James' at the New Princes Theatre, whose personality and methods of getting his effects from his team of Australian jazz musicians is, to most members of the audiences, one of the outstanding features of the show, introduces a newer and more sympathetic school of conducting and claims attention for the merits of the much maligned jazz music.
>
> 'Jazz music is the expression of modernity,' declares Mr Webber. 'Twenty years ago the music of Debussy was cried down by the traditional school of musicians. Its innovation caused a revolution in their circles and was resented. But the innovation of today is the anachronism of tomorrow. Jazz music has been decried by the academic musical heads

who live in the past, but they do not move with the spirit of the times. A great artist like Kreisler is all the greater for his recognition of the spirit of the times. He accepts it and brings it into his music. Kreisler is too big not to realise the importance of modern music, and to adapt it, whilst still paying tribute to the music of the past.

The innovation of a purely jazz orchestra in 'Little Jessie James,' in place of the traditional theatre orchestra, was greeted with the usual cold shower given to the adventurous, but, as I was privileged two years ago to be in close touch with Paul Whiteman and Isham Jones, the two masters of jazz music, I banked on its success when applied to musical comedy. Paul Whiteman has an international rather than an American reputation. He made a great impression on me. His outstanding success is his exploitation of departments of jazz music hitherto neglected. Previous to Whiteman, jazz had been merely negro syncopation, but his musician's touch grasped the vital tone contrasts and beauty of its musical phrasing, and adapted it to the needs of music. He brought them out and eliminated the raucous, blatant effects on drums, trombone and trumpets, cat-calls, etc., which had been associated with jazz, until he realised the underlying beauty of the noise which was striving to express something. He found the soul of undine-jazz, and has given it to the world in the new jazz music. He applied the musician's standpoint to the tone contrasts at his disposal in the jazz music and added musical perspective, making the instruments which had previously been merely noise makers subservient to the song solo, and thus overcame the difficulty of adapting the jazz band to the needs of the theatre. The jazz orchestra meets the requirements of musical comedy more than did the theatre orchestra of tradition.

'A few years ago', added Mr Webber, 'the saxophone was regarded as a noisy curiosity, but it is expected and has its accepted place in the orchestras of today, for the wonderful effects that can be obtained from it. It can laugh, talk and sob in human-like tones. There is so much juggling with the instruments to get the required effects from them, that it is necessary that each musician shall be an artist and master of his own particular instrument. The jazz orchestra instruments are made by masters who study scientific acoustics in arriving at the best means of making the 'mutes,' which are used in obtaining the effects from the trumpets and trombone. An old time cornet player, no matter how good he may be, would be lost in these days with the trumpets of which there are three in a jazz orchestra. The trumpets in the jazz bands are the cornets of today, and each have a different set of 'mutes' for getting the various effects demanded of them.

Whiteman realises the full significance and superiority of the arranger of jazz band music. He retains a jazz band arranger, whose business it is to take a simple melody and weave it into the artistic tone fabric for every instrument in the orchestra, by symphonic arrangement, adapting it to the needs of the whole jazz band. In the skilled musical arranger a new art and a new avenue of employment has been created in the musical world. [215]

This article accurately expresses how the typical 1920s dance-band musician thought, especially in relation to the type of jazz-influenced popular music made famous by Paul Whiteman. While Whiteman was certainly one of the best-known exponents of this style of music, he was certainly not the first or only bandleader to adapt different styles of music in this way. However, he was pre-eminent in popularising the symphonic jazz style, and it became popular all over the world. The visiting American violinist, Jan Rubini, recorded some titles for *Vocalion* in Melbourne during 1929 with his 'Symphonic Dance Band' which demonstrate the influence of this style in an Australian context.

SOUND BEGINNINGS

The acceptance of symphonic jazz was also greatly facilitated by Whiteman's association with George Gershwin during the 1920s. At the famous Aeolian Hall Concert of 1924, he gave Australians their first hearing of Gershwin's 'Rhapsody in Blue'.

> The musical world is discussing keenly the *'Rhapsody in blue,'* written by Mr George Gerchwin [sic]. This remarkable composition may be accounted unquestionably the 'last word' in jazz music as far as it has been developed. Alike in quality of themes, in ingenuity of treatment, in variety and resourcefulness of instrumentation, and in the brilliant musicianship which distinguishes it throughout, the work exceeds anything of this kind which has been produced previously. Music that might have been danced to by blood-mad Indians or wild Hungarian gypsies, crescendos which surge like waves of elemental passion, passages ranging from shrieks of disembodied souls to the soft croon of waves lapping the shores of dim-lit lagoons, with a climax crashing like the union of all the destructive forces of the universe – is the best way to describe this extraordinary production. No wonder exponents of jazz rejoice to be able at last to point to a work which can be taken seriously by musicians.[183]

More usually the pieces despised as 'jazz' by many commentators were in fact the popular songs of the period. Apart from being dismissed out of hand, there is little discussion of these passing fads. One article from 1923 titled 'Present favourite jazz songs' asks:

> What do Melbourne flappers sing? The manager of a popular music store, smiling enigmatically, replied: 'What London sang yesterday. Look here,' and he picked a bundle of songs off his desk. 'All these without exception were London's favourites six months ago. "Georgette" and

THE DISTRESSING EFFECTS OF SYNCOPATION

"Mimi" were whistled by every street urchin long before Melbourne had ever heard of them. But I venture to prophesy,' and his eyes twinkled, 'the most popular songs in Melbourne in three months' time will be "Thru the night", "Dearest", and "Red moon".' 'Selling songs is an interesting business,' he continued, 'and selling songs in Melbourne particularly so. The musical taste of Melbourne has increased enormously in recent times. I don't mean that there is any demand for highbrow stuff, the trade in Wagner and Beethoven being dead as mutton, but, owing to the advent of the gramophone and pianola, everybody has become more musical. Why, the symbol of respectability in the home used to be a large and solemnly-bound Shakespeare, which nobody read, but now the outwards and visible sign of prosperity and right living is the gramophone or pianola, which everybody uses and enjoys.'

Asked what he considered made a song popular, the song-seller threw up his hands expressively. 'If,' he said, 'I could, amongst the hundreds of manuscripts submitted to me, spot the winner, I should be a millionaire in a week. But the man who does so has yet to be born. The chances of a song becoming a favourite are infinitesimal. If the newsboys whistle it and the flappers hum it, then there are hopes. But the taste of newsboys and flappers are difficult to gauge...'[167]

The above article is unusually perceptive, even while it is very general. Another rare piece of commentary is titled 'A popular hit':

Often critics in the newspapers speak disparagingly of popular numbers of such 'fool songs' as 'Horsey keep your tail up,' 'Yes, we have no bananas,' and 'It ain't gonna rain no more,' all of which have been extraordinary successes. Why they should try to condemn them is mysterious. It is impossible for everyone to appreciate Beethoven's Choral

SOUND BEGINNINGS

Symphony No. 9 (which, no doubt, is very delightful) – just so it may be impossible for these judges to enjoy the fool songs mentioned.

Not everyone enjoys drama – some prefer the lighter class of entertainment. Just so, tastes in the 'nut' songs and classical numbers vary according to musical education, environment, etc.

It seems as though the popular song craze goes in cycles, each period bringing its distinctive type of song. One remembers the old hits, 'Shoo fly, don't bother me,' 'Get your hair cut,' 'Down went McGinty to the bottom of the sea,' 'Where did you get that hat?', ' What ho, she bumps,' 'How de do dee,' and a host of others.

The most recent to reach Australia is 'Don't bring Lulu.' It is one of the big hits in Sydney and soon will be in Melbourne the catchword ditty... [165]

These snippets may not seem very informative by today's standards, nor do they represent any deep analysis. The relatively small number of outlets for publication of such material is part of the reason why so little of interest survives. Another is their brevity. News items in daily newspapers in the 1920s were normally very short; even prominent events often rated only one or two paragraphs.

It is even more difficult to find contemporary comment on the relation between musical taste and the production of gramophone records. Although by the mid-1920s recorded music had been commercially available in Australia for over 30 years, it was still a sufficiently new means of entertainment for opinions to differ on the relative merits of recordings and live performance. *Edison* records capitalised on this by promoting a series of 'Tone Tests' during the early 1920s. Audiences were invited to compare a selection from an *Edison* recording with the same selection sung live by the same artist, for the purpose of demonstrating

THE DISTRESSING EFFECTS OF SYNCOPATION

how 'life-like' the recording was.

In 1926 Peter Pindaret prefaced his new column in the *Triad* called 'The records of a plain man' with the pronouncement:

> Three months ago, when this page was first discussed, I... was one of those queer persons who turn up their noses at gramophones... I loved music, but I was afflicted with the peculiar form of snobbery exhibited by the music-lovers who sniff at the people who haven't heard Galli-Curci's voice issuing from her own throat. One such music-lover, who also poses as a great critic, used to make capital out of the fact that he consistently refused to listen to 'mechanical music.' That his knowledge of music and musicians – the most important part of a modern man's knowledge – is twenty years out of date, doesn't seem to trouble him in the least. His colossal vanity still allows him to rest secure in the belief that he is an Authority because in 1819 or 1919 (I forget which) he heard Signor Pincha da Fisho sing the aria from Rippa d' Atmosfero's opera, '*Glooma Pongalooma*,' at Chicago.
>
> For a very long time I was under the influence of the Great Critic's wonderful bluffing powers. Thank the God of Music, I am now free. I believe in the gramophone. I believe that it is the greatest educative force in the world (except monthly periodicals). For thirty years I have been listening to good music, whenever there was any to listen to, in this dear land o' mine, and I am now convinced that an Australian home, minus a gramophone and a stock of records chosen with discrimination, is a home more seriously handicapped than if it had not water laid on.
>
> Music is the water of life. Music says all that words can say, and all that words cannot say. The gramophone brings music – the very best music – into the home. It's your own fault if you allow it to bring the very worst music...

> I have no patience with the people who think jazz is ephemeral. One might as well speak of the waltz as ephemeral. Jazz will last; it will have its periods of eclipse, of banality, of monotonous repetition. But it will persist, because it has forcibly restored to humanity a keen delight in rhythm, which is not a thing of today or yesterday, but a thing eternal... [162]

This article demonstrates that as late as the 1920s there were still people who refused to listen to 'mechanical music'. This view was understandable, considering that the gramophone had originally been promoted as a novelty. And later when this was no longer the case, the poor standard of recording and the fact that the overwhelming majority of recordings were of little enduring value, led to a continuation of the view, in some quarters, that 'mechanical' music was not to be taken seriously by the discerning listener. But by the 1920s recording techniques had improved greatly and the range and variety of material recorded was much wider. By the time the record industry in Australia was established, those who sneered at the gramophone were a tiny minority and generally regarded as eccentric.

Certainly, when the electrical recording process for making commercially-released records became widespread after 1925 there was a noticeable improvement in the quality of most recordings, and this further increased acceptance of recorded music. The *Australasian Phonograph Monthly* of 10 December 1926 is typically optimistic about the future of the record trade. It enthused: 'The almost unbelievable superiority of the new type of phonograph, and the equally wonderful improvement in the new process of recording will be considered, if it is not so already, one of the shining attainments of this decade.' Obviously, part of this enthusiasm was derived from the well-founded belief that it would also increase record sales:

THE DISTRESSING EFFECTS OF SYNCOPATION

There can be no question but that electrical recordings will give a big spurt to record sales during the next few months. For the past year we hear trade in America has been slow, and companies have been hit by the drastic wiping out of obsolete stock. Gramophone dealers need not have any fear of the prospects of the 1926-27 season, however, for it is considered that the improved quality of the new records will create thousands of new gramophone users. [109]

The improved quality of the new recordings is discussed in another article a few months later:

A luncheon was held in London recently to demonstrate a new gramophone, made by the firm of Columbia. New 'electrically made' records were played on an old machine (1923), and on the new model... and in each case the improvement in the tone was obvious.

Sir George Croydon Marks, chairman of the Columbia Gramophone Company, who presided, said that it was somewhat unfortunate that the first introduction of the gramophone was regarded by the public as a mechanical freak or wonderful toy. This prevented any great change being made either in the machine for reproducing the sounds or for processes and methods for recording them. Yet, from no other instrument could a reproduction of speech or music in all its phases be obtained under the direct control of an unskilled user. The nearest approach to anything giving similar results was connected to the new art of wireless sound transmission. Wireless devices and instruments, however, were concerned solely with sound transmission or sound transference in a manner that was transient, while the gramophone effected the translation or immediate reproduction of sound in a manner that was permanent.

This important factor of permanence, he said, had naturally led to the keenest attention, being directed towards the improvement and perfecting of the instrument itself,

SOUND BEGINNINGS

and also to the methods of obtaining the original record. The basic method of recording and reproducing music by gramophone manufacturers was almost stationary for about 40 years, but new lines of originality had led to important advances during the last few years. In these new efforts the friendly co-operation and technical assistance of our great musicians was happily secured. The Columbia Company, having determined to undertake original investigations and scientific research in fields previously unexplored, set apart large sums of money to be spent year after year on details and features connected with the methods of producing the records and the manner of constructing the machines.

Sir Henry Wood said that he used to have a deep-rooted antipathy for gramophones and all forms of mechanical reproduction, but a very great change had lately come over recording, especially over the recording of orchestral music. The result was that the playing of the gramophone today was one of his greatest pastimes. The making of orchestral records had been one of the most trying things that one could ask a musician to do. The room used to be so small that he himself had often given members of his orchestra raps on the head with his baton. But now, under the system of 'electrical' recording, the whole scheme of things had been changed. Instead of playing in an attic, they now played in a fine large studio. Even the atmosphere had improved, and there had certainly been an amazing improvement in the recording of the bass. People had realised the harm of trying to force tone. Loudness made for monotony, and monotony was the death of art. They could now use a large orchestra and produce recorded work that was 'stereoscopic' in character. [176]

A press report of some remarks by the singer Peter Dawson makes a fitting conclusion to this survey of contemporary views on the gramophone and recorded music:

THE DISTRESSING EFFECTS OF SYNCOPATION

Addressing members of the Good Companions organisation, of which he has been appointed patron, Mr Peter Dawson last night gave his views on broadcasting and the phonograph as factors in the life of the present-day musician...

The time had gone by, said Mr Dawson, when a singer could achieve fame by singing for the phonograph. It was broadcasting nowadays which made a musician quickly famous. But public approval won by this means did not last. Only by hard work, and by frequent appearances, appearances in person on the concert platform, could a singer build up a lasting reputation. When he himself first went to London, he had decided to sing whenever and wherever he could. It was all fine experience. He had sung as Masonic Lodges – four, five, and even six in the week. He had taken three engagements in the one evening, when this was practicable. In addition, he had spent the hours between ten and one and between two o'clock and five in recording for the phonograph. In those days, it took three weeks to make a record. The singer kept on singing and singing the same thing over and over again until he felt that he wanted to cut his throat from sheer boredom.*

Phonograph records, he considered, were much too dear. If the price was reduced to a shilling in some instances, sales would become so tremendous that the distributing companies would make a handsome profit. It was a golden rule for a singer to be content with a financial reward which was reasonable, instead of holding a gun at the head of the people he sang for, and demanding something exorbitant. He said this as a singer whose voice had been issued on ten million records. Australia was extremely lucky to be able to hear splendid music on discs which had been recorded under perfect conditions. Nowadays it was to the phonograph that

---

* Peter Dawson is here speaking of the early recording practice where each recording had to be made separately, before a process was developed which enabled a large number of copies to be made from each 'master' recording.

students turned when they wanted to make the acquaintance of works which were new to them... [103]

The industry was at its height in 1927, and the *Sydney Morning Herald* of 12 January summed up the popularity of the 'new industry':

> From a thousand music shops talking machines blare the syncopated musical nonsense of the hour; from a hundred others issue the quieter, more arresting, strains of the classics of music and song; elsewhere the talking machines explain music, teach languages, and even direct how the 'daily dozen' gymnastic exercise should be carried out. Indeed, the talking machine and its sine qua non, the phonograph record, have brought music to almost every home and sleepless nights to many a suburban street.
>
> But more amazing, and as interesting, as all these things, is the growth of the manufacture of phonograph records in Sydney – the only Australian city where factories have been established. Although the Brunswick-Balke-Collender Company has been manufacturing records for only three years, and the remaining two companies, the Columbia Graphophone Company, Ltd., and the Gramophone Company, Ltd., opened their factories only last year, the three firms are now producing more than ten million records annually, a total that will be increased, and even doubled, very shortly, it is expected.
>
> Each of the companies has found such an amazing demand for their products that they have been working more than one shift, and the Brunswick Company claims that their machines never stop during the whole twenty-four hours. This company within a few weeks will be manufacturing its own compound or composition for the records, a departure that will shortly also be made by the Columbia Company.
>
> Another company, the Parlophone Company, is about to enter the field of phonograph record production. It is

THE DISTRESSING EFFECTS OF SYNCOPATION

gratifying to note that, without exception, the manufacturers pay a tribute to their Australian workmen. Each at first imported experts from overseas, but the Australians, it was found, acquired a knowledge of the intricate processes with remarkable facility.

The Columbia Company is the first to begin actual recording in Australia* and this is being done by the new electric process – a development of the wireless microphone. By this method music at the Town Hall or the Conservatorium may be conveyed to the factory at Homebush by land line and recorded there. In future Sydney people will be able to obtain a lasting record of local artists, great visitors, and possibly of the speeches and the enthusiasm at historic gatherings.

But the usefulness of the phonograph record is not confined to music and song. One of its most interesting uses is teaching. In the interpretation of a classic the teacher will stop the student and say, 'Now just listen to Kreisler's phrasing of the same subject,' and the student will be led to appreciate – even if he cannot emulate – the masters. Then there are courses of physical exercises and wireless courses.

Some of the companies believe that the future of the phonograph lies along the road of classical music. The Gramophone Company, makers of His Master's Voice and Zonophone records, are particularly insistent upon this.

This opinion is not generally held, however, and at least one of the manufacturing firms believes that the greater demand will always be for the popular song and musical 'hits' of the hour; for jazz and saxophones. [16]

During the 1920s sales of sheet music, previously the accepted measure of the popularity of a composition, were being overtaken by the sale of gramophone records – and

---

* Less than a year after the collapse of Pemberton Billing's World Record venture in Melbourne, it has already been forgotten.

probably also starting to be affected by radio broadcasting. The following article analyses the factors at play in the music trade:

> There is no question of doubt that the sales of [sheet] music during the last two or three years have materially dropped off, and that the publishers are faced with a very serious position. What are the reasons for this shrinkage of business? There are many causes. The player-piano, gramophone and wireless broadcasting have made the most serious inroads into the vitals of the business. Fees paid for mechanical royalties and broadcasting rights have helped to a certain extent to balance the shrinkage to the publishers, which may have the effect of relieving the pressure as far as they are concerned, but what of the music seller who does not collect any royalties? Is that business doomed, and why should the sales of popular and standard music have fallen away to such a large extent?
>
> Other factors must be at work. The picture theatre, which provides cheap entertainment, and the jazz palais, which has almost entirely supplanted the private dance, are factors which account for the position of the music trade just as much as the mechanical change. Now the question arises, will the trade ever revive, or have we arrived at the stage when the public no longer wants music? I think not. The sale of music, with the exception perhaps of the educational side of the business, is what one might term a luxury, and is an item which can be done without. It is noticeable at present, and has proved itself to be correct, that during periods of financial stress in the past, the trade has materially suffered, while when business generally is prosperous it is reflected in increased sales of music and instruments, thus proving that given favourable conditions, the trade is in a sound position.
>
> After having spent the greater part of my life in the music business, and having watched the fluctuations and phases of

THE DISTRESSING EFFECTS OF SYNCOPATION

it for over thirty years, I feel forced to be optimistic of the future. What appeals more to the best that is in us but music, or stirs us more than a strain of a good melody played or sung by a good artist? It has appealed in the past, and will again take its place as an uplifting force in the world. We have had our periods of coon song, descriptive ballad, comic and sentimental songs, ragtime and jazz music, while behind it all stands the solid foundation of standard and classical works. It therefore rests with those of us who have the welfare of the musical public at heart, and the uplifting of the trade generally, to do all that lies in our power to bring this better state about. Those who should find themselves in the forefront of any movement to this end unquestionably are the musical profession, schools and those employed in the various branches of the music business. From their combined efforts should spring an awakening of the soul and a quickening of the musical pulse of the people. Let us make for our slogan, 'Music for all. Sing it, play it, and talk it.' Take on the spirit of optimism and I feel confident that success will be achieved. We are all tired of ragging and jazzing and want something better... [147]

Finally, here are some observations by a leading member of the British music industry during a visit in 1928, published in the *Australian Musical News* under the heading 'Australia's musical outlook':

A visitor to Australia during the past three or four months has been Mr Arthur Ferdinand Bosworth, son of the late Mr Arthur Edward Bosworth, who founded the well-known London music publishing house bearing their name. Mr A.F. Bosworth regards the musical outlook in Australia as a particularly interesting one. The sheet music trade has, of course, been hit to a considerable extent by the increase of interest in mechanical means of reproducing music, just as in other countries, yet he has been able to gather in the course of his investigations here that on the teaching side there is an improved outlook. Especially in New Zealand since the beginning of the year has there been quite a revival in the demand for good standard numbers and teaching pieces.

Naturally, Mr Bosworth has not neglected his opportunity of observing how we take to music as provided by leading interpreters, such as the Williamson-Melba opera company, Moisewitsch, and Shura Cherkassky. It had greatly impressed him to see the big audiences for the operas and the two pianists mentioned, and to find how discriminating they were. 'I think the standard of appreciation is very high out here,' he remarked... He also heard various musical comedies, and 'what struck me was that the singing of the choruses, and of the principals for that matter, is very much better than what we get in England.' [78]

It was in this climate of optimism that a series of enterprising individuals set about the task of developing a new Australian industry.

Chapter 3

PEMBERTON BILLING AND WORLD RECORD

… a factory is to be opened in May in Bay Street, Brighton, Melbourne, at which records of the singing, instrumental work, and so on of Australian artists will be taken and completed. The World Record (Australia) Proprietary Ltd. is thus initiating a new industry so far as Australia is concerned. This company controls the Pemberton Billing record patents throughout the world. It will be recalled that Mr Pemberton Billing, formerly a member of the British House of Commons, arrived in Australia a few months ago, in connection with the project. It is claimed that by the records and a special 'controller', continuous performances lasting from ten minutes to half an hour can be given. [73]

This entry from the *Australian Musical News* of 1 February 1924 was the first published reference to the company which was to produce the first disc records recorded in Australia.

World Record (Australia) Pty. Ltd. evolved directly out of World Record Co. Ltd., which was established in Britain

SOUND BEGINNINGS

From Sun News-Pictorial, *1 August 1925*

PEMBERTON BILLING AND WORLD RECORD

in 1922 to exploit the patent obtained by an Englishman, Noel Pemberton Billing, in October 1921. This patent related to extending the duration of the conventional recording process by utilising a method of constant linear speed recording. To play discs using this process a 'controller' was needed which was fixed to the gramophone beside the turntable, and which regulated the speed at which the disc revolved (ranging from about 30 rpm at the beginning to about 80 rpm at the end) so that the needle was always travelling at the same speed in the groove of the disc, whatever the length of the groove at that point.

Pemberton Billing's development of the constant linear speed process was brilliant in conception, but fatally flawed in its application. The discs recorded by this method could not be played on a conventional gramophone, and the 'controller' could only be used for the recordings made by the World Record process. The early history of the gramophone is littered with similar examples of recording techniques which failed because they were not universally adaptable. World Record simply followed their example with the same inevitable result.

This seemingly impetuous and strangely ethereal approach to invention was characteristic of Noel Pemberton Billing. He was one of the most colourful characters to be involved in the early record industry in Australia but this venture, like so many of his other attempts to put his unconventional ideas into practice, was bound to fail. His early life demonstrates a strong streak of nonconformity in his character. At the age of 13 he stowed away on a merchant ship and ended up in Durban where he joined the Natal Mounted Police, and went on to fight in the Boer War before returning to England in 1903. He developed an early interest in aircraft (where he did some pioneering work), and by 1908 had designed and tested his own monoplanes. He was also active in such diverse fields as writing, land speculation and yacht broking, and by 1913 had amassed sufficient capital to begin construction of an early version of the flying boat which he called a 'supermarine'. With what has been described as 'characteristic bravado' he obtained a pilot's certificate with a total of four hours and two minutes flying experience.

After service with the Royal Naval Air Squadron in the World War I, Pemberton Billing was elected to Parliament in 1916. These eventful years as the member for East Hertfordshire included a famous trial for criminal libel, of which he was eventually acquitted. He retired in 1921. It seems that with time on his hands, he was able to indulge his interest in inventing: he claimed to have taken out 500 patents. These included a miniature camera, and a two-sided stove.

Despite its relatively brief life span, World Record holds an important place in the history of the record industry because it was the first company to make commercially-released disc recordings in Australia. Pemberton Billing was also instrumental in bringing to Australia a number of individuals with experience in the British record industry who remained active well after the collapse of the World Record venture. Significant as this was for Australia, biographical information on Pemberton Billing mostly fails to mention these activities. By coming to Australia he seems to have effectively disappeared from view in Britain – perhaps not unintentionally. In order to establish the background for his Australian venture, we need to go back to his fledgling attempts to establish the World Record operation in Britain during 1922. Despite an initially favourable reception when the first constant linear speed records were released in October that year, the company was undercapitalised and record sales failed to reach the anticipated levels. In December 1922, soon after the release of the first World Record discs, Pemberton Billing went

PEMBERTON BILLING AND WORLD RECORD

Above: The earliest known photograph of a recording session in Australia. The Big Four, an Australian vocal quartet appearing at the Tivoli Theatre in Melbourne in 1925, are photographed at the World Records recording studio.

Left: The studio of the World Record broadcasting station at Brighton. The floor is divided into squares numbered so that a table can be prepared to show the effect of placing instruments in different positions in relation to the microphone.

Right: A Wocord Condor label. From the author's collection.

to the United States to try and establish an American outlet for the new process, but he does not seem to have succeeded as no recordings were produced there during the 1920s. The only practical result of his visit was that in early 1923 he obtained the rights to use masters recorded by the Emerson Phonograph Company. Some of these appeared on World Record issues credited to the 'American Jazz Combination'.

In May 1923, he applied for another patent and, despite World Record's far from promising start, a new company called the Featherweight Flexible Records Co. was incorporated on 22 June 1923 to develop the patent for a flexible, unbreakable disc record. The first *Fetherflex* records were released in November 1923, but poor sales and production difficulties combined to sink the venture almost from the start. Within six months the company had gone into voluntary liquidation.

Against this background of business difficulties, Noel Pemberton Billing decided to come to Australia. It has been suggested that he left England to escape his creditors; but exact details of his financial position at this time are not known. He certainly had sufficient capital to be planning to establish a record factory but this may have been at the expense of his creditors. The official reason for his departure was medical advice that his wife's health required a warmer climate; this was rapidly confirmed by a notice in *The Times* of 1 December 1923 under 'Imperial and foreign news items', stating: 'An Exchange telegram from Melbourne announces the death of Mrs Pemberton Billing, who accompanied her husband to Australia a few weeks ago.' [110]

Pemberton Billing probably chose Melbourne for his factory because an associated company was already active there. This was Controlaphone Ltd., set up in May 1923 by Alexander Knapp to act as a distributor for the World

Record discs and the controller apparatus necessary to play them. Presumably as a result of Knapp's activities, some publicity had been generated in Australia including an article in the *Australian Musical News* of August 1923 which is a good example of the type of promotion at the time for the 'new device':

> One of the latest inventions dealing with the phonograph promises to make two or more words or sounds grow where but one has been recorded before. It is a device that has claimed for it the possibility of giving half an hour's entertainment on a 12in. record. What can be done with it, if the claim works well, can be seen in its application to dance programmes, in the recording of entire acts from operas, and in numerous other ways that can be readily imagined.
>
> As is commonly known, the ordinary phonograph record consists of a very small continuous groove, cut spirally on a flat disk. The sound is reproduced by the needle coming in contact with projections on the side of the groove. If this groove were strung out in a straight line it would reach a length of approximately 900 feet. On the ordinary record, the needle travels this entire distance in about 3½ minutes, the revolving table making 280 revolutions in that time at a constant speed, about 80 revolutions a minute.
>
> It may be readily seen that, although the speed of revolution is constant, the speed of the needle's passage over the record varies. In other words, when the record is started with the needle on the outer edge, more than 50 inches of groove is passing under the needle each second, while when at the end of the record, which is the nearest groove towards the centre, only about fourteen inches passes the needle per second. The former is regarded as too fast, and the latter as too slow for perfect reproduction by the manufacturers of the new controller.

SOUND BEGINNINGS

The speed of recording as well as of reproducing being constant, it can readily be seen that the amount of music or sound on each circle, no matter what the circumference may be, is the same. As a result, it is claimed, records made on the ordinary plan cannot be made larger because so much groove will have to travel under the needle every second that the 'surface scratch' and 'needle wear' become too great.

The new record is manufactured in such a way that there is the same amount of music or sound in each 'foot run' of the groove, no matter what the diameter of the circle may be, with the result that three to five times as much entertainment is put into the same length of groove, and a correct and constant needle speed is obtained by fitting the controller, which regulates the revolutions of the revolving table, so that the speed of the groove past the stationary needle is constant, no matter what the diameter of the circle around which the groove is cut. [145]

World Record (Australia) Pty. Ltd. was registered in Melbourne on 5 October 1923, prior to Pemberton Billing's arrival, by Knapp. He found a suitable location for the proposed record factory in Bay Street, Brighton, a Melbourne beachside suburb. However, it apparently took some time for their pioneering plans to be put into effect. The optimistic forecast that the factory would 'be opened in May' seems not to have been met; the specialist staff required were not yet available, and no further publicity concerning the developmental activities of World Record (Australia) appeared until mid-1925.

World Record's 'long duration records' continued to be advertised during 1924, pronouncing that 'the outstanding feature of this invention is that it produces three to five times more music from a 12in. World Record than is contained on any other 12in. record.' [223] The advertisements also stated that the records cost 5/6 for 10in. discs and 7/6, 10/- and 12/6 for various classes of 12in.

discs. The 'controller' was priced at £2/17/6 for the plated model, or £3/7/6 for the gilt model. The original outlet was at 211 Elizabeth Street, Melbourne (opposite the General Post Office). There is no mention of any locally produced records, which suggests the factory was still under construction.

Two of Pemberton Billing's staff from the British World Record venture are believed to have joined him in Melbourne during 1924: Frederick George Mitchell and Herbert Goody. It seems likely that record production at the Bay Street factory began around November 1924, as the *Austral* trademark was registered at that time. But there is no evidence to confirm exactly when the *Austral* records first went on sale – it may not have been until some time early in 1925.

During 1925, a *Wafer* record was made available issuing the same titles as *Austral*. This was an unbreakable flexible record, apparently a further development of the *Fetherflex* label produced in Britain. The selling price of *Wafer* records was 1/6. World Record publicity also mentions *Gold Label Wafer Duplex* records, but as none of these has yet been discovered there is no evidence that they were ever issued.

The full range of World Record products was never produced in Australia. The first discs produced here were certainly the 10in. *Austral* records, which used the Emerson masters to which Pemberton Billing had obtained the rights. Test pressings exist of 12in. World Record constant linear speed discs which were produced at the Melbourne factory but, despite various statements to the contrary in contemporary publicity, local commercial production did not proceed. There was also a 5in. disc sold only in Australia as a children's record under the *Wendy* label. These discs have 'Wocord Australia' on the label, but they were pressed in Britain for export. No presses for 5in. records were available in Australia.

SOUND BEGINNINGS

According to company papers dated 13 August 1925, World Record (Australia) was reconstructed as Wocord Limited. But the Wocord name had already been used in company advertising prior to this date, and the record labels continued to refer to World Record (Aust) right up to and including the production of the *Condor* label in late 1925. So, whatever the company papers say, both names seem to have already been in use and for all practical purposes they were interchangeable.

One of the most innovative aspects of Pemberton Billing's venture was his plan to set up a radio station at the Brighton record factory to broadcast the company's products. The station was registered as 3PB (with typical élan Pemberton Billing used his initials for the call sign) and was on the air from September 1925 to January 1926. The new station attracted useful press coverage – radio was just becoming established as an entertainment medium and there was a high level of public interest in any new developments. An article in the *Listener In* of 6 June 1925 headed 'Should radio be used for advertising?' provides the first news of Pemberton Billing's latest imaginative scheme:

> The original type of 'B' class stations is passing, and a new is arising in its stead. 3UZ, for so long known to amateurs as an experimental station, and latterly as a 'B' class station, has intimated that in a short time it will close down. A new 'B' class station, 3PB, conducted by the World Record Company, of Bay Street, Brighton, of which Mr Pemberton Billing is the manager, has applied for a licence.
>
> The cost of maintaining the station is given by Oliver J. Nilson and Co. as the reason for closing down 3UZ. Besides the cost of the upkeep of the studio apparatus, power, and the payment of engineers and artists, which they were prepared to stand, the question of royalties on music, which

amounted to approximately 3/6 for every number broadcast, and the £50 royalty for patent and other rights, were found so far to outweigh any return received by the station that the operation of the station was a dead loss.

No direct advertising was broadcast on 3UZ. Oliver J. Nilson and Co., who conducted the station, preferring to run it on the principles of the Westinghouse and other companies in America. But things have changed rapidly in the Australian broadcasting world. In the old days, when Oliver J. Nilson and the Associated Radio Co. were the only people broadcasting, it was essential for them to carry on, otherwise no one would buy their sets or parts. Now that there are two good stations operating constantly every day, there is no need for these old stations to broadcast.

The latest 'B' class licence is for the World Record Company, and will be used in an entirely different manner. This company has just been established here, and is manufacturing World and Austral records. These are of a special unbreakable type, similar to the standard gramophone record and a thin wafer-like record, double-sided, and made from paper, which can be rolled up into a small cylinder. These are not affected by a needle scratch, and give numbers with a clarity and volume equal to any record. Mr N. Pemberton Billing, who brought the patent to Australia, is a well-known ex-member of Parliament in England.

'We will broadcast dance records', he said, 'from our station every night between eight and ten o'clock. The numbers will be of the best, and consist of specially selected jazz and orchestral items from America, England, and Europe, which have not been heard here yet. Before each item, when announcing the number, we will mention that the record is manufactured in Australia by the World Record Co., and can be obtained at our dealers. Our records will be the cheapest on the market, and will be for sale in about a

SOUND BEGINNINGS

fortnight.'* The call sign of the new station will be 3PB, and [it] will operate on a wave of 290 metres. The power will be 1500 watts, with 2500 watts on the plate. The aerial is a hundred and fifty foot five wire cage, eighty feet from the ground.

A 6-wire fan type of counterpoise is employed. Mr Maxwell Howden installed the plant.

A novelty in broadcasting programmes will be given from there when artists intending to have records made visit the factory to have reproduction of their voice made. At the same time as the trials are made the singer's voice will be broadcast. A large special type of air-driven gramophone will be used, and a player piano and organ are about to be installed in the studio.

A new departure in the arrangement of the studio in relation to the instruments and kind of music has been made. The studio floor has been cut up into squares by a number of white lines. Each of these squares is numbered, and a table has been written showing the results obtained with certain types of music from the gramophone when that instrument is placed on each of the squares.

Advertising by indirect methods presents many opportunities for success. The World Record Company has probably struck one of the successful methods. Most indirect advertising aims to create goodwill for the firm or person advertising. 3PB, by giving a good programme, aims not only to create this goodwill but to give listeners an idea of the quality of their productions. [188]

The reference to the production of 'World and Austral records' is apparently in error, as *World* constant linear speed records were not commercially manufactured in Australia. The article goes on to say that the records are

---

* Perhaps this is a reference to the imminent release of the Austral Duplex record.

'similar to the standard gramophone record', and this was certainly not true of *World* records. It further describes records 'of a special unbreakable type', which is clearly a reference to *Austral* records. The *Wafer* disc – 'a thin wafer-like record' – also produced by World Record gets a mention, but it is noticeable that no mention is made of Australian recordings. The locally-recorded *Austral Duplex* does not appear to have been in production at this time (though the fact that recordings could be made is noted).

It is not known exactly when 3PB began broadcasting. An article of 6 June 1925 in the *Listener In* states that 3PB 'will shortly open'. However, although the photographs which illustrate that article depict the aerial in place at the factory and show a fully equipped studio apparently ready for transmission, it was to be over three months before 3PB was making regular transmissions. Another short item in the *Listener In* of 22 August 1925 reads:

> The station will be on the air between eight and ten, broadcasting gramophone music, the idea being to enable listeners in to hear the records and make their selection. A special attachment fixed to the tone arm of the gramophone allows the playing of a certain type of record for 15 minutes, which makes the station a convenient one for dancers, who it is expected will take advantage of all 3PB has to offer them. The station will operate on a wave length of 290 metres with a power of 1500 watts. Coils of 25, 35, 35 are necessary to tune the station in. [84]

Parts of this item are reproduced verbatim from a longer article published in the same periodical in June 1925. The mention of 'a special attachment fixed to the tone arm of the gramophone [which] allows the playing of a certain type of record for 15 minutes' is a reference to the use of the 'controller'. The instructions provided 'to tune the station in' suggest that 3PB was making test broadcasts by this time. These test broadcasts seem to have continued for some weeks, as they are also referred to in an article in *Punch* of 24 September 1925, which mentions that 'a "B" class transmitting station under the call signal of 3PB has been erected. From this station gramophone dance records and programmes will be broadcasted in the evenings. The management has received many congratulatory messages on its "test" broadcastings, not only from this State, but from New South Wales and elsewhere.' [117]

In yet another innovative move, World Record was to make the first commercially-released disc recordings in Australia. Once again, there are no sources which establish the exact date these recordings were made. However, by examining published reports about the artists known to have recorded for World Record it is possible to establish a fairly narrow period for production.

The *Austral Duplex* label, on which the first locally-recorded disc records were released, was of the same composition as the *Austral* record (pressed from American masters) but of 8in. instead of 10in. diameter. All issues on *Austral Duplex* were Australian recordings made in the World Record studio at the Brighton factory. The artists known to have made recordings are Ralton's Havana Band, Ray Tellier's San Francisco Orchestra, Yerke's S.S. Flotilla Sextette, Lee White, and Maud Fane (all of whom were British or American artists), as well as Australian artists the Big Four (a male vocal quartet), Fred Moore, and Dudley Glass. There are unconfirmed reports of other Australians having also recorded including the Jimmie Elkins' Orchestra, Jack O'Hagan, Jack Lumsdaine and a vocal group called the Harmonizers. It may be that these recordings were never released, but sometimes not even a single copy of those *Austral Duplex* records known or believed to have been issued (such as those by Maud Fane, Fred Moore, or Dudley Glass) is known to exist. However, it shouldn't be assumed that the absence of identified copies means that none will ever be found. The rarity of some of these issues more probably indicates that certain records had much lower sales than others, which is hardly unusual.

It can be deduced from press reports of the performers' presence in Melbourne that these recordings were made between May and September 1925. Ralton's Havana Band had a season at Carlyon's night club in St Kilda from 2 May to the 28 August 1925; Ray Tellier's San Francisco Orchestra were playing at the Palais de Danse, also in St Kilda, from May 1925 until November 1925; Yerkes' S.S. Flotilla Sextette was playing at the Wattle Path Palais from May to September 1925; Lee White (with Clay Smith) was starring in the revue *Back Again* at the Athenaeum Theatre in Collins Street between August and October 1925; and Maud Fane was in Melbourne from June to August 1925, starring in the musical *Primrose*. Of the Australian performers, Dudley Glass left Australia in early September 1925 for America, and later went on to London.

The probable date is narrowed down even further by an advertisement dated 1 August 1925, announcing that 'to-day for the first time in this country's history an All Australian Record is on sale.' [146] This full-page advertisement promotes all of Wocord's products – *Austral*, *Wafer*, and *World Record* – and (without mentioning *Austral Duplex*) also lists 'Australian recordings' by all the artists mentioned above except Lee White. This confirms that recordings had been made prior to August 1925; but it is unlikely that they were made more than a month or so before the *Austral Duplex* records were released. This would suggest that the first Australian disc recordings were made by World Record (Australia) in June and July 1925.

The new recordings, and the release of a new label, resulted in a burst of activity by World Record; an unusual amount of publicity appeared during August and September

1925. Advertisements on 1 August give the addresses of World Record outlets as Howey Place, Melbourne; 155 Chapel Street, Prahran; and Memorial Hall, St Kilda; and add 'other shops opening shortly in Malvern, Brunswick, Elsternwick, Collingwood, etc.' The same advertisements promote the availability of World Record's recording studios for making personal records, promising: 'If you possess talent either as vocalist or instrumentalist, or are desirous of securing a permanent record, either of your own or of your children's voices, the resources of our studio are at your disposal for a moderate fee. Write for full particulars.' [146] No evidence of private recordings has yet been found.

A similar full-page advertisement appeared in the Melbourne *Punch* on 24 September 1925, by which time some new outlets had been established at 237 High Street, Malvern and Moorabool Street, Geelong. There is also, for the first time, a specific reference to *Duplex* records. The issue which carried this advertisement also contains a short article on the 'World Record Coy.' which seems to have been written from publicity material supplied by the company:

> The problem of fostering and encouraging every form of local industry is exercising the minds of our statesmen today, and must be the deep-felt desire of every patriotic Australian. It is, therefore, most encouraging to know that a factory has been built at North Brighton for the manufacture of an article which is a complete novelty in the gramophone world, namely, an unbreakable gramophone record. This record is manufactured by the World Record Coy., and is sold under the title of 'The Austral'; it is a double-sided record, in appearance identical with the ordinary standard record, but in addition to being unbreakable, it is marketed at the low price of 3/-.

PEMBERTON BILLING AND WORLD RECORD

Another novel type of record manufactured by the Company is 'The Duplex Austral;' this is also unbreakable, but differs from 'The Austral' in that it is 8in. in diameter instead of 10in. By a special process of recording, however, the 'Duplex' contains as much music on its 8in. surface and will play as long as any standard 10in. record. 'The Duplex' record is retailed at 2/6.

The Company has also acquired the Australian rights of 'The World Record', which, although no larger than an ordinary record, contains upon its surface three times as much music as any other. This record is also being manufactured at Brighton.

The factory provides for every process of record manufacture from the grinding of the raw material, which is all Australian product, to the printing of the multi-colored label on the face of the record. Between these two processes many skilled trades are employed: wax mixing, moulding shaving, polishing, the recording of the sound wave upon the wax, graphiting, electro-copper depositing, silver plating, nickel plating, steam and hydraulic pressing. Among the plant employed in the manufacture of the raw materials are steam rolling mills, wet and dry grinders, and vaporising machines.

Everyone employed in this factory has been trained to the work, in preference to importing special workmen...

The factory contains recording studios, which are of great value to the Company, in so much as it enables them, within 24 hours of a melody becoming popular, to record it by the best dance bands. Thus the Company will be enabled to place these records upon the market within as many days as it now takes months to import them from England and America.

Private recording is also carried out, so that at a very reasonable cost, the public may have their voice or playing recorded as a gift to their friends.

A number of retail branches have already been opened in Melbourne and the more important suburbs. A shop will be opened at Geelong on October 1, 1925 and it was proposed to eventually extend branches throughout Australia. [117]

Austral, *Wafer* and *Austral Duplex* records sold poorly, and few have survived, largely due to the porous nature of the cardboard base on which they were pressed. Once they became damp they rapidly fell apart, and although 'unbreakable' they probably had an even lower survival rate than conventional shellac records. Many were discarded as unplayable because the heavy reproducers and steel needles then in use quickly tore through the record grooves into the soft material underneath. In fact, many of these records probably sold simply as a novelty. Another factor which affected the viability of this venture was the limited production capacity at the Brighton factory, which kept the long-term profitability of the company open to question. Added to this was competition from the new electric recording process introduced in the second half of 1925.

After this brief flurry of activity there was no further publicity. The *Austral*, *Wafer* and *Austral Duplex* labels seem to have been discontinued around October 1925 and in their place a conventional 10in. shellac pressing was launched: the *Condor*. This trademark had been registered at the same time as the *Austral* trademark (20 November 1924), but remained unused until this point. The 'indestructible record' so proudly promoted only a few months before was now quickly abandoned.

The last few recordings made locally by World Record were released only on the *Condor* label. These recordings (six more titles by Ray Tellier's San Francisco Orchestra, and the same number of titles by the Hawthorn Salvation Army Citadel Band) were made in October 1925 and probably released in November or December of that year. In the event, the change to conventional records came too late. World Record was almost certainly in dire financial straits.

Towards the end of 1924, Pemberton Billing invited Charles H. Gendle, who had formerly been on the staff of World Record in Britain, to visit Australia. Gendle had joined the Vocalion Gramophone Company in 1924, and may have been involved in that company's brief attempt to use the Pemberton Billing patents after it acquired the British rights in 1924. Pemberton Billing no doubt hoped to gain Charles Gendle's support for Vocalion investment in the Brighton factory: the large reserves and powerful promotional capabilities of the Vocalion Gramophone Company would have transformed World Record's struggling operation. Gendle was apparently impressed by the potential of the Australian record market, but declined to recommend that Vocalion take an interest in the World Record factory; instead Vocalion began construction of their own factory in Richmond exactly a year later.

There are certainly no known World Record releases after 1925, and 3PB did not make any further broadcasts after January 1926. Pemberton Billing left Australia in early 1926 via America where he learnt more about the new electrical recording process which had contributed to the downfall of World Record. However, he did not pursue his interests in the record industry after his return to Britain and turned his energies elsewhere. In 1928 *High Treason*, a play written by him, was performed at the Strand Theatre. He went on to make several unsuccessful attempts to re-enter politics, but was never again active in the record industry.

When Pemberton Billing died on 11 November 1948, his obituary in *The Times* focused almost entirely on his earlier activities in the aviation field:

He was among the earliest Englishmen to realize the potentialities of aircraft. So far back as 1908 he constructed an airfield at Fambridge and designed three aircraft, the last of which flew... He foresaw the vital role that aircraft would play in future wars. From 1914 to 1916 Pemberton Billing did useful service in the R.N.A.S. In 1916 he retired with the rank of squadron commander in order to seek election to Parliament. After a reverse at Mile End he was elected for East Hertfordshire as an Independent. Attacks in a paper published by him on alleged treacherous activities led to his arrest on a charge of criminal libel, but he was acquitted. In 1921 Pemberton Billing resigned his seat for health reasons, and his subsequent attempts to enter Parliament were unsuccessful.

There is no mention of his activities in the record industry and the obituary ends on a negative note: 'His constant and dismal appearances in the Courts had begun to pall, and the public found little to admire in a man so persistently combative.' [150]

In 1927 the World Record factory in Brighton was sold to a group of investors for use as a production facility by the newly-formed Unbreakable Disc Records [see Chapter 9].

Chapter 4

BRUNSWICK

The Brunswick-Balke-Collender Company was established in 1845 in Chicago as a manufacturer of a variety of products including furniture, carriages and bowling balls. In 1916 it entered into an exclusive agreement with the Pathé Frères Phonograph Co. Inc. of New York to distribute their disc records in the United States, in return for an undertaking from Pathé to stay out of the American gramophone market. At the same time it began to produce the first *Brunswick* records which, in accordance with this agreement were sold only in Canada. The agreement lapsed in 1919 and from 1920 *Brunswick* records were marketed in the USA.

Brunswick records first appeared in Australia in 1921 when 'D. Davis & Co. Ltd., of Queen Victoria Buildings, secured the agency'. [132] The Australian agents had been publishers of sheet music since 1885 and by the early 1920s the founder of the company, David Davis, had handed the day-to-day running of the business over to his two sons, Jack and Herbert Davis. In his evidence to the Tariff Board hearings in 1927, Herbert Davis declared:

SOUND BEGINNINGS

Brunswick advertisement, c.1925.

BRUNSWICK

My company was the first factory opened for the manufacture of phonograph records in Australia. We established our plant here [at 30-34 Hutchinson Street, Darlinghurst, Sydney] in July 1924, and commenced operations in September of the same year. We were, however, unable to produce a payable quantity of records before the beginning of the year 1925, on account of us having to train about 100 workmen, who, at the start, knew nothing of the industry, into the technicalities of record manufacturing. [45]

The major record companies were closely monitoring the activities of their competitors, and a letter dated 26 November 1924 from Messrs Hoffnung, Sydney agents for the Gramophone Company, to its London head office includes a paragraph headed 'Brunswick Factory':

We have heard recently that the Brunswick people have been up against some trouble in running their factory having had difficulty in keeping the water at the right temperature, but they have put in a large refrigerating plant which overcame the difficulty. A number of the matrices arrived broken and owing to the inexperience of the people they employ many of them have had to be destroyed and also some of the records are of imperfect production. The principal difficulty they have to contend with as far as we can understand, is that they have inexperienced people; they have only one expert and it is of course impossible for him to look after everything... Notwithstanding this, however, we understand they are gradually getting shipshape and are turning out a large number of records. [23]

The Messrs Hoffnung were a well-established music business in Sydney who had moved into the record business as retailers and agents for overseas companies. A further letter dated 7 January 1925 from the Gramophone Company to a Mr Williams states:

It is satisfactory to learn that there is little likelihood of a duty imposed on records at the present time, and that the Brunswick Company are apparently not... applying for such a duty. We understand from your cable that they are satisfied with their present position which enables them to produce American 'hits' ahead of ourselves and others, they being of the opinion that the imposition of a duty would lead to further local manufacture and so nullify the advantageous position which they now hold... There has recently been a slight check in the volume of our business with Australia and Hoffnung's sales figures for October, which have just reached us, show a very sharp decline on the previous months. This Messrs. Hoffnung ascribe to the influence of radio, but in part to the fact that the Brunswick Company can now give quicker deliveries on popular numbers than we can. [23]

In April 1925 Herbert Davis visited the United States to buy additional machinery for the Brunswick factory. His interview with the American trade journal *Talking Machine World* at the time provides some useful background:

> H. Davis, known to his friends in the trade as 'Bert' Davis, managing director of D. Davis & Co., Ltd., Queen Victoria Buildings, Sydney, New South Wales, Australia, spent several days at the offices of the Brunswick-Balke-Collender Co. during the latter part of April. Mr Davis' organization represents and acts as distributor for Brunswick phonographs, Brunswick radiolas and records on the continent of Australia and in New Zealand. In addition, arrangements have just been completed which will extend the territory to include India, South Africa, Dutch East Indies and the British Straits Settlement. Singapore, the leading port of the Settlement, is a British naval base and at the present time millions of dollars are being expended by the government in enlarging the base and increasing its

facilities. This project should greatly increase the white population and bring about a stimulation of trade in that section.

... Mr Davis stated that the Australians are ardent lovers of music. Popular hits and dance selections seem to be in greatest favor in the Antipodes at the present time, but the fact that music of the better type holds a place of high esteem in the minds of the people of the land is shown by what might be termed national sorrow at the departure of Henry [sic] Verbrugghen, conductor of the New South Wales Conservatorium Orchestra. Mr Verbrugghen had risen to be by far the most popular conductor in Australia and concerts by his orchestra brought forth overflow crowds. He is now conducting the Minneapolis Symphony Orchestra, and while his loss is keenly felt by Australian music lovers, they feel recompensed in some measure by being able to hear selections by the last named organization upon Brunswick records.

D. Davis & Co. received a Brunswick pressing plant in July, 1924, and immediately began operating on a twenty-two-hour-a-day schedule. On March first of this year Mr Davis states that his firm was one quarter of a million records behind on orders, so over-whelming is the demand in his country. He arranged for the shipment of another pressing plant while in Chicago, and with this additional equipment the output will be greatly increased.

D. Davis & Co., Ltd., is one of the oldest music houses in Australia, having been founded by D. Davis, father of the present managing director, forty years ago. The founder is now retired from active business, and acts only in an advisory capacity. The firm is one of the largest of its kind on the continent, maintains several branches, and covers its territory in a very complete manner. [104]

The Darlinghurst factory was duly extended in July 1925 to incorporate the new machinery from America and, as

SOUND BEGINNINGS

there was no serious competition at this stage, *Brunswick* records were selling very well. The British newspaper, the *Daily Guardian*, published an article on 10 July 1926 giving some details of the Brunswick operation:

It is interesting to study the birth of new industries in the Commonwealth: to mark the subsequent growth provides a mass of fact showing the adaptability and enterprise of the Australian type.

Consider the growth of the Brunswick phonograph record business in Sydney...

Looking ahead the management secured the right, when the business was developed sufficiently, to build an Australian factory to make records in Australia. At this factory in Surry Hills 138 Australians pace fast machines every week from 11p.m. Sunday until midnight the following Saturday. Each machine makes a record in 31 seconds. There used to be an expert American staff, but after instructing Australians, the experts were sent home. Australians now carry on.

One of the heads of the firm, Mr J. Davis, is in India in connection with distribution work. From there he will go to the Straits Settlements and Java.

Records are manufactured by the company from plates imported from America. The Brunswick interests would long ago have installed a recording plant were it not for the shortage of first-class world talent in Australia. Australians get the best quality of music on records where, to limit recording to artists in Australia, would limit the selection.

Founders of the record-making industry in Australia, Davis and Co. are planning daily to extend the field of operations. It is another phase of successful business endeavour backed by foresight and Australian workmanship.[132]

As indicated above, *Brunswick* had no recording studio and all the records pressed in Australia were recorded in

America. Most Australian *Brunswick* issues used the same catalogue number as the equivalent American issue; however some pressings were coupled differently from their American equivalents. Regular 10in. popular records were priced at 4/-, and popular 12in. records at 6/-. There were also various special series for classical music that sold from 5/- (and up to 10/- for the 12in. gold-label series).

Not all issues released in the United States were pressed in Australia, however. Such popular artists as Al Jolson, Marion Harris and Nick Lucas were extensively featured; but Brunswick's policy was unusual in also releasing a large number of fine jazz recordings at a time when most locally-available record labels released very little other than the best-selling 'hits' played by conventional dance orchestras. This was probably because *Brunswick*'s management was American-backed; most of the others were subsidiaries of British-owned companies. Some of *Brunswick*'s jazz artists produced best-selling records (like the Mound City Blue Blowers, or Red Nichols and His Five Pennies) but *Brunswick* also released in Australia many recordings by some of the greatest early black jazz artists such as King Oliver, Duke Ellington, Andy Kirk, Clarence Williams, Johnny Dodds, and others almost totally unknown in Australia at that time.

According to contemporary reports, an agreement between D. Davis & Co. and Brunswick-Balke-Collender was finalised on 1 October 1926, and the *Brunswick* trademark was registered in Australia on 19 November 1926. As D. Davis & Co. had been pressing *Brunswick* records since July 1924 the delay is puzzling. Perhaps this agreement gave D. Davis & Co. more direct control of the business.

Production figures for the Australian factory from the time local pressing began in 1924 until mid-1927 [Appendix 2] show that 1926 was the peak year for sales of *Brunswick* records, and figures for the first half of 1927 are much less than half the sales for the previous year. Later sales figures are unavailable, but the paucity of later *Brunswick* records suggests that there was a steep decline in their sales after 1927.

There is little published material on the activities of Brunswick during 1928 and 1929, although an article in the Melbourne *Age* of 3 October 1929 reports that the Davis family's problems were not confined to business:

> The hearing was resumed today of the case in which Herbert Davis and his brother, John Davis, are contesting the will of their father, David Davis Klippel, who died recently, leaving estate valued at £131, 930. The sons allege that when their father made the second and third codicils to his will, tying up their full share in the estate till they had reached the ages of 50 and 48 years respectively, he was not of sound mind and understanding. [192]

The same article mentions that Herbert Davis had started a gramophone factory with his brother at Woolloomooloo. This was a reference to Clifford Industries [see Chapter 12]. A short item in the *Australian Phonograph News* of March 1930 appears to be of a more promotional nature:

> We called the other day at the Brunswick factory, Sydney, and were shown round by Mr H.V. Cohen (the genial manager); things are very busy there and the factory has been working overtime since the first week of January. There are plenty of orders on hand at the present moment, and several records proved an enormous success, such as for instance, those by Sandy Macfarlane. Another tremendously successful number was by Nick Lucas in *The Gold Diggers on Broadway*.* Mr H.V. Cohen comes from a very musical

---

* The record referred to here is actually a coupling of 'Tip-toe Through the Tulips With Me' and 'Painting the Clouds With Sunshine' – both of which were from the stage show *Gold Diggers of Broadway*.

family, his father Rabbi Cohen, being a recognised authority on traditional Hebrew music. Harriet Cohen the talented English pianiste is a cousin, and there are several other members of the family who are distinguished musicians. Mr Cohen has had a wide experience in handling men during the Great War, and at the factory everyone is happy and contented. Mr Cohen is very fond of his work, and takes interest in every phase of it. The factory is run on a very efficient basis, being very compact. The... factory possesses most up-to-date automatic presses, which do not require any shifting of levers. All the operator has to do is to place the 'biscuit,' (out of which the record is made), and the press does the rest. The work of the men consists therefore of putting the labels and the raw material 'biscuit', and within a few seconds the press automatically closes down. In a few seconds later it opens out again when the record is to be taken out...

A more significant development was reported in the *Australian Phonograph News* of May 1930:

Brunswick (Aust.), Ltd., was registered last week, the objects of the company being to purchase, take over, and acquire from D. Davis and Co. Ltd., all the rights and benefits made between the latter and the Brunswick-Balke Company, of America, in 1926. The new Company will carry on the business of manufacturers of records, phonographs and radios under the famous Brunswick trade mark, the products to be sold in Australia and New Zealand. Five directors were appointed: Messrs. Alfred Joseph Morgan, James Alford St Clair Walker, James Murphy, Herbert Davis and Jack Davis. The offices of the Company will be in Hutchinson Street, Sydney, where the factory is situated. Extensive alterations were made during the last few weeks to accommodate the office staff...' [86]

SOUND BEGINNINGS

Brunswick (Australia) Ltd. was registered on 1 May 1930. The directors each held a nominal share; the bulk of the shares (39,997) were held by D. Davis & Co.; Brunswick-Balke-Collender of Chicago, USA, was the only other significant shareholder with 19,996 ordinary shares.

However, the ink was barely dry on the documents setting up the new corporation when the American parent company (Brunswick-Balke-Collender) sold its record division to Warner Brothers Pictures and the American branch of the company became the Brunswick Radio Corporation. An article in the show-business newspaper *Variety* details the ensuing legal action:

> Warner Brothers and its Brunswick subsidiaries and directors have been named by Abeles & Green, attorneys, as defendants in a suit for $2,000,000 brought by D. Davis & Co. Ltd. of Sydney, Australia.
>
> Davis & Co. allege the exclusive right to manufacture and distribute Brunswick records in Australia and New Zealand. A contract between Davis and Brunswick, the attorneys state, was for eight years, starting in 1926. It agreed to pay a royalty to Brunswick over here of 5c. per record, amounting to $100,000 or more yearly.
>
> Abeles & Green charge that prior to Warners taking over Brunswick, in May 1930, they unsuccessfully attempted to gain control of Davis in Australia.
>
> It is charged Brunswick for more than six months stopped shipping matrixes to Davis and it was unable to make and distribute records over there. Later the two sons of D. Davis, deceased, agreed to sell to Brunswick after E.C. De Villaverde, export manager for Brunswick and also named in the suit, promised a profitable share in the new company which would be formed.
>
> Abeles & Green allege that since Warners took over the Davis business, it has earned nothing, whereas previously it

had made $300,000 a year profit. It is also alleged that Davis's contract direct with Brunswick specified that if Brunswick sold Davis would receive as much per share as Brunswick. Davis received nothing from the Warner buy of Brunswick, it is claimed. [101]

It seems evident that during 1930 serious legal and other problems began to plague what had previously been a profitable business.

On 22 January 1931 an application was made by Brunswick (Australia) to register the name *Melotone*. However, Davis's Clifford Industries, who had produced such a label since 1928, had already lodged an application to register it. Brunswick's application was withdrawn about six months later. Without doubt, Brunswick was planning the release of some 'budget priced' discs on the *Melotone* label, as Brunswick in America had been using this label since November 1930. A month later, a report in the *Australian Phonograph News* of April 1931 stated:

> At the end of February, Brunswick (Aust.) Ltd., released a new record on the Australian market, and the name 'Panachord' at once identifies it with that of the world-famous product of Brunswick, the 'Panatrope' [gramophone].
>
> The ever-increasing demand for a low-priced record of high standard has resulted in the production of the Panachord record, which should retail at 2/6...
>
> The Panachord records cannot fail to be at once noticed in a shop, because of the attractive deep royal blue label with gold lettering. The quality is excellent and the surface is quite free from scratch. So far the releases consist of popular dance numbers, vocal duets and songs. Several Sydney metropolitan dealers have expressed themselves as highly satisfied with the records, both in regards to the excellent quality and the sales. [148]

An item in the 'Trade notes' section of the same issue mentions that:

> ... the trade reports considerable interest in the Panachord records, whose high quality has pleased everyone. It will naturally be several months before the records have become very well-known. There is no need to fear a shortage of good titles, for Warner Bros., who acquired Brunswick some time ago, possess unlimited facilities to record all the best titles, and have recently purchased a large factory in England, where operations will commence at once.

At this time Brunswick also produced the third (and last) *Embassy* label which was made specifically for sale by Coles Stores. Production began in early 1931, and its catalogue was made up of selected titles – mainly 'hits' – from the *Panachord* catalogue. *Embassy* issues, however, were issued under pseudonyms to prevent customers discovering that the same recordings already released on the Brunswick budget-priced *Panachord* label could be bought even more cheaply on the Coles label. The price of *Embassy* records was originally 1/11d, but they were later reduced to 1/9d.

Despite the extra business which resulted from sales of the *Panachord* and *Embassy* labels, by September 1931 Brunswick was in serious difficulties. On 7 September 1931, James Murphy, Manager of Brunswick (Australia), wrote to the chairman of the Commonwealth Tariff Board:

> I was present at a meeting of your Board held at the Commonwealth Bank Building, Sydney, on Monday 31st August 1931, in connection with an enquiry being held into the duty on stamping matrices for use in connection with the manufacture of records for gramophones, and I, at that time, indicated that I would be giving evidence on behalf of this Company at a later date.

> For your information I have to advise that an action is now pending in the Equity Court, in which application is being made by D. Davis & Company Limited for the winding up of this Company.
>
> It was hoped that this case would have been settled today, and in that case the writer would have been leaving Sydney this evening, in order to give evidence for the Board on Wednesday next. You will realise, therefore, that it is impossible for me to leave Sydney until this case is disposed of by the Courts, and it is not anticipated that the hearing of same will be completed before Friday of this week... [2]

On 10 October 1931 the *Sydney Morning Herald* reported that the Equity Court had ordered that Brunswick (Australia) be wound up:

> Judgement was given on the petition of D. Davis and Co. Ltd., for an order for the compulsory winding up of Brunswick (Australia) Ltd.
>
> Following the death of David Davis Klippel, managing director of D. Davis and Co. Ltd., which distributed Brunswick records, an agreement was come to between the American company, Brunswick-Balke-Collander Coy. (manufacturers of the records), the executors of Klippel's will, Messrs. B. and J. Davis, and others, for the flotation of a new company to be known as Brunswick (Australia) Ltd., for distribution of Brunswick records. The agreement provided for the rescission of an old agreement and for the settlement of all claims thereunder. The new company was to have a capital of £60,000 in 60,000 £1 shares, half to be ordinary shares and the remainder to be 8 per cent cumulative preference shares, guaranteed both as to dividend and to return of capital by the Brunswick-Balke-Collander Coy. for a period of two years. Of the shares issued, Davis and Co. Ltd., received the 30,000 preference shares and

10,000 ordinary shares, the Brunswick-Balke-Collander Coy. 20,000 ordinary shares. Though Davis and Co. Ltd., held the greater proportion of the capital of the company, the articles of association placed the management of the company under control of the Balke-Collander Coy.

From July, 1930, to June, 1931, the company's losses were £7,033, and the petitioner sought an order for compulsory liquidation on the ground that the company was being carried on at a loss, and that its position as a trading concern was practically hopeless. The company resisted liquidation, mainly on the ground that the Court would not force liquidation where the only matter complained of was that a company was being carried on at a loss; that the petition was presented by shareholders who at a general meeting had the right to determine whether the business should be carried on or not.

His Honor said that there were some peculiar circumstances in the case. One was that a minority of the interests of shareholders had voting power in the company, and control of the directors. Another was the provision that the B.B.C. Coy. had to repay Davis and Co. Ltd., the total amount of preference shares in the event of the company being wound up within two years. In his opinion the problem the Court had to consider was whether the B.B.C. Coy., which controlled the voting, honestly and sincerely believed that there was a reasonable chance of carrying on the business in future, or had it merely used its voting power for the purpose of carrying on a business which it knew to be hopeless, in order that it might escape liability to pay the value of the preference shares in the event of liquidation? Taking into consideration the fact that the domestic forum was controlled by the B.B.C. Coy.; that a large part of the preference capital had practically disappeared; and that the prospects were hopeless, it appeared that the case was one in which it was just and equitable that the company should be wound up so that the shareholders might recover what was left of their capital before the company got into deeper difficulties.

His Honor made the winding up order asked for, operation of the order to be suspended for seven days, and in the event of notice of appeal being filed operation of the order to be stayed until the appeal was disposed of, or the Court otherwise ordered. [219]

In a further letter to the Tariff Board dated 29 October 1931, James Murphy wrote: '... we have to advise that an order has been made for the winding up of this Company by Mr Justice Harvey, in the Equity Court. An appeal has been lodged, which we trust will be heard within the next few weeks. It was on account of this that the writer was unable to attend on the 16th Sept., to give evidence at the adjourned enquiry relative to the duty on stamping matrices.' [2]

It seems that Brunswick may have continued to operate for a short period after the date of the order. There is evidence that the *Panachord* label continued to be released after the *Brunswick* label had been discontinued, but the company was almost certainly out of the record business before the end of 1931. A provisional liquidator was appointed on 5 September 1933, and the company was finally wound up on 10 March 1936; but an order to formally dissolve it was not made until 21 May 1941. Brunswick's parent company in the United States was also sold off to another syndicate, the American Record Corporation, at the end of 1931, although there was no apparent connection between the two events.

So it happened that, the first company to press disc records in Australia was to become one of the most prominent victims of the Depression, and its failure closed another chapter in the early history of the Australian record industry.

SOUND BEGINNINGS

Zonophone supplement cover from 1918.

Chapter 5

HIS MASTER'S VOICE

The Gramophone Company was established in Britain in April 1898 as a branch of Berliner's American Gramophone Company. It was reorganised as the Gramophone Company Ltd. on 23 August 1899. With commendable alacrity, the company decided to establish an Australian branch and Peter H. Bohanna was dispatched to Australia on the *RMS Omrah* in February 1900, with 25,000 recordings and a large quantity of gramophones. On arrival he was faced with a host of unexpected difficulties, including the threat of being quarantined because of a plague outbreak in Sydney; State customs duties; and what he described as 'a Colonial characteristic' of people making promises which they failed to keep. In the event he established an office in Pitt Street, Sydney, and began appointing agents around the country. [225]

It was an uphill battle. January 1901 saw Australia become a federation and the company name changed to the Gramophone & Typewriter Ltd. Bohanna reported that the business was slowly becoming established despite delays caused by the continuing plague, a prolonged drought, slow cash collections (people were 'in the habit of paying in four

SOUND BEGINNINGS

months') and an unusually large number of public holidays, about which he was driven to comment: 'They are demons for holidays here'. [225]

Later in 1901 the first shipment of 500 *Monarch* records, the first 10in. records issued by the Company, arrived and 300 were sold within ten days. These 10in. discs were easier to sell than the 7in. discs previously available, but the biggest problem was a shortage of both discs and machines. The shipment of Lambert typewriters, on the other hand, was not successful. They did not have a conventional keyboard and were twice the price of typewriters directly imported from America. In consequence, the first two years' figures did not meet expectations and brought a peremptory response from the London office. A letter of 20 March 1903 from W.B. Owen proposed that Bohanna:

> ... close up this business within, say, two or three months after you receive this letter, and hand over the agency to Hoffnung or make such other arrangements for the disposition of it as you, in your judgement, think best... It would be better in the end, that you... return here.
>
> From the experience we are having I am very frank to say I think you are selling as many goods as can be sold to four million people – an average of 600 to 800 pounds a month wholesale – but it is certainly enough to make it worth our while to conduct the agency there, as 400 pounds of sales per month, as an average, free of expenses would probably be much better for us than an average of 800 pounds with all the expenses of the agency...
>
> I will, in conclusion, make a very important addition to the letter and say I do not, in any possible way, mean that this letter shall convey to you that you have failed in the doing of everything that it was possible to do in that territory... I am only recognising the fact, which we have learnt from past experience, that 4 millions of people will not buy more than 1000 pounds of gramophones a month,

HIS MASTER'S VOICE (HMV)

at the very outside, and this is hardly good enough to have the burden of the full expenses of an agency. [225]

Bohanna resisted. He believed that the introduction of the 12in. record, the first of which arrived in June 1903, would change their fortunes. A further eighteen months, however, did not persuade his masters, and in a letter dated 3 December 1904 the London office wrote directly to Hoffnung's:

> We have for some time been considering the advisability of closing some of our colonial branches, and continuing to do the trade through the Home Shippers; our object in sending our own representatives to establish our trade on a firm basis has been attained and a healthy demand has been created for our goods at a very great cost to ourselves.
>
> We consider it good policy in remote territories to withdraw our capital so far as possible, and to place the conduct of our business in other and capable hands on the basis of a remunerative contract. We think if you seriously entertain the matter a very simple contract will meet the case. We would suggest for instance that you take over our stock in Australia at a reasonable and fair valuation, that our book debts be placed in your hands for collection against payment of a percentage on the amounts to be collected, that we hand over to you the entire good-will of our Australian and New Zealand business without consideration, and that we enter into a contract with your good-selves for a period of years based on the minimum turnover per annum.
>
> The most vital question is that of price, and we would suggest that the ruling London retail prices be made the basis of the contract, subject to a liberal discount, which would enable you to do a very profitable business. We would turn over to you all enquiries from Australia, and we should be happy at all times to give you any information which might be of assistance to you in the development of the

Australian business, and we believe with the large organisation at your command you should be able to expand the business to far greater extent than we ourselves can afford to in a large territory like Australia. We are compelled to work from one centre, and we have not the facility for reaching out-lying territory which you possess.

We feel sure that the arrangement would be a mutually advantageous one, and that whatever sacrifice we may be prepared to make in regard to profit will be more than recompensated by the increased trade which you will be in a position to do. [225]

Hoffnung immediately acquired the existing stocks of 88,500 records held by Bohanna (although about 50,000 of these were described as 'obsolete') and Hoffnung impressed on the London office the need to fulfil orders promptly. They also recommended that Gramophone & Typewriter make more records suitable for the Australian market, such as comic songs by the music-hall artists Gus Elen, Harry Lauder, G.H. Snazelle, and Harry Tait; Gregorian chants (about one third of the Australian population was Catholic) and, interestingly, some Chinese records.

Once Hoffnung had taken over as local agents, Peter Bohanna withdrew. It is thought that he returned to London. There is little further mention of him in company correspondence, but a letter of 8 November 1906 refers to 'the late Mr Bohanna'.

In June 1903 Gramophone & Typewriter acquired the business of one of their competitors, the International Zonophone Co. and they continued the label as a lower-priced subsidiary. When double-sided records were introduced in October 1908, the label was re-named the *Twin*. In June 1911 the *Twin* name was dropped, and the records were once again released under the *Zonophone* label.

At this time a separate corporate entity was created as the British Zonophone Co. Ltd., and the legal fiction of no connection with the parent company was maintained from this point onward. All the various incarnations of Zonophone were available in Australia as imported products up until the 1920s. In 1912 a special 3000 export series was introduced, and the majority of the releases in this series were made specifically for Australian release. The series included a wide variety of popular and standard repertoire, amongst which were one of the earliest recordings of 'Advance, Australia Fair' (1915), 'Boys of the Dardanelles' and other patriotic songs of World War I and a number of selections by Australian composers. One unusual variation from the practice in Britain, where *Zonophone* was sold at 2/6, was that in Australia and New Zealand these records sold for the same price as issues on *His Master's Voice* label, namely 4/- for 10in. records. There was also a Celebrity series of *Zonophone* records which sold for 5/- while 12in. *Zonophone* records were 6/-.

Despite strong competition from *Columbia*, and from cylinders produced by the British Sterling Company, the Gramophone & Typewriter Co.'s business seems to have gone well under Hoffnung's management. The typewriter side of the business had long been abandoned, but the name of the Gramophone & Typewriter Co. was not officially dropped until 18 November 1907 when the original name of the Gramophone Co. Ltd. was restored.

However, by July 1908 the sales situation in Australia was less than happy and the London office wrote expressing concern that sales for the year just ended had dropped by a third from the previous year. The letter continued: 'We are very much afraid that this retrograde movement may continue. This we should be very sorry to see. All we ask you is to join us in measures for the protection of your interests.' [225]

A short time later it was decided to send Mr Sheard, manager of the Gramophone Company's Overseas Department, to Australia to assess the situation. On his return to London, Sheard produced a 21-page report (dated 15 June 1909). He recommended that much larger stocks of records be carried by Hoffnung, that better use be made of catalogues and press advertisements, and that additional attention should be paid to the more remote regions such as Tasmania and New Zealand.

After these changes had been implemented, it was agreed that Hoffnung would continue to represent the Gramophone Co. This arrangement continued until 1922 without any significant attempt to review the situation. On 23 October 1922 the London office prepared a report in relation to the current contract with Messrs Hoffnung & Co., due to expire on 25 April 1924. This concluded:

> ... in considering whether a Branch in Australia should be established, or whether another agreement should be entered into with Messrs. Hoffnung, a study of the figures seems to show that the prudent course would be to avoid the risk that would be run in establishing a Branch of The Gramophone Company so far from Headquarters and where so little control could be exercised. Everything would depend on the man selected as Manager; a mistake in this respect would have dire results and lead to a set back that might take years to make good.
>
> Though the figures put forward are not unfavourable to the establishment of such a Branch, they presuppose that the Branch would immediately step in and occupy the position created by Messrs. Hoffnung and take over their organisation. There is no certainty that such would be the case. The possibility of Messrs. Hoffnung taking up another line, active opposition to us with their present organisation would have to be faced. In such a case the profits now

HIS MASTER'S VOICE (HMV)

estimated for would be largely curtailed, or perhaps be non-existent, for some time. Would not the Brunswick Company, or Columbia, jump at the chance of securing Messrs. Hoffning's co-operation in the Australian trade?

In considering the Australian problem the present protectionist policy of the Australian Government should not be overlooked. Did they place a higher tariff on records, as it is understood they would be willing to do if any company were prepared to put down a plant which would give employment to a sufficient quantity of labour, the opening of not only a Branch but a factory would be forced upon us so that if the final solution of the problem as it exists today is continued co-operation with Messrs. Hoffnung the contract would have to provide in some way for such a contingency arising; that is to say, that we should not bind ourselves for a long period without taking powers to get out on adequate notice. [22]

The general manager, James Muir, however, was not letting the grass grow. His cable to the board on 23 April 1923, the day before the deadline to extend the Hoffnung contract on the existing terms, read:

IMPERATIVE SEVER NEW ZEALAND FROM HOFFNUNGS APRIL 1924 EARLIER IF POSSIBLE RECOMMEND CREATION AGENCY FAVOUR HYAMS RECOMMEND PROLONGATION HOFFNUNGS AGREEMENT EXCLUDING NEW ZEALAND APRIL 1925 OR SUCH SHORTER TIME AS NECESSARY FOR FORMATION AUSTRALIAN COMPANY... [23]

A sales committee document dated 4 September 1923 states:

It appears from the knowledge that Mr Muir has gained that Messrs. Hoffnung have not been in the habit of keeping sufficient stock of records to meet the full demand, and that the advertising of the company's products has been insufficient and defective in Australia and non-existent in New Zealand.

... it was apparent from the present position that we ought not to continue to leave our interests in this part of the world wholly in Hoffnung's hands as the importance of the trade is very great and likely to become still more important as the years go on.

For these reasons it was therefore decided to recommend to the Executive Committee that the present contract with Messrs. Hoffnung's, which expires in April 1924, should not be renewed, and to recommend to the Finance Committee that the question of forming a company, to which Messrs. Hoffnung's would be invited to subscribe capital... be considered.

The question of the erection of a pressing plant with machine erecting shop and possibly a cabinet factory was carefully considered.

Though the business might be continued for some years by import of records, as now, from England and possibly facilitated by importing direct from America the American numbers now pressed in this country, the [Sales] Committee were of the opinion that the provision of a factory would ultimately become necessary and might be forced upon us at any time were a move made in this direction by a competitor, and that the company should undertake the supply of such manufacturing facilities now and not wait until action were forced upon [us]. It was pointed out... that the sales of records in two or three years would no doubt reach 1,200,00 per annum, and that with the starting point of an Australian pressing industry it was expected the Commonwealth Government would give tariff protection.

... it was therefore decided to recommend to the Executive Committee that it was advisable to erect a pressing and machine assembling plant in Australia to begin with... [22]

Accordingly, at a meeting on 6 September 1923 the executive committee decided to form two new companies:

(a) One for Australia, the object of which would be to carry on the selling agency now held by Messrs. Hoffnung and to erect and equip a record factory with accommodation for the assembly of machines. The latter portion of the building to be constructed with a view to the manufacture of mechanism parts, should this become advisable. The capital of this company to be fixed at £200,000 with 200,000 ordinary shares of £1 each, 25% of such shares to be taken up [by] Messrs. Hoffnung and the remainder to be held by the Gramophone Company Limited.

(b) One for New Zealand, the object of which would be to carry on the sub-agency now held by Mr E.J. Hyams from Messrs. Hoffnung and Co. Ltd., and carried on under the title of The Gramo-phonium Company Ltd. The capital of this company to be fixed at £25,000 ordinary shares at £1 each, 25% of such shares to be taken up by Mr E.J. Hyams, the remainder to be held by the new Australian company. The necessary capital of the New Zealand company to be provided for by the proposed Australian company.

[It was also decided] that land be acquired in Australia to the extent of about six acres for the purpose of building a record and machine assembly factory and the possible accommodation at a later date of a cabinet factory, saw mill and timber yard [and] that a record factory be erected in Australia and equipped on the land mentioned... with the necessary plant for a capacity of 100,000 records per month. [22]

Hoffnung declined to accept the offer to subscribe 25% of the shares in the new company, and suggested instead that they would continue to act as sole distributors in Australia.

SOUND BEGINNINGS

This was apparently agreed to, as there is no further mention of Hoffnung providing capital for the company; but they continued to act as sole distributors.

A further report dated 30 April 1924 gave details of the proposed factory with 'provision now for an output of 150,000 records monthly' and suggested that:

> ... the most urgent need at the present time is that a representative of The Gramophone Company should proceed to Australia as soon as possible for the following purposes:
>
> (a) Ascertain definitely whether the proposed factory should be erected in the vicinity of Sydney or that of Melbourne,
> (b) Select a suitable site providing sufficient land to cover the building scheme with ample area for extension, due regard being paid to factory requirements for water, light and power, and with access by rail to the ports of Melbourne or Sydney,
> (c) Select and instruct an architect to prepare drawings, specifications and bills of quantities for buildings, and obtain competitive prices,
> (d) Ascertain what class of machinery and equipment can be purchased in Australia,
> (e) Approach the Customs Authorities with a view to obtaining free entry of specialised machinery from this country and America on the ground of their being required for the establishment of a new Australian industry,
> (f) Investigate the possibility of obtaining suitable raw materials in Australia and see the Customs Authorities as to the possibility of importing raw materials not obtainable in Australia free of duty,
> (g) Report by cable to Hayes [London Head Office] on above points and subject to their approval.

HIS MASTER'S VOICE (HMV)

... Mr Lockley, who has been selected for the position of Factory Manager, should reach Australia when the building contract is placed and be in constant touch with the progress of the building, receive and install the plant, and make arrangements for labour and the staff necessary for running the factory... When the factory is nearing completion the additional staff, to be sent from Hayes, consisting of one Matrix man, one Mixer, 2/3 Foremen Presshands, should be sent out. These employees should be ear-marked for these duties as soon as possible.

... With the completion of the factory it will be necessary to have a Commercial Manager to act as a link between it and Messrs. Hoffnung and Messrs. E.J. Hyams Ltd., and watch our interest generally, and who would take over the duties which devolve upon a Branch Manager, that is advertising, printing and the issue of Monthly Supplements, and the provision of catalogues, duties which are at the present time handled by Messrs. Hoffnung and Messrs. Hyams. [22]

An undated memo from around this time headed 'Approximate estimate for proposed Australian factory' showed progress was being made:

As the price of factory sites in Australia has been quoted at the low figure of £200 an acre, it is recommended that consideration be given to the purchase of an area of 7 acres, which would be sufficient to meet our needs...

Estimated cost of land, 7 acres @£200 = £1,400.
Record factory with... an output of 100,000 records monthly: £71,770
Record factory with... an output of 150,000 records monthly: £87,000
Cabinet finishing & erecting. Output 9,000 machines per annum: £23,225
Branch offices (provisional): £3,100

The above estimates may require revision when the actual site is fixed, and the local conditions have been investigated... There is an amount of approximately £4,000 included to cover import duty on machinery, but it may be possible to obtain a concession on this. As information has been given that electricity supply is cheap, no generating plant has been included... [22]

A sales committee report of 13 May 1924 debated the comparative benefits of manufacture versus importation:

It has been suggested that the building of a factory might be deferred and the imposition of a duty met by raising retail prices to the level of those current in New Zealand, where our records pay an import duty of 20% and 1% on the Home Consumption value plus 10%. This would be of no avail, however, in meeting the competition of a Brunswick factory in Australia. At the present time three-fourths of our trade is done in American titles pressed from Victor shells at Hayes. It is this trade that the Brunswick Company are out to capture, and they will capture it by service alone and irrespective of price and even of a duty if they can deliver records pressed in Sydney 5 to 6 weeks before we can deliver those made at Hayes. On a careful review of the position the Committee decided... that the situation is critical, and the resulting loss of a profit which... would result from the installation of an Australian factory will have to be faced if we are to maintain our Australian trade. [22]

Brunswick's rising position in the market place was stimulating the company to push forward:

The Managing Director reported that a competing company [Brunswick] had now installed a record factory in Australia, that there was every prospect that the Australian government would grab a protective tariff on records, and that, in his

HIS MASTER'S VOICE (HMV)

opinion, it was desirable we should proceed to erect a record factory in Australia capable of turning out at least 150,000 records per month. He submitted estimates showing that for an expenditure of approx. £160,000 a record factory of this capacity could be erected and installed together with a cabinet finishing factory and sufficient land secured for future extensions if necessary... After careful discussion the Board resolved that... the Chairman be granted six months leave of absence and authorised to proceed at the company's expense to Australia with full powers to act at his discretion and make all the preliminary arrangements for a factory in Australia and to purchase a site or suitable factory buildings. [22]

Three months later:

... the Chairman had found a factory building in Sydney within 15 minutes of the centre of the city, containing an area of 40,000 square feet on two storeys, and admirably suited for a record factory of fifty presses and complete mixing plant. Alterations required [were] estimated to cost £2,000 and that he had made an offer of £17,500 and hoped to secure [the property] for £18,000. [22]

The following month, on 26 March 1925, a letter from the London head office announced that 'as already intimated, we are furnishing 24 10in. & 12 12in. semi-automatic presses. The body parts of these presses will be shipped direct to Sydney from Victor Talking Machine Company, Camden, N.J., U.S.A. The balance of the presses, with exception of stands and counterweights, will be sent from Hayes.' [23]

Work on the new factory was progressing rapidly and a memo of 28 May 1925 instructed the manager, A.E. Lockley:

... as explained to you, our Chairman, Mr Trevor Williams, when in Australia, engaged the services of Messrs. Fyvie &

SOUND BEGINNINGS

Stewart with regard to advice in connection with the Sydney factory. With regard to any matters arising on the building, you may consult [them] on the same lines as you would an architect. You will also, no doubt, find their knowledge of Australian conditions very helpful... [23]

Less than a month later, Circular No.180 from the London office advised:

We desire to inform the trade that, in order to cope with the company's large and increasing business in Australia and New Zealand, we began some months ago the erection of a factory to supply that territory. It is now nearing completion, and this has necessitated us sending out a member of our Executive Committee, Mr William Manson, who... has lived in both Australia and New Zealand, and has seemed to us particularly fitted for this work. He has consented to go there, and consequently will relinquish the management of our English Sales Department at the end of this month. [23]

The *Australasian Phonograph Monthly* gave some background on the new general manager:

Mr William Manson, who until quite recently was manager of His Master's Voice English Branch, and is now general manager of the new Australian and New Zealand Branch, arrived recently in Sydney. Mr Manson has been connected with the talking machine industry almost since its inception, for, prior to joining His Master's Voice Company some eighteen years ago, he was connected with the cylinder industry, which was later displaced by disc records. A cultured man with the charm and manners of the perfect English gentleman, Mr Manson, who is particularly interested in the gramophone's educational development, is responsible for many important policies of His Master's Voice Company, such as the introduction of the double-sided

HIS MASTER'S VOICE (HMV)

disc, the formation of the Virtuoso String Quartette, the first recording of complete instrumental works, and many others. It was also he who carried out the negotiations for the King and the Queen to make the famous 'Empire Day' record, and more recently still the Prince of Wales record.

In England [said Mr Manson] the gramophone is playing a very important part in education and thousands of schools have instruments, and we are the only people who have devised a school model at a moderate price... I have been connected with His Master's Voice Company for eighteen years, prior to which I visited both Australia and New Zealand, so I do not feel like a 'new chum'. During that period the development has been simply marvellous. I well remember the astonishment of the late Hon. W.F. Massey, Premier of New Zealand, to whom I showed His Master's Voice huge factories at Hayes, at the sight of thousands of employees flocking out of the buildings at lunch time. He could hardly credit the development which had taken place in an industry only 25 years old.

'Hayes [Middlesex], where we employ between four and five thousand people, is the great centre from which have sprung several factories in various parts of the world, the youngest of which will be in Sydney. We have been induced to build our factory owing to the increased demand for records, so that we shall be able to cater satisfactorily for the Australian public and supply records at or about the same time as in England or America. That is our principal object, and the business will be exclusively confined at first to making records.

'I had the honour of superintending the recording of their Majesties the King and Queen, the result of which was that charities benefited by many thousands of pounds. After the recording session I asked the King whether he would like to hear some records. "Yes, certainly," he answered with great interest. "Where are they?" I informed

SOUND BEGINNINGS

His Majesty that I had a machine in an adjoining room. At the King's request to hear one of Caruso's records, I put on Handel's *Largo*, which made a great impression. "Why, this is marvellous!" exclaimed the King, "is it the artist himself singing?" As the Queen expressed a desire to hear Melba, I put on her record of *Lo, the gentle lark* [sic]. Since then instruments have been installed in the Royal Palaces, and the Prince of Wales and his brothers are also His Master's Voice enthusiasts...

'During my long association with His Master's Voice I have met most of the great artists of the day, many of whom I have known intimately for many years. Chaliapine is one of the most interesting men to talk to and a supreme artist. The Australians will have one of the greatest of treats when they hear his wonderful singing...' [218]

But on 20 July 1925 Lockley notified head office:

It is essential that before commencing operations we should be registered as a foreign company doing business in Australia. Messrs. Minter Simpson & Co. have gone as far as they can in this matter. The Registrar must be supplied with true copies of the memorandum, Articles of Association and latest Balance Sheet. I hope you will have... forwarded immediately these documents as at the present time I am taking a certain amount of risk in carrying on business without proper registration. [23]

The August 1925 issue of the British trade journal the *Sound Wave* carried an item headlined: 'His Master's Voice factory for Australia: Mr William Manson to develop Antipodes', which seems to have been based on Circular No. 180, but also added that 'Mr Manson will be accompanied by Mrs Manson, known to the concert public in two hemispheres, who, to the regret of her many friends, has now retired from the concert world. Under her professional name, Miss

Mabel Manson, she enjoys a wide reputation as an accomplished soprano, and her numerous admirers in the Antipodes, of which she is a native, will be delighted to see her again.' [122] An article in the *Talking Machine and Wireless Trade News* the following month adds that Mr William Manson 'sails from Liverpool... on the 19th inst.' and that he will not go directly to Australia, 'but will spend three weeks in America first'. The same item also specifies that 'Mrs Manson is a native of New Zealand.'

The social superiority of the Mansons was clearly becoming a concern to Lockley. On 4 November 1925 he wrote once more to head office:

> Referring to your letter notifying me of the approaching arrival of Mr Manson and asking me to prepare for his accommodation, I would say that his accommodation has been booked for him at his request at the Wentworth Hotel, and included in his suite is a sitting room. I think it extremely unlikely that Mr Manson will want to stay at the factory. It is exceedingly inconvenient for anyone having to spend much time in Sydney, and I do not think Mr Manson would be satisfied with any accommodation that could possibly be arranged for him. Should he desire it, however, the general office is as yet untenanted, and he will be able to make use of this pending other arrangements being made.
>
> I received a visit yesterday from Mr Davis and his associates of the Brunswick Company. These people are getting rather nervous on the labour question, as all their workers have decided to leave them and work for H.M.V. Most of them have in fact applied here for jobs. We are agreeing reciprocally not to engage one another's employees except in certain special circumstances. Mr Davis was hoping that we could come to an agreement with regard to rates of wages, but that is a question which requires much consideration. He also broached the subject of a trading agreement with a view to eliminating certain competitors.

SOUND BEGINNINGS

This, however, being a question beyond my ambit, I have asked him to leave the matter over until a later date, to be considered by Mr Manson. [23]

Matters were proceeding apace. Lockley wrote again on 15 December 1925:

There are today 16 presses all complete and ready for production. We have tried these out today with scrap matrices, and everything appears to be in good order for normal running. The remainder of the presses are being completed, but I am giving priority to the completion of other departments.

The edge grinding machines are ready for running, with the exception of the final connecting up of motors. The tables for cleaning and inspection are installed; the audition boxes are completed with the exception of painting. The refrigerator plant has been given a trial run today.

We have experienced some little difficulty with the Municipal Electric Light inspectors' by-laws with regard to wiring, and controls are somewhat antiquated and very cumbersome. The inspectors wanted fuses and switches put in every case in addition to our Ellison starters, and there were several other requirements of a similar nature. The authorities insist on inspecting all the internal wiring and gear before they will allow current to be put on. We have now got over most of these difficulties, and I do not anticipate any further hindrances to the completion of our electrical installation.

The hydraulic pump and the press-cooling pumps seem to be quite satisfactory. Some difficulty was experienced in making the correct adjustments to get the contactor panel working properly for the hydraulic pump, but that is now all right.

The box making plant is running satisfactorily, and we have during this week created a sufficient stock of boxes for present needs.

HIS MASTER'S VOICE (HMV)

The roof over the yard will be completed before the end of this week, and the shipping platform is being erected today.

In the Matrix Department the gas is now laid on, and we are making the final connections to the various motors in order to have the cleaning machines and the various lathes running by Thursday of this week.

We have not yet received all the goods from the 'Euripides'; you will recollect that there was some essential material on this boat required for the matrix plant. The cathode clip supports and anode supports are on the 'Chitral', which is due to arrive here at the end of this week. With this shipment to hand the matrix plant should be complete. There still remain various water connections to be made. This is rather a long job, and has been awaiting the completion of the gas fitting. In connection with plumbing, it will be of interest to you to know that it is illegal for anyone other than a licensed plumber to make any connections, extensions, etc. to the water supply. The same thing applies to the gas. I consider that we have about a good week's work before the whole of this Department will be in working order. We still have the shells to unpack and put in order, and the index for some to be written out. At the present time we are writing out the card index for matrices and putting the matrices in their racks; also the card index for label stocks. These are very big jobs, but until they are completed we are not in a position to give any definite information to our distributors as to what and when we can supply. I note that the matrices received from the Victor Company are not ready for use, as they have to be stepped down and the centres recessed.

No decision has yet been made by the Tariff Board regarding labels or record bags. I have paid a deposit on these and am having them withdrawn from bond. [23]

SOUND BEGINNINGS

Everything seems to have gone according to plan, and the official opening of the Gramophone Company's factory at Erskineville was held on 18 January 1926. The speech by J.T. Lang, nationalistic Labor Premier of New South Wales, gives a characteristic insight into the climate of the times:

> Gentlemen – I have been asked by the Management just to say a word or two on the occasion of the opening of another factory for the manufacturing of Australian goods in this country of ours. I want to say quite frankly to you, friends, that it gives me very, very much more pleasure to be here, opening a factory in this our country for the manufacture of our own goods, than to be elsewhere, as many of you think I would like to be, engaged in political business. I can see smiles on the faces around me, and I want to say that it is true, and that all that I strive to do, and all that the Government strives to do, to develop the resources of this country is given very little prominence in the newspapers, while any little political wrangle is given a great deal of prominence, and from this it is natural for people to conclude that we are mostly engaged in political wrangles. This is not so. Nevertheless, party feeling is running very high at the present time; never has it run so high, and I believe that during the next 12 months or so it will run very much higher; after that, I hope, our enemies will be worn down, they will be tired out, and will give us a chance to settle down, to shew what we are doing for this State of New South Wales.
>
> I am not going to say any more about politics than that. I hope our friends of the press are not going to be disappointed. They generally are disappointed when I talk, but I am not going to give a bad example of myself by talking party politics.
>
> The present Government of this State stands solidly, stands steadily, stands earnestly, for local industry. I said so

often upon public platforms before I was elected, and I have acted upon those lines ever since. There is no protection which we could give to help local industry which we do not give; there is no encouragement which we could give to start Australian industries which we do not give; there is not a penny piece of public money sent out of the State unless we have a written certificate from our officials that the article required cannot be manufactured in Australia. There are many thousands of pounds that would have left Australia and New South Wales for other markets if the Government had not kept a tight hand in that respect. And I have adopted this course simply because I realise – because it is my conviction and I firmly believe it – that you can never build up a nation if that nation is going to rely upon the importation of foreign goods

All of our people throughout the State are not of the same way of thinking. A lot of people imagine that Australia is a country of primary products. It is largely, but it is not solely so. If you relied upon primary products alone, you would not find markets for our goods. We want local markets that will take all our primary products and make it possible for men to live upon the land in a state of comfort and decency. So I feel that we should all help our primary producers by endeavouring to turn our raw products into the finished article, for our own use. The finished articles that we are going to use ourselves at least ought to be manufactured in our country by our own people; and that is the first step, which will do more to help the man on the land, the primary producer, than all our talk of finding markets overseas...

Just at this moment I believe our orchardists are bewailing the fact that they produce the finest fruit in the world and have to leave it rotting upon the ground because if they sent it to the local markets they would not get enough to pay the freight. On the other hand, there are men, women and children in this great metropolis of ours, hungering for fruit. It is the local market that wants developing, wants looking into, to see why the man who wants the fruit cannot get it, while the man who grows it sees it rotting. This is the kind of thing that wants watching, and the Government are watching it, and intend to remedy it.

Turn your attention for a moment to the astounding strides that have been made in the manufacturing industry of New South Wales. Some people would have led you to believe that because my own or my Government's ideas about how this country should be run do not agree with theirs, then the country must perish. But we have heard that before, and the country has not perished. As a matter of fact, in 1915 the output of our manufactories in New South Wales was about £68,000,000, while in the last official year – 1924 – the value of that output was £146,395,260. There you are; in round simple figures, from the year 1915 to 1924 – exactly ten years – the value of our productions has increased one hundred per cent. They have doubled – and there is nothing to fear in this country of ours.

Our people are today, I think, more contented, more prosperous, perhaps not as well paid as people in some other parts of the world, but taking them as we find them here, for the last ten years their conditions have gradually improved. Their hours of work have been made shorter, their conditions of employment more congenial, their wages are gradually rising, and the things that they buy, the clothes that they wear, their home surroundings, are one hundred per cent better than they were ten years ago. The people have benefited, and the manufacturers have not suffered. That steady progress, friends, I feel will go on, so that in the next ten years the improvement in the people's condition will have increased by more than 100 per cent, and the prosperity of the manufacturers the same.

Remember, friends, what has been told to you here this afternoon. You went around with the Management, and you

HIS MASTER'S VOICE (HMV)

know that one of their chief prides and boasts was of the beautiful surroundings they have endeavoured to obtain for their employees. They have tried to make the conditions of work as healthy and congenial as possible, because they know it will improve the health of their employees, and result in better work turned out for the employer.

You have seen how production increased from 1915 to 1924. During the same period the number of factories in New South Wales increased from 5,269 to 7,321. When you read that, I hope you will not let the newspapers or their employers mislead you into thinking that this country is going to fade right away. You will have seen a statement in the press today that a certain lolly-shop was going to close and the work was going to Victoria. That may be so. There may be reasons behind the amalgamation that make it more economical to work in one centre of Australia rather than another; but this is completely counterbalanced by the opening of these works for the manufacture of 'His Master's Voice' records this afternoon.

I find on looking up the number of employees in this State that they increased from 116,611 in 1915 to 159,674 in 1924; and if you turn from the number of employees and value of manufactures and look at the salaries and wages that were paid to the office staff and employees generally in our manufactories, you will find that salaries and wages increased from £12,627,200 to £29,722,999. There again is an enormous increase in the production of wealth, in manufactories, in the prosperity of the manufacturers themselves and of their employees, so that everywhere you go you see the same thing – advance, progress and prosperity in this State of ours.

I want to thank the Management for the opportunity and the pleasure it has afforded me to be here this afternoon. The works opened here will be finding employment for a large number of people. Both the gramophone and wireless have practically revolutionised society today. It is another

SOUND BEGINNINGS

step forward. Whether they are used educationally or for amusement there is no doubt whatever that all men recognise we have made wonderful strides.

The high standard of efficiency and the integrity of our people, as well as the way they have adapted themselves to surrounding circumstances, and their eagerness to take advantage of all scientific developments, have made our people what they are today. Because of their efficiency, we can say that the Australian-made article today has got no superior, right throughout the length and breadth of the world; and I am proud to be here, because you must remember that although voices will be recorded in other parts of the world, the works will be brought out here and the Australian artisan will manufacture records from them.

I thank the Management most heartily, and I do hope that when the records are on the market of this country of ours, they will reap the reward of their enterprise. I wish them all sorts of prosperity and success, and I hope that in 12 months they will not only have turned out their ten or twelve million of records, but will actually have doubled that number, and have set out on the high road to success. [30]

Immediately after the ceremony Manson sent the following cablegram to Hayes:

HIS MASTERS VOICE AUSTRALIAN FACTORY OFFICIALLY OPENED AT SYDNEY TODAY BY PREMIER OF NEW SOUTH WALES RIGHT HONORABLE J.T. LANG Stop REPRESENTATIVE GATHERING INCLUDING LORD MAYOR OF SYDNEY AND SIR MARK SHELDON Stop FIRST RECORDS PRESSED WERE THOSE OF THEIR MAJESTIES THE KING AND QUEEN AND H.R.H. THE PRINCE OF WALES MANSON. [23]

HIS MASTER'S VOICE (HMV)

The following day Manson wrote a more detailed account, giving the background to Premier Lang's comments:

> I have to report that the official opening of our Australian factory took place yesterday, and proved to be a highly successful function in every particular. Fortunately the matrices of the Royal records arrived a few days before the ceremony, and we were thus able to get the greatest possible publicity out of them. Everyone congratulated me on having been successful in getting the Premier of New South Wales to preside. He is a very difficult man to get hold of, and I have not been able to trace his attendance at any similar function. His presence also ensured that of quite a large number of Sydney pressmen. The majority of them are not at all fond of Mr Lang's politics, but he is so much in the limelight at present that they are very glad of any opportunity of reporting him. The only thing I have been afraid of is as to whether in reporting Mr Lang fully they would rather smother our interests.
>
> When Mr Lang accepted my invitation he set the hour of 3 for the ceremony, but later on his Secretary told me that as he would have to attend a very important meeting at 3 our ceremony would have to take place at 2.30. The guests for the most part arrived very punctually, and were conducted to the General Office, which is our largest room on this floor. I hired a number of chairs for the occasion, and a caterer attended to supply refreshments. While we were awaiting the arrival of the Premier I had a number of records played so as to keep our guests from feeling impatient. Although Mr Lang has the reputation of being always punctual, on this occasion he was 25 minutes late, and I felt very worried. However, Sir Mark Sheldon had arrived, and in the event of the Premier not coming I would have got Sir Mark to preside. In order that the visitors might learn as many interesting particulars as possible in their tour

of the factory, I had arranged for six guides and divided the guests up into small parties in charge of these guides. We had previously gone all around the factory, and our men were supplied with typed particulars, so that they could all tell the same tale to the visitors. This proved very satisfactory, and the various groups found their way back to the General Office very soon after the Premier got there.

The proceedings commenced by the Premier proposing the toast of 'His Majesty the King'. He then followed with a speech, which unfortunately was more of a political nature than one containing facts suitable for the occasion. I had supplied the Premier's Secretary with quite a lot of material which I hoped he would make use of, and I asked the Secretary if he would endeavour to get copies of Mr Lang's speech so that I could distribute them among the reporters who were present. Unfortunately, however, this was not done, but Miss Norman took a full report, which I will endeavour to enclose with this letter, together with a copy of a few words I said in reply...

You will be interested to hear that through the courtesy of Broadcasters (Sydney) Ltd. the proceedings were broadcasted.

Every guest was presented with copies of the Royal records, and I am sending others to the Governor-General of Australia, the Governors of the various States, the Governor of New Zealand, the Premiers and principal Ministers, and the editors of all the leading papers throughout Australasia. I am hoping by this means to get a lot of very useful publicity, and I have asked our jobbers to look out keenly for any notices that may appear.

... Matters in connection with production in the factory are gradually getting into a satisfactory state, but where practically every member of the staff is new to the work it will be quite some time before we can rely upon getting an adequate output. We hope to make our first delivery to

Hoffnungs this week. I have given them an estimate which was furnished by Mr Lockley as to the number of records we hope to be in a position to deliver during the months of January, February and March; and I have asked Hoffnungs to furnish me with estimates of the number of records which they anticipate they will require in that period.

We have to meet very great difficulties in the transition period, and I have been desirous that no trade should be lost owing to either Hoffnungs or Hyams being short of stock through depending too much on our new factory. This cautiousness may cause their orders to be somewhat small at first, but in the course of a few months I hope that we shall be able to take care of all their requirements... [23]

The running of the factory seems to have quickly settled down into a routine, and there is little significant correspondence until 23 September 1926 when William Manson wrote to one Alfred Clark, c/o Victor Talking Machine Co., Camden [USA]. The letter is marked 'PERSONAL', which explains his unusual directness:

I specially want to write to you on the copyright question. In England, the music publishers have for the most part been friendly to the Company, and it has been comparatively easy to work with them, but in Australia they are all out to try and fleece us if they can, and if they find we are not ready to give in to them on all points, they are likely to make things as difficult as they can.

I gather from conversations I have had with them, that American publishers have found their sales of sheet music growing smaller, while mechanical royalties have provided them with sums which have more than compensated for the shrinkage in their sheet music sales. The publishers here depend mainly on America for 'hits', and they work together so as to get the greatest possible results from their mechanical and performing rights.

As a result of negotiations which took place some little time ago with Allans, who, by the way, are very well-known to me personally, and have been comparatively well-disposed, I succeeded in getting them to permit us to print facsimile stamps on records of compositions which they control. A letter I have received today informs me that after November, this concession will be withdrawn. Albert was willing to give us this privilege if we were prepared to pay him even money instead of the fraction, which, according to the Act, the owner of the copyright is legally entitled to (eg. 2¼ d instead of 2⅛ d).* If we had agreed to this, the publishers in England would have been sure to put forward a similar claim, which, if acceded to, would cost the Company a very considerable sum annually. Albert has just returned from America, and I believe it is owing to his influence that Allans have withdrawn the permission they gave us.

It occurs to me that it should be possible for The Gramophone Company, and the Victor Company to come to some arrangement with the leading American publishers for the control of mechanical rights throughout the world. Brownsden informs me that several American publishers have written to Hayes at various times offering the Company the control of the mechanical rights of the compositions in their catalogues. If this is correct, it looks as though it should be possible to make a deal with all the principal publishers. You might consider it advisable on broad grounds to get a few of the opposition record concerns to combine with us, and so eliminate competition from inside the industry, and it might be found easier to deal with the publishers if such a combine was formed.

---

* Royalties to the copyright owner were paid via a stamp supplied by the copyright owner to the manufacturer. The music publisher Albert & Sons are here attempting to gain a higher royalty in return for allowing the stamps to be facsimile printed instead of pasted on by hand.

HIS MASTER'S VOICE (HMV)

I am convinced that this is a question which has got to be tackled seriously sooner, or later, and it is such a big one that I feel I need not apologise for bringing it to your notice at this particular time. In this country, the publishers, like a good many other people here, are imbued with the idea of getting rich quickly, and if they have a chance, they will threaten and squeeze for all they are worth.

American publishers could continue to give them publishing rights for sheet music, but we ought, without doubt, to secure mechanical rights. This would greatly strengthen our position and make us independent of English and Australian publishers of American 'hits'.

After experience of the difficulties of opening a factory where everyone was new to the game, we are now settling down here, and the outlook is more satisfactory than it has been since we commenced. I have not worried you with all the troubles that have had to be faced because they were such as our new enterprise was bound to encounter, and simply had to be overcome when they arose, but I believe that when I leave Australia, I shall have the satisfaction of knowing that the branch here will be one of the best assets of the Company. My only regret is that it is not a branch in the true sense of the word, with everything under our direct control, but in view of our agreement with Hoffnungs, this, of course, is not possible. My task has been much heavier, and in many ways very much more unsatisfactory than if you had sent me to a place where the Company could work direct with the trade, who, by the way, as far as the Australian section is concerned, would like nothing better. I am very friendly with all the Directors of Hoffnungs, and have nothing but the best to report of them personally, but they have run in a rut so long that without having the right to dictate to them, the results I wish to obtain have to be laboured for with a patience worthy of Job. I hope, however, that you are not disappointed with what has been accomplished, and while I am here, I shall strive to so improve things that the Company may benefit to the fullest extent.

You must have had a very anxious time over the general strike, and also with the coal strike. The latter looks as if it is going on for ever, but it is splendid to see that our shares continue to be quoted at such a high figure, and to know that in spite of national troubles, our business is doing so wonderfully well... [23]

Another matter preoccupying Manson was the production capacity of the Australian record factory. In a memorandum to Manson, Lockley (the factory manager) wrote:

The question which you raise as to the capacity of our factory, and the possibility of increasing the number of presses, is one that embraces the whole question as to the size and suitability of our present building.

I consider that without overtime it is inadvisable to count on an output from our present plant of more than two and a half million records per annum. We have sufficient space in our present press-room to put down a further 12 presses. This addition to the presses calls immediately for a proportionate increase in the consumption of steam, water and hydraulic power. Of these three, we can at once dismiss the hydraulic power, as a second hydraulic pump is actually under construction, and this second pump would take care if necessary of the extra requirements.

We should not, however, have sufficient steam; an additional 12 presses would require approximately an additional 30 per cent. steaming capacity, and this our present boiler is unable to supply. Given suitable coal and good working conditions, our present boiler will supply our present actual requirements; even now, however, we never have a real feeling of security, as there is practically no margin of reserve. In this connection, I would add that I

HIS MASTER'S VOICE (HMV)

have already started enquiries, and am making a lay-out to see the possibility of installing a second boiler. This second boiler would of necessity have to be a vertical one, owing to the lack of floor space...

Thirdly, the cooling water is probably the most important of all. When we commenced operations here, most of our calculations were based on the consumption of 5,000 gallons per hour. Considerable difficulty was experienced in getting the Water Board to agree to supply this amount. It is as well to record here that the whole of the Sydney water supply is derived from a semi-artificially constructed reservoir in a catchment area, and depends solely upon the annual rainfall. In cases of excessive heat, serious curtailment of the water consumption has to be made throughout the district, and frequently in summer time the supply is totally cut off from at any rate residential areas during certain hours of the day. These conditions render the Water Board very reluctant to supply a large quantity to any one consumer, particularly in a district where the mains are none too big for the demand... The increase in the number of presses would only intensify these difficulties. Again, the water has to be disposed of, and the difficulties that we encountered in obtaining a supply of water were also met with when the Sewerage Board had to make arrangements for taking away the waste...

To sum up; increasing the number of our presses would necessitate a second boiler and a second refrigerator. The refrigerator compressor could be easily installed, but it would be costly and very awkward to install a further boiler and the necessary condenser tower for the refrigerator. [23]

It seems that Manson's enquiries about increased record production capacity were the result of concerns expressed by head office. On 1 October 1926, Manson wrote a letter to James Muir:

SOUND BEGINNINGS

I am in receipt of your letter of August 20th. I can quite understand that you and the other members of the Executive have been considerably perturbed at the apparent inability of the factory here to cope with the Australian and New Zealand orders for records; but the figures which have reached you since that letter was written will have shown that the output has improved to such an extent as to make it fairly certain that our difficulties have greatly diminished, and it should be possible to deal satisfactorily with the demands that are likely to be made upon us for some considerable time to come.

At the beginning of the year, I asked Mr Lockley to give me a conservative estimate of the output we might expect in January, February and March, so that I might be in a position to know what orders we should ask for. You will see by our Management Minute No. 62 that the following estimate was given:

> January   68,000
> February 80,000
> March   100,000

With these figures in mind, I approached Hoffnungs but only succeeded in getting orders for 30,350 records during the whole of January as they had been buying heavily from Hayes, and had continued to cable orders up to Christmas, with the result that they expected to receive regular shipments for some time to come.

At the beginning of February, the outlook for the factory was serious for although they had not succeeded in living up to their estimates, Mr Lockley considered such progress had been made that the estimates for February and March could stand. I, therefore, felt that in order to provide sufficient work, it would be necessary to get some orders from New Zealand. Before asking for them, however, I called a special meeting of the Management Committee on

HIS MASTER'S VOICE (HMV)

February 1st, and produced figures of the sales in Australia and New Zealand for the period July 1st, 1924 to July 31st, 1925. After these had been carefully examined, Mr Lockley expressed the opinion that the factory could deal with all the orders we were likely to get from both Australia and New Zealand, and I notified Hyams accordingly...

The total quantity of records ordered up to the end of March was 207,856 from Australia and 14,473 from New Zealand, or 222,329 in all, against the factory estimate of deliveries amounting to 248,000, but which as a matter of fact only reached 88,814.

On March 10th, at the meeting of the Management Committee Mr Lockley was asked to furnish his estimate of deliveries for the months of April, May and June. It was pointed out that the wide discrepancies between the estimates and actual deliveries for the months of January and February made it necessary to consider whether the factory would really be in a position to satisfy Hoffnungs and Hyams requirements, and that, in the event of the factory not being able to do this, Hoffnungs and Hyams must be immediately advised so that they could arrange to obtain necessary supplies from England. After giving the matter consideration for a fortnight Mr Lockley furnished the following estimate:

April	100,000
May	120,000
June	125,000

Once more we were disappointed, and in view of the conditions here, I wrote to the Managing Director suggesting that a good Assistant Factory Manager should be sent as I felt that it was impossible for Mr Lockley to cope with all the detail, and he had no reliable man to help him. Fortunately, my plea was successful, and Farr was sent out, and you have seen what a great improvement has taken place since his arrival.

SOUND BEGINNINGS

The orders (including August Supplementary) received to June 30th amounted to 646,631, and if the factory had delivered in accordance with their estimate, viz. 593,000 for the period, we should have been in an excellent position. Unfortunately, the deliveries only amounted to 374,628. To relieve the situation, I simply had to advise Hoffnungs and Hyams to cable certain orders to Hayes, and after a few men had been trained, a night-shift was started to reduce the outstandings as quickly as possible. As a consequence of this, we were able to deliver 394,204 records in July and August, and although there are still a lot of small orders and balances which have been in hand for a considerable time, these are being rapidly reduced so that the outlook today is more satisfactory than it has ever been.

After reading the foregoing, you will see how difficult it is to gauge with any degree of accuracy the probable demand which will be made upon us in the future. I think, however, we can take the sales in Australia and New Zealand during the twelve months ending June 30th, 1925 as a basis, and allow for the normal increase which would have taken place if records had been imported from England. To this we should add the increased business we shall get from the quick supply of 'hits', and also from the larger turnover our distributors should enjoy owing to our being able to supply stocks in a much shorter time than they could get them from Hayes.

According to the figures given to me, the sales of His Master's Voice and Zonophone records in Australia from July 1st, 1924 to June 30th, 1925 amounted to 1,321,403 records. During the same period, sales of His Master's Voice records in New Zealand were 201,677, making a total for both countries of 1,523,080, or an average of 127,000 records per month... Taking everything into consideration, I feel we are safe in anticipating the receipt of orders at the rate of 2,000,000 records per annum, with a strong probability of an increase to 2,400,00 within a year provided there are no manufacturing difficulties or big slumps in the general trade.

There is every reason to believe that the population of Australia will grow rapidly during the next few years, and with this growth, we can expect a large increase in the demand for our records which we should not be able to cope with in our present premises... It is regrettable that we did not purchase the factory which the Columbia Company acquired as it would have given us all the accommodation we are likely to need for many years to come, and it has certain features which make it very superior to our factory.

By the way, I have been informed that the Columbia Company is going to float an Australian company. Apparently, they have found the expense of buying the factory &c. rather too heavy for them, and they wish to raise capital here. The whole question is under discussion at their Head Office at present, and is kept very quiet. It was only quite by accident that I gained my information, and I have found it impossible to get any further particulars up to the present.

[Wilhelm] Backhaus has paid a return visit to Sydney after a triumphal tour through New Zealand. He has evidently been 'got at' by the competition because he told me he felt he was only one of a crowd with us, and believed that if he went to another company he would be treated as the bright particular star, so far as pianists are concerned. I see that you have exercised the option on his services for another year, and I think it is very advisable to secure him for a much longer period. He is just reaching his prime, and is right in the front rank. Indeed, his playing gave me greater pleasure than that of almost every other famous soloist I have heard. As a record maker he has always enjoyed an exceptional reputation, and from what I recollect his sales have been excellent. He will be in London early in the new year, and is desirous of doing a lot of recording.

SOUND BEGINNINGS

I am delighted to hear that Zonophones are going ahead in the Old Country. The new recording [the electrical recording process] has doubtless been a great help, and, apparently, the starvation policy with regard to money for artistes and printing has been changed. Properly catered for, there is, as I have proved in the past, a splendid market for Zonophones... [23]

Manson had already received a report from Hoffnung's on the 'New Process Recording':

The Columbia Company have placed quite a few records on the market, Sydney pressings, and have also recorded two or three numbers, one vocal by a man by the name of [Walter] Kingsley, two orchestral numbers by [Sydney Simpson's] Wentworth Hotel Orchestra and some others, all by the old method of recording, and not too good. As a matter of fact, the ones that we heard took us back to the time when the phonograph was predominant. However, we understand that it is their intention to get out the newest and latest method of recording (electrical), and then probably there will be some little competition – competition in the nature of some of the Australian composers giving these people the first right to record, and if it is a big hit then we are out of it.

We, personally, do not think there is a great deal of talent in Australia – talent that would interest the public – but it is just the publicity which the Columbia Company would gain by recording here that we would like.

We think that you should give serious consideration to the advisability of putting in an installation for recording in Australia, and as you are in the best position to judge of this necessity we await your views with some interest. An electrical recording installation will be very costly, not only in the initial outlay but also in upkeep, but we should not allow this to influence our opinion to too great an extent when judging the necessity for such recording facilities.

HIS MASTER'S VOICE (HMV)

The point raised by Messrs. Hoffnung re Australian compositions is important, and obviously without a recording studio we could not compete in the trade in such titles. We are unable, however, to judge as to how much importance is to be attached to such Australian compositions. Further, there is the fact that the competition with a local recording studio could be first with hits in instances where the sheet music is available before you are in possession of shells, and in some instances such shells will not be available where the title has not been recorded in either America or this country. How far the fact that recordings are made locally will influence sales with the Australian public can only be judged by the success achieved by Columbia with such recordings, and perhaps you may soon be able to give us some information on this point. [23]

William Manson again wrote to James Muir at Hayes:

I am in receipt of two letters from you dated September 6th and 9th respectively. In the former you venture the opinion that we are losing ground in the record trade in Australia, and that our competitors are relatively doing better than we are. Since you wrote, you will have received later figures of Hoffnung's sales, which show us in a very much better light, and bear out what I stated in connection with the June figures, namely, that sales had been affected by inadequate supplies from the factory. I have not yet received particulars of the September sales, but have been informed that the gross figures show that the business done in that month is the biggest on record. No doubt the machine sales will show up particularly well as the first deliveries of the new Bungalows and Studios were made last month.

Until I have been around all the states, I cannot write more fully on our position as compared with other companies, but I have in front of me particulars of the sales of 'Valencia', which has been the biggest 'hit' of the year.

His Master's Voice advertisement, c. 1920.

HIS MASTER'S VOICE (HMV)

We have issued two His Master's Voice records of this title, and one Zonophone, and our total sales have been 59,379. The Columbia Company, as you know, have had to purchase stamps from us, and they have issued 'Valencia' on five different records, and have called for a total quantity of 35,584.* There appears to be very good evidence that Brunswick sales have been considerably affected both by our advent and that of the Columbia Company...

I am interested to hear what you have to say about the new Columbia machines, and I am glad that, in your opinion, the reproduction is inferior to ours. Their cabinet work, of course, never has compared with ours.

... I shall leave for Brisbane on Tuesday, and while I shall probably visit two or three different towns in that direction, I do not feel justified in staying away from Sydney for more than ten days at the outside. I hope, however, that at the beginning of the year everything will be running sweetly here [so] that I shall be able to pay my promised visit to New Zealand, and afterwards visit all the Australian States...

The Columbia Company had an official opening of their factory yesterday, when the Governor of New South Wales presided. I am posting to you newspapers with an account of the opening, and also containing the Columbia advertisements. No doubt it will appear strange that the Governor should have consented to open our competitors' works after he had informed us that he was 'precluded from opening a commercial enterprise'. I have, of course, written drawing his attention to this, and if he replies it will be interesting to see what explanation he gives. [23]

James Muir then returned to the question of local recording. Manson by now had reconsidered and his response was tetchy:

---

* The purchase of royalty stamps was the only way a copyright owner could gain sales figures on rights sales.

SOUND BEGINNINGS

It is pretty certain that while we might make a few friends by recording locally, the sales of the records would be very limited, and we should certainly incur the enmity of those whose efforts we were not prepared to perpetuate on our records.

The expense of installation and upkeep would probably be very heavy, in addition to which a large recording allotment would be necessary. The Recorder's salary and expenses would also have to be taken into consideration. The instrumentalists and vocalists here do not compare favourably with the best English and foreign artistes, and local jealousies would militate against sales. Bad feeling would result if we were to decline to make records of Victorian, South Australian, Queensland or Tasmanian artistes, while if we were to agree to a number of such artistes coming to our studio, the expense of bringing them to Sydney would be prohibitive.

Then again, one has to consider the general policy of Australia, namely, to declaim loudly the necessity of buying everything Australian but in their private life to buy imported articles and to 'swank' amongst their friends that these are the only ones good enough for them. This attitude obtains even with the working classes. In fact, I believe that it is very strong with them.

As regards Australian compositions which develop into 'hits', Hoffnungs cannot say definitely how many are produced in the course of a year, but during the past twelve months, Australian 'hits' appear to have been very few and far between, and certainly there have been none of very great importance. Opera, musical comedies, and other musical shows achieve popularity in other countries before they are produced here, and, consequently, we shall, as a rule, have matrices of all popular numbers in time to cater for the demand in Australia.

Altogether, a recording studio here can but be a stunt show which would cost a lot to establish and maintain, and

HIS MASTER'S VOICE (HMV)

from which we are not likely to get sound commercial results. There is not much prestige to be gained from recording Governors or politicians here. The ordinary public would only smile at them, and certainly would not pay money for such records. Therefore, it would be only the individuals themselves and perhaps their families who would be pleased, and as they are as a rule on the lookout to get everything they can for nothing they would probably suggest that if we recorded them we should also give them machines to play the records to their friends. Teachers of music in its various branches would flood us with applications for their pupils to be recorded and refusal would cause bad feeling which would be prejudicial to our trade.

In the course of time, change in conditions may warrant the establishment of a recording laboratory, but we do not feel we would be justified in recommending the work to be undertaken at present. There may be instances where an Australian artiste may spring into sudden fame, and the Columbia Company with a recording apparatus might profit by recording such an artiste, but these cases are very rare. I shall carefully watch any move the Columbia Company may make with regard to recording, and will send you a report if, and when, anything of an interesting nature occurs.

The musician who has been engaged to conduct any orchestra which the Columbia Company may use in their recording here is very well known to me, and he informed me that the Columbia Company intend to record dance music mainly. If this is correct, I cannot see how it will pay them, except on odd titles which might spring into popularity, and may not have been recorded by either English or American bands. The dance bands here certainly will not compare with Jack Hylton's or the Savoy Orpheans. [23]

Meanwhile, William Manson was still feeling snubbed by the King's representative:

SOUND BEGINNINGS

In my letter of October 15th, I informed you that the Governor of New South Wales had presided at the official opening of the Columbia factory. I immediately wrote to him drawing his attention to the correspondence which took place when we were arranging for *our* opening ceremony, and when, in response to an invitation to preside, he stated that he was 'precluded from opening a commercial enterprise'. In reply to my letter, I had a note from the Governor's Secretary stating that His Excellency was going away from town, but on his return would communicate with me. Yesterday morning, the Private Secretary telephoned to me, and asked if I could go to Government House this morning at 11.30. I went there, accordingly, and was received very graciously indeed by the Governor.

I spent about three-quarters of an hour with him, and he informed me that he felt he had been deliberately misled as to the nature of the ceremony at the Columbia factory. The Official Secretary, who was present at the original interview, backed up the Governor's statement that he was invited to visit the factory for the purpose of inspecting the new machinery. It was further stated that Australian capital only had been used in the purchase and fitting up of the works, and the staff were entirely Australian.

I had with me a Status Report which Mr Wise procured... This made it very clear to the Governor and the Secretary that the company was a branch of the English company of the same name, and it was reported that all the capital would be provided from overseas... The Governor informed me that it was not until two days before the opening ceremony that he received information to the effect that the visit was not to be an ordinary one of inspection, but it was too late then to make any change.

I spoke at some length on the damage which had been caused, and our loss of prestige both with the trade and the public. His Excellency assured me that he was most desirous of doing everything in his power to do away with any bad

HIS MASTER'S VOICE (HMV)

impression which may have been created, and he suggested that he should come and visit our works and make a eulogistic speech, which would clearly indicate that he appreciated our pre-eminent position in the industry. He would have been prepared to come almost immediately, but it occurred to me that such a visit would at once give the Columbia Company a handle to say that we were jealous, and perhaps it would not look very dignified either for His Excellency or for us. I suggested, therefore, that he should pay us a visit on the anniversary of the opening of the works, and he thought this would be an excellent way out of the difficulty. Upon turning up his books, he found, however, that he could not come here until February 1st. This date, therefore, has been definitely booked, and he will be here at 2.30 in the afternoon.

In order that we might get the utmost value out of the visit, the Governor asked if I could get a number of representatives of the press to be present. He said that if I thought there would be any difficulty in getting them, he would see to it himself.

The whole interview was as friendly as possible, and there is no doubt that His Excellency is genuinely sorry at having done anything to upset us. [23]

On 19 November 1926 William Manson wrote once more to James Muir on the subject of 'Australian recording':

I have recently written at some length on this subject, but will reply to the various points you raise where it is possible I have not made the position clear...

Cost of Installation: You say that the initial expense would be very heavy while the yearly cost of operating it would at a moderate estimate be not less than £2,000. To this should be added the fees and expenses of the artistes which would undoubtedly amount to a large sum...

... The proportion of local recordings would be small, and you will therefore see that the loss which would be sustained if a recording laboratory were to be installed here would be exceedingly heavy, and the amount of kudos or advertising value gained would not warrant me in recommending the scheme.

You ask what would be the position if the Columbia Company were to record numbers from sheet music, which you say is available as a rule before matrices arrive, and were to place records on the market six weeks to two months before we could... Possibly you have been informed that sheet music is shipped over here in bulk from America, but from the information at my disposal, I understand that sample copies only are sent, and the music is printed locally when required. Publishers here do not as a rule issue the new compositions immediately they are received, and in any case, the earliest date about which they could produce stock would be one month after receipt of a sample copy. If they were to print stocks of all the new compositions immediately samples arrived, they would pile up unwieldy and unsaleable stocks, and would make heavy losses accordingly. As I understand it, they try over the music as soon as possible after arrival, and then await suitable opportunities for introducing it in musical productions or music halls. When these are forthcoming and everything has been done to engineer the novelties into the position of 'hits', the publishers print stocks. In some instances, they do not publish sheet music here until records have created a demand.

From all I can gather, it does not appear that there would be many instances where the Columbia Company local recording would enable them to get ahead on titles. The artistes, both vocal and instrumental; and orchestras, both symphony and dance, are very inferior to those who record for us in England and America, and as a rule they are not likely to appeal to more than their own narrow circle of acquaintances, although, of course, there might be an exception occasionally. There are hardly likely, however, to be a sufficient number of such exceptions to seriously affect us.

HIS MASTER'S VOICE (HMV)

If the Columbia Company use their laboratory here to any extent, they will not be able to issue so many records by European, or American artists, and their lists will naturally deteriorate, while the value of ours will be enhanced in proportion.

The question you raise about Australian compositions was dealt with in a previous letter. When Hoffnungs were asked to give details of Australian compositions which had become 'hits' during the past year, they were not able to produce any, so apparently we are not likely to sustain a very heavy loss over this. [23]

By now Muir had become the repository of Manson's impatience:

With regard to my expression of hope that the growth of the Australian population would be rapid in the next few years, it seems to me that with the eyes of the world on this vast and sparsely populated continent, great developments must take place. We have had a number of distinguished visitors here lately who are all impressed with the necessity of providing British population for Australia, and I understand that Mr Bruce went very carefully into this subject on his recent visit to the Old Country.

There is a growing feeling amongst the best class of people here that if we do not people this country with Britishers within the next few years, Japan may be tempted to help in this direction. In any case, I cannot help but feel that the unsatisfactory state of affairs which seems to have obtained during the past year in Great Britain will induce numbers to come here. The temptation of coming to a country where wages are big and hours are short must be very great to people who are struggling against adverse conditions at home, and much as the few who are here would like to keep this great country to themselves, I cannot see how in the long run they can possibly be successful in their 'dog in the manger' policy. [23]

SOUND BEGINNINGS

The first anniversary ceremony planned for 1 February was the occasion of the next letter:

> I am sure you will be pleased to hear that our anniversary celebration passed off most successfully, and without a hitch. His Excellency the Governor asked me to call for him at Government House and escort him to the works. Before leaving, he chatted about the industry, and apparently both he and Lady de Chair are keenly interested in records.
>
> We arrived at the factory punctually at 2.30 p.m. A crowd of people had gathered outside, but we had made arrangements for the Police to be represented so that everything should be orderly.
>
> His Excellency went to the Office floor first of all and sat in my office for some time discussing the address which he was to give. When he was ready to proceed on the tour of inspection, I went into the General Office where the other guests were gathered and told them that we were about to start and that I had arranged for them to be split up into small parties and had allotted a guide for each. I may mention that these guides had received special instructions about the information that was to be imparted to our guests and they were prepared with answers to any questions which were likely to be put.
>
> I had arranged for a photographer to be present to take a picture of the arrival of the Governor, and also one in which he is shown pressing a record. The newspapers were also well represented with photographers so that a regular battery was turned on when His Excellency was ready to be photographed. He particularly requested me to stand there with him, and quite an excellent result was obtained...
>
> After thoroughly inspecting the factory (and I am pleased to say His Excellency was exceedingly interested in all he saw, and asked innumerable questions during the tour), we returned to the Office floor and as soon as the guests were settled down, His Excellency went into the General Office

HIS MASTER'S VOICE (HMV)

and delivered an address, which was listened to with rapt attention by all present. He concluded by asking those present to charge their glasses and he then got up and toasted the Company. I, of course, had to reply, and I took the opportunity of forcibly stating several facts which I felt ought to be generally known. As soon as I had finished, His Excellency had to leave to catch a train for the country. I should mention that he really paid us a great compliment as he came to town from Moss Vale specially to attend our function. When leaving, he thanked me very much indeed for the attention he had received, and said he had been intensely interested in everything he had seen, and in fact I had given him a very happy afternoon.

About half-an-hour later, his Aide-de-camp, Major Lloyd, telephoned me and informed me that the Governor had asked him to ring up and tell me once again how much he had enjoyed the afternoon. As a memento of his visit, I asked His Excellency to accept a parcel of records which I had specially selected and he told me how delighted he would be to receive them.

Mr Lockley had gone to a lot of trouble to have every part of the factory looking as bright and clean as possible. Our guests were most enthusiastic about the works and the results which had been obtained...

Just as I was dictating this letter, a telephone message came through informing me that Dame Melba will pay me a visit tomorrow afternoon... [23]

A copy of the Governor's speech was enclosed, with its fulsome praise for the company and the educational value of the gramophone:

> To offer children the best of music by the medium of the gramophone is not a difficult task. The proportion of good music to merely popular music is very large in the catalogue of 'His Master's Voice' records. I do not think too much praise can be given to the Gramophone Company, who have

renounced the possibility of the easy money that would result from production of cheap records of popular music only, and whose chief aim has been to provide the people with the best of all music in record form. I am sure they will reap their full reward in time. Wherever good music goes it creates its own large public. I believe the low standard of musical taste that has disgraced many communities in the past has been the result of musical starvation.

Twenty-five years ago, the man who lived far away from the great musical centres of the world might be many years without the opportunity of hearing a piano well played or a classical song well sung. Today he who is most distant from civilised communities can have whatsoever music he desires. He can hear a Melba or a Galli-Curci sing. He can hear a Backhaus at the piano, or a Kreisler on the violin. He can even have that which would be denied him on any concert programme – an Elman playing the violin obbligato to a song by Caruso, for instance...

The British Museum has quite recently begun to store the matrices from which can be made records of the great voices of our own day. The matrices are supplied by the Gramophone Company. They are stored in hermetically sealed brass containers which must not be opened till 50 years after the death of the man or woman whose voices they represent. Thereafter they shall remain the property of the British nation in perpetuity.

How will future generations receive the records made in their time from the matrices that are being stored in ours? It is an interesting speculation. At first, I think, such records will be considered curiosities, but our descendants will soon learn to treat the records that our time has bequeathed them as splendid gifts from which the fullest advantage should be gained. The gramophone will allow the establishment of a national library of interpretive music, a library which will contain the works of musicians now living and yet to live. [121]

The following day, the *Sydney Morning Herald* carried a report of the Vice-Regal visit, and a photograph of Manson with the Governor, captioned 'Sir Dudley de Chair examining a record'. [204] In fact, he appears to have just pressed the record, as Manson noted, because he still has one hand on the press.

On 26 April 1927, William Manson wrote to Alfred Clark in Britain:

> Before commencing a recital of any Antipodean news, I must congratulate you most heartily upon the Royal visit to Hayes. It was most thrilling to hear of the very great interest which the King took in everything he saw, and my one regret is that I could not be there to witness it. The publicity connected with the visit will prove of very great value to the Company in Great Britain, and on our side of the world New Zealand people especially will be delighted to hear of the signal mark of Royal favour with which the Company has been honoured. It is improbable that the Australian public will react to the same extent. They need the actual presence of the great personalities in their midst to draw out their expressions of loyalty, while New Zealanders have it in their bones and think the world of our Royal Family and all they mean to the Empire.
>
> The papers in the Old Country will, no doubt, have followed very closely the adventures of the Duke and Duchess of York. I had the good fortune to see quite a lot of them in Rotorua (N.Z.) where their visit coincided with my own, and I witnessed the elaborate ceremonial dances with which they were entertained by the Maoris. Sydney gave the Royal Couple quite a warm welcome, and my wife and I were honoured with an invitation to the Garden Party given at Government House. The Duchess was escorted by Sir Dudley de Chair, the Governor of New South Wales, and when he caught sight of me, he brought the Duchess over

and introduced her to my wife and self. Naturally, we were exceedingly delighted, and we found the Duchess the very embodiment of charm.

In response to an invitation from Lieutenant Commander Hodgson, I visited the 'Renown' and inspected the 'His Master's Voice' electrical model in the Royal apartments. It was in perfect order, with only a mark on the cabinet after its long voyage. I was informed that it had been played regularly, and that for dances on deck, one of our portables was always used, and gave great satisfaction. A Brunswick 'Panatrope' was also in the Royal apartments, but looked in a disgraceful condition. The lid had warped badly, the polish had sunk, and the cabinet altogether looked cheap and nasty. I asked Lieutenant Commander Hodgson if it had been used, but he told me it had seldom, if ever, been played. The 'Panatrope' has been very extensively advertised in Australia and New Zealand, and has been useful to the Brunswick Company from a prestige point of view. Hoffnungs say that several sales have been made, but they have not been able to learn of any experiences of the purchasers...

Brown has spent six weeks with us, and had an exceedingly busy time. His recommendations, with which I am in agreement, will have already reached you. I am convinced that this market is going to be one of the best served by the Company, and we should certainly take steps now to secure such land and erect such a factory as will enable us to cater for Australian requirements for many years ahead. I regret that we did not secure the factory which the Columbia Company eventually purchased, but the site at Lidcombe, which is under offer to the Company, should give us all the space we shall require for many a long day. Sydney cannot help but develop in that direction and the value of the site will be enhancing all the time...

You will be sorry to hear that Mr E.F. Broad has been very ill for some time. I took Brown to see him in the nursing home where he is staying, and he gave us quite a lot of exceedingly useful information... Incidentally, he has a very poor opinion of our distributors, whom he dubs 'the Jew boys', but he says he has observed a great change for the better in the advertising, and also in shop window displays, since I came here.

Melba had a great success in her farewell concerts in Sydney, and must have made an excellent profit out of them. This will be so helpful to her in her old age, poor thing! She told me she intended coming to see our factory in May if it was at all possible, and she also kindly invited me to call upon her in her Melbourne house if she should happen to be there when I visited Melbourne.

Record orders continue to come along satisfactorily, and it looks as though we shall have to continue employing a night shift for some months... [23]

Following these recommendations, the Board minutes of 15 July 1927 confirmed:

The Managing Director reported [on] the position in Australia – that he had obtained an option on land suitable for a new factory and, although he was not desirous of undertaking the erection of a new Australian factory at the present time, he thought it advisable to secure land as a precautionary measure, and the Board authorised the M.D. to purchase 9 acres of land at Lidcombe, Sydney, N.S.W. at a price of £500 per acre. [22]

Factory manager Lockley was actively pursuing matters. In a letter to Hayes dated 17 August 1927, he mentions that 'we have now received a favourable reply from the Metropolitan Water Board in regard to the question of a water supply to the Lidcombe premises', and that 'the Electricity Department have also intimated that the necessary supply can be made available at the site...'. [23] But despite this evidence, construction work never actually began. As the business environment began to deteriorate, it seems that plans to erect a second factory were abandoned. Sales figures for the first year of local production [Appendix 3] show a great deal of variation in sales from month to month, but there is a gradual overall increase during the short period covered.

The above correspondence has been quoted at some length because it gives a unique account of how one company, the Gramophone Company, planned and managed the establishment of a record factory in Australia. These letters cover a wide range of topics which bring to life in a very graphic sense the character and attitudes of some of the players who established Australia's record industry; and also sheds considerable light on how business was conducted during the 1920s. As well, it vividly portrays the attitudes of the day towards society and politics.

No unusual problems seem to have disrupted the normal operation of business once the factory was up and running. Like their competitors, Gramophone were beginning to perceive a general decline in sales; but exact sales figures are not available for the late 1920s. There were no major changes in operations until William Manson left Australia and returned to Britain in July 1930, having been the general manager here since 1925. Whatever his private thoughts may have been, Manson courteously said his farewells in the 'Trade notes' section of the *Australian Phonograph News* of October 1930, writing that 'it was a very great wrench to tear myself away from Australia and all the good friends who have helped me to make my sojourn there so enjoyable' and revealing the hope that he might one day revisit 'the land of sunshine'. The subsequent general manager was John Ritchie.

In January 1931 Ritchie reduced the price of *Zonophone* records to 3/- for 10in. records (except the *Celebrity* records which were 4/-), and to 5/- for 12in. records. In Britain

Zonophone had always been a lower-priced label; only in Australia and New Zealand had it been sold for the same price as the prestigious *His Master's Voice* label. It is an indication of how difficult things had become that Gramophone finally acknowledged that they needed a 'cheap' label to compete with Columbia's aggressively-marketed *Regal* label. The decision to lower the price of *Zonophone* must have been a sudden one because the supplementary catalogue of *Zonophone* Records, published in January 1931, still showed the old prices but was overprinted in red with the new ones and a banner proclaiming the 'New Reduced Prices'.

A few months later the factory was closed. The Board minutes of 15 July 1931 abruptly declared:

> The Managing Director reported that after a very thorough investigation of the factory facilities rendered available on account of the merger with the Columbia Company and with a view to effecting considerable economies, he applied for authority... in Australia to transfer the record manufacture from the company's factory at Erskineville to the Columbia factory at Homebush, Sydney. [22]

Once more, the decision was taken on the other side of the world. A merger had taken place in Britain on 20 March 1931, to create the giant EMI (Electrical and Musical Industries) [see Chapter 9]. Following an agreement for the amalgamation of Columbia and the Gramophone Company to create the new entity EMI, *HMV* and *Zonophone* records began to be pressed at Homebush.

For the consumer this meant that from 1931 all releases on these labels – and any repressings of earlier records – had the same fine laminated surfaces as did *Columbia*, *Parlophone* and *Regal* records. It also meant that the Gramophone Company, for the first time, had access to Columbia's recording studio at Homebush. The results were the first Australian recordings to be released on *HMV* – all made in a short burst of recording activity in late 1931 and early 1932 by Columbia's recording engineer, Reg Southey. The issued recordings from these sessions include several by the visiting British comedian John Henry (among them 'Captain Cook discovers Australia' and 'The Harbour Bridge'), and discs by two Australian pianists, Isador Goodman and Molly De Gunst. No further local recordings were released on *HMV* until the mid-1930s.

The Board minutes on 23 December 1931 note that:

> ... terms for an agreement with the Radio Corporation of America, International General Electric Co. Ltd., Westinghouse International Company, The Gramophone Co. Ltd., Columbia Graphophone Co. Ltd., E.M.I. Ltd., and the Amalgamated Wireless Australasia Ltd. had been settled for the unification of the entire entertainment field, except wireless valves, in Australia. The terms, which provided for the formation of a new company to take over the various assets in exchange for shares were reported. The Board approved the action taken and authorised the preparation of the agreement. [22]

By 1933 the price of *Zonophone* records had been further reduced to 2/6 for 10in. records and 4/- for 12in. records. The Celebrity series had been discontinued. Shortly afterwards *Zonophone* was merged with Columbia's 'budget' label *Regal* to form *Regal-Zonophone*. *His Master's Voice* continued as an EMI label.

Chapter 6

COLUMBIA

The Columbia Phonograph Company General was established in London in 1900 as a subsidiary of the American Columbia Company. While it is frequently mentioned as a competitor to other record companies in Australia during the early 1900s, there is little specific information about Columbia's early activities in this country.

In January 1913, the British branch of the company was re-named the Columbia Graphophone Company and remained a subsidiary of the American company which adopted the same corporate identity on the same date. The newly-formed company was in turn succeeded by the Columbia Graphophone Company Ltd. in February 1917, when it was incorporated as a British company.

On 23 January 1923 Louis Sterling, the American-born managing director of the British branch of Columbia, acquired the shares of the British entity from the American stockholders. When he learnt that an electrical recording process developed by Western Electric had been licensed to the American branch of Columbia he sailed to New York and succeeded on 31 March 1925 in purchasing the American firm. In this way he gained control of their

SOUND BEGINNINGS

Above: Gil Dech and his Syncopators record Don Bradman's 'Every Day is Rainbow Day' at the Columbia recording studio 4 February 1931. Dech is standing at rear left, Jack Lumsdaine (vocalist) is at the microphone, Bradman is holding the wax master. Photo courtesy of Mike Sutcliffe.

A section of the Columbia factory at Homebush, Sydney. Photo courtesy of Mike Sutcliffe.

options from Western Electric and made the British firm the parent company. Some years later, in 1931, Sterling was to become a director of the new EMI conglomerate and in the same year he became the first person from the recording industry to be knighted. He retired in the late 1930s and died in 1958.

After Sterling's purchase of the American Columbia, the final step was to bring the branches together under the umbrella of Columbia (International) Ltd. The news was reported in the February 1927 issue of the Melbourne record-industry publication *Music Trader*:

> An important transaction has recently been completed by the Columbia Graphophone Co. Ltd., of London, by the purchase of shares and option certificates in Columbia (International) Ltd. in exchange for shares of the Columbia Graphophone Ltd. For the purpose of the transaction, the capital of the Company has been increased from £600,000 to £800,000 by the creation of 400,000 additional ordinary shares of 10/- each. The London company recently purchased the minority shares of the Columbia Phonograph Co. of New York, and now, as a result of the latest transaction, the London company owns practically the whole of its American subsidiary, together with the remainder of the foreign holdings held by Columbia (International) Ltd. It is expected that by bringing the various branches of the company under one control, it will be possible to have much closer and more economical co-operation than would be the case so long as the interests of the company were not identical. At the meeting of the shareholders, at which the agreement for purchase was ratified, the managing director (Mr Louis Sterling) explained that the earnings from the companies which were being purchased would be sufficient to maintain a 40 per cent. dividend on the whole of the issued capital of the London company. [97]

SOUND BEGINNINGS

Compared with the wealth of material on file concerning the Gramophone Co. in the EMI Archives, there is relatively little relating to Columbia. According to Ruth Edge, the Chief Archivist at EMI Music Archives, 'our Columbia information pre 1931 [when Columbia merged with the Gramophone Company to form EMI] is virtually non-existent'. Among the few items found relating to Columbia's Australian operations are letters offering positions at 'the Australian factory about to be installed under our control' which are dated 27 June 1925. [6] Sidney Power was appointed as factory manager, John Cole as assistant factory manager, and Donald G.C. Hawker as factory office manager.

The first published report of a new Columbia factory in Australia appeared in the British journal *Talking Machine and Wireless Trade News* of September 1925:

> The luncheon given at the Savoy Hotel [London] on August 18th to inaugurate the new gramophone and record factory to be opened by the Columbia Graphophone Co. (Ltd.) in Sydney, New South Wales, is a sign of the times, for not only is it an indication of the enterprise and prosperity of the company, but it is likewise an indication that Great Britain does not intend to lose trade by the imposition of excessive tariffs in the way of import duty upon musical or other goods.
>
> The Hon. Sir Arthur Cocks, Agent General for New South Wales, presided... Sir George Croydon Marks, C.B... said that the luncheon was an historic occasion in that it marked not only the inauguration of a great industrial enterprise, but it signified the closer knitting of Empire interests. Australia was farther away from the Motherland than from America, but despite distance she insistently called for British products which she knew had secured supremacy in the world's markets. It was not very long since the Columbia Graphophone Co. was but an English branch of

an American company, but it so grew and prospered that it not only bought itself out of the American company and so became an independent British company, but it later on bought out the original American undertaking, and so may be said to have devoured its parent.

The new step now being entered upon was an important development in British policy which should have far-reaching effects, for it was the establishment of a factory in Australia for the production on a large and developing scale of British gramophones and records. [94]

Within a few weeks, the news was also published in Australia. On 31 October 1925 the *Music Trader* published an item headed 'A new Australian industry':

> The announcement of the plan of the Columbia Grafonola [sic] Company, closely following that made by The Gramophone Company to establish record pressing plants in Australia, is a move that will meet the trade's hearty approval. Already The Brunswick-Balke-Collender Company is pressing records in Sydney, and judging from reports we shall have these three big companies pressing records within the Commonwealth and employing close upon one thousand trained artisans. The number will grow, of course, and if the records are up to the standard established by the 'Brunswick' record, the companies will be well rewarded for their progressive step. [139]

When the Gramophone Company's competitive new manager, William Manson, reached Sydney in December 1925 one of his priorities was to inform head office in London of Columbia's activities:

> I have now received a few particulars, also a rough plan, which I am sending you, together with a photograph of the building.

The property is known as Gold's Hosiery Mills Ltd., Parramatta Road, Homebush. The extent of the property is about 2 acres... and it adjoins the railway and is close to a station. The factory buildings comprise two structures of reinforced concrete and brick, with ground floor measurements of 190 x 66 and 155 x 60 feet respectively; fitted with motor driven lifts. There are also two offices adjoining. There is a main road water supply; the roof is of concrete, and two additional floors can be added if desired.

The sum of £45,000 was asked for the whole property, but my informant believes that a smaller price would be accepted. The insurance cover was for £35,000, but has recently been reduced to £30,000. The total area of the factory building is 43,680 feet, excluding passages, the area of our factory being 35,900 feet, excluding passages.

Although the building is further away from the centre of Sydney than ours, it has an excellent railway service, and in addition there is a very good bus service, while we depend on trams which run every quarter of an hour. There are good factories in the neighbourhood, and it would probably be very much easier to get good class labour than is the case in the district where our factory is situated. There will be very much less dust to contend with, and the better water supply will be a very great convenience.

The building was erected two years ago, and there is plenty of room for extension if necessary, while if we desire to extend it would be necessary to purchase the cottage property adjoining our works.

Altogether, it appears to me that they have very great advantages over us, and this opinion is shared by Mr Lockley.

I am endeavouring to find out the exact price paid by the Columbia Company, and will advise you directly I get this information. [23]

A 'Commercial Report' dated 12 July 1926, also found among the Gramophone Company papers, added:

> This company is to be registered at an early date, and is a branch of the English company of the same name. No details in regard to capital or directors are yet available, and the local representative H.A. Parker of H.A. Parker Ltd., 283 Clarence Street is now awaiting information from England. The company has purchased land at Homebush. A factory has been erected, the value of the land and buildings being set down at £31,000. Stocks and plant at present are valued at £9,000, and further plant is now coming forward. It is estimated that the value of the building, land, plant and stocks will at the end of the present year be worth £100,000.
>
> It is reported that all the capital will be provided from overseas. The company will specialise in the manufacture of Columbia records &c and is quite good for its undertakings. Their bankers are The Commercial Banking Company of Sydney. [22]

By late June 1926, the Columbia studios were making the first Sydney disc recordings. The first two recordings – selections by Sydney Simpson and His Wentworth Café Orchestra (issued on *Columbia* 0514) – were placed on sale during September 1926. On 20 September 1926, an advertisement headed 'Dance Supplement No.1', referred specifically to:

> ... songs by Walter Kingsley, the eminent English baritone. These were recorded and made entirely in *Australia*. Attention is directed also to the two dance records [that is the two sides of Columbia 0514] by the famous Wentworth Cafe Orchestra, Australian recordings of popular interest. [99]

Although recording and processing had obviously been under way for some time, the factory was not officially opened until the following month.

The acoustic recording equipment originally installed in the Columbia studio was quickly superseded and replaced after a few months by the latest Western Electric cutting head brought out from Britain by Reg Southey. On 12 October 1926, just two days before the official opening, the Jimmie Elkins' Orchestra made the first local electrical recordings.

The official opening of the Columbia factory in Parramatta Road, Homebush, took place on 14 October 1926. The opening address was given by the Governor of New South Wales, Sir Dudley de Chair KCB, MVO, who congratulated the management on having 'achieved already quite remarkable results':

> It is of interest to learn that this new factory, so conveniently located in the heart of Homebush, possesses 20 pressing machines of the most modern kind, which are capable of producing nearly 11 million records a year between them. This is an impressive figure. But the Company have so little doubt that their output will be readily absorbed, that they have set up this factory, with a floor space of 50,000 square feet, merely as a first unit, and have made arrangements to expand.
>
> The Company may well be proud of the up-to-dateness and efficiency of their equipment, since not only have they had the benefit of the very latest improvements from London in the manufacturing plant, but they have here the only recording plant in Australasia. In this connection Mr Parker has requested me to ask Lady de Chair and Miss de Chair to come out to the factory at some time convenient to themselves so that they may each make a record. This will be an interesting memento of their visit.

What is of especial interest and importance, we must all feel, is that this enterprise is backed entirely by British capital, the sum involved being £100,000. By the linking up of industrial concerns throughout the Empire, we forge ever stronger links binding us together all over the world. Furthermore, by establishing this new factory, in which all measures have been taken to ensure that the products will be fully equal to those manufactured in Columbia factories in any other country, the Country is taking another step forward in the development of Australian industries. For the factory will shortly be employing 350 highly-trained Australian workmen. Their work is extremely specialised and one of its two branches has never been attempted before in Australasia. It is obvious, therefore, even to the most casual observer, that this undertaking is to be regarded as something more than a commercial one.

The interest shown in it by the Australian-Made Preference League, several of whose officials and members are present, and by the large number of representative Australians interested in the development of Australian music, is a happy augury for its success. [144]

It is not known if the recordings by Lady de Chair and Miss de Chair referred to were ever made. The comment by the Governor that 'one of its two branches has never been attempted before in Australasia' suggests he was unaware that the first Australian disc recordings had been made in Melbourne the previous year – not to mention the cylinder records produced before World War I. Reference to the Australian-Made Preference League can be explained by a contemporary press report which mentions that Sir Dudley, 'during his two years in New South Wales... had visited nearly 30 representative factories under the guidance of the Australian-Made Preference League, of which he was the patron.' [91]

Label of the souvenir record made for the opening of the Columbia factory. From the author's collection.

COLUMBIA

The *Music Trader* reported that:

... to commemorate the official opening... a special record was taken of the speech of his Excellency at the luncheon which was tendered by the company to the visitors. This record, a copy of which has been received by Wertheim's, Melbourne, is a fine example of the products which may be expected from this factory. His Excellency's speech is recorded with perfect clearness, and one can even hear the clinking of glasses, waiters removing dishes from the table, and the comments of those sitting near the recording instrument. [125]

No copy of this recording seems to have survived.

The Governor's presence to grace the occasion was not lost on William Manson of the rival Gramophone Company; the Governor soon found himself in a predicament [see Chapter 5]. Today's event, however, continued untroubled. A series of speakers heaped fulsome praise upon Columbia. The following excerpts taken from contemporary reports give an insight into the confusion of Anglophile and nationalistic attitudes.

Mr R.A. Marks, President of the Chamber of Manufactures, said the factory was a very fine addition to the secondary industries of Sydney. 'The secondary industries were sure to be a good foundation for the expansion of the Commonwealth. Australia was handicapped by large distances from the chief centres of the world, and for that reason the establishment of secondary industries was very necessary.'

Mr Peter Board, representing the Australian-Made Preference League, commented that the opening of the factory was another example of Australia starting to take her place as one of the manufacturing countries of the world. 'In the past Australia had been considered solely a primary producing country, the Australian-Made

Preference League maintained today that the prosperity of Australia depended to a very large extent upon immigration and that depended largely on secondary industries.' It was unfortunate that Australia still had to go to foreign countries for her amusement, he said. He looked forward to the day when the picture shows would be Australian both as regards to films and producers. He concluded by saying that Australia was indebted to the Columbia Company, which had forged a new link between Australia and the Motherland.

Sir John Vicars said he had not expected to see such a well-organised unit of industry, and 'it will help to keep our own gold circulating in Australia a little more. It is an industry that should appeal to all of us. The Australian workman is very adaptable to an industry like this, for his hands are clever and his brain is keen. Work is a misnomer for an industry like this; it is an interesting occupation.' A great change had come over Australia in the last few years, he said. Formerly it was popular to say you imported what you wore or used. Today we were satisfied to use and to wear what we produced in Australia.

Sir Thomas Henley, MLA, said he was pleased to know that in his electorate a big institution had been established for the creation of harmony in Australia. 'If some gramophones were put into Macquarie Street it would be a good thing for Australia. Our secondary industries would afford a tremendous fillip to our primary production.' He thought if Parliament could only be equipped as efficiently as the Columbia factory, then Australia's future would be entirely assured. 'If more technical gentlemen and men of business ability would devote their talents to Parliament, there would be less interference in industry, and Parliament would be a better place.' It was very pleasing that the factory had been built with British capital. He put forward as a suggestion that the words 'British-Australian' Columbia

COLUMBIA

Graphophone Company should be printed on each record, so as to induce the public to give full support to the enterprise.

Mr Arundel Orchard, Director of the Conservatorium of Music, spoke of the value of records in education. He had always been partial to Columbia records and was exceedingly anxious to hear the new process records. He said he frequently used the graphophone to illustrate his lectures to his advanced students. This added immensely to the interest of the students. He hoped the Columbia Company would produce the complete works of well-known composers without any omissions. He looked forward to the day when some means would be found to avoid the breaks which occurred in orchestral and similar pieces when the record had to be changed. However late he returned from his labours at night, he was never too tired to hear good music on his graphophone. He also hoped that the company would continue to maintain their policy of producing only good music.

Mr H.A. Parker spoke of 'the great advances made in the improvement of the graphophone since its inception'. The irritating scratch had been entirely eliminated by a device invented, and as a result there was an increased demand for orchestral records. The sales of records exceeded the sales of any other class of musical instrument. The profits from popular records enabled them to encourage the popularity of serious and orchestral musical records, which otherwise they would be unable to produce. Thanks to the Columbia factory, Australia would be able to hear the reproduction of the latest musical comedy, as well as the compositions of Australian composers and the voices of Australian singers. Australian musicians should reap the benefit of this new industry. He paid tribute to Mr Power, the factory manager, saying that Australian workmen had proved themselves adaptable and intelligent in the new industry. The new process of musical reproduction on records was called electrical recording, which enabled a great volume of sound with proper stereoscopic results. Thus Mr Orchard's orchestra could be recorded at the factory while playing at the Conservatorium.

Mr Leo Rogaly (Grafonola) appealed to the press 'to find sufficient space for reviewing graphophone records, then the graphophone companies would be able to spend more money in advertising their products'. In this way, they would assist those who needed guidance in the choosing of good graphophone records.

Before leaving each guest was presented with the 'Columbia Company's latest record', 'Land of Hope and Glory', sung by the young Australian, Harold Williams, with full chorus and with the Band of HM Grenadier Guards. [91] However, the record presented to each guest was not the Columbia Co.'s latest record but a special pressing in a souvenir cover with a label which commemorated the opening of the factory. The recordings were made in London, but the disc was pressed at the new Australian factory.

A special four-page advertisement in the *Australasian Phonograph Monthly* gave the company's version of the development of recorded music, including comments by the general manager, Mr H.A. Parker, on 'Topical Music for Australia':

> Naturally it is in the lighter kinds of music that we expect to do the greatest business, here as elsewhere. The latest dance and the latest musical comedy 'hits' have the readiest sale. No sooner is a musical comedy staged here than its catchiest numbers are immediately asked for. Hitherto the Australian public has only been supplied with records of the London or foreign artists' performances. Depending on supplies from overseas we have sometimes been in danger

of being a little late for the market or of not meeting the demand in full. Now we shall be able to give the public prompt records of the actual performances it has enjoyed so heartily.

Since we are now able in our new factory to record and manufacture within a week or two, we shall be on the spot in more senses than one to give the Australian public what it wants.

Furthermore, we can encourage our own musicians. Hitherto, a piece of music composed in Australia has had to be sent to London to have a record taken and discs manufactured. Similarly our own concert artists, of whom we have a constant succession who go abroad and achieve fame on the other side of the world, have had to wait until they have left us to get records taken of their renderings. [92]

Columbia used their local recording facilities not only to make versions of the latest hits, but also to record topical material with particular appeal to an Australian market. A good example is Columbia 0539, *3OL – A Radio Fan's Dream*, which nicely uses public interest in a competing medium to promote record sales. This recording was made on 1 December 1926 and released about two months later. The 15 February 1927 issue of the *Music Trader* contained a review headed '3OL broadcasting sketch':

> One of the most amusing talking records which has been heard for a long time is the Sydney manufactured Columbia *3OL*, or *The Radio Fan's Dream*. It is composed and performed by Rupert Hazel, who appeared on the Tivoli stage in Melbourne recently, and is a burlesque imitation of the various forms of entertainment which are sent out by the broadcasting stations. There are blaring noises by the Woop Woop Brass Band, racing results and descriptions from the Moonshine Valley Racecourse, wrestling from the Stadium, a Salvation Army meeting, and many other items,

concluding with the announcer's angry discovery that he has 'done his last train in again.' One of the most amusing incidents is when the Stadium becomes mixed up with the Salvation Army and instead of a message of peace and goodwill, barrackers are heard shouting, 'Tear his ears off', 'Kick him in the shins,' etc. [195]

This record was so popular that a sequel was recorded in 1928, issued on *Columbia* 01274.

Columbia's enterprise and imagination in using its local facilities include the earliest 'original cast' recordings made in Australia. The first set were made by Reginald Dandy and Harriet Bennett, both of whom were members of the cast of *Rose Marie*, which had opened at Her Majesty's Theatre in Sydney on 29 May 1926. This production was so popular that it had already been running for nine months when the recordings were made in February 1927. The two records released as a result (*Columbia* 0580 & 02503) must have sold reasonably well as in June 1927 three more recordings were made by the stars of the production of *Madame Pompadour* which had recently opened at the Theatre Royal in Sydney. These 'original cast' recordings were by Vera Spaull, Arthur Stigant, Frank Webster, and Beppie De Vries (*Columbia* 0686, 02509 & 02510). The following month a further batch of original cast recordings were made by Arthur Clarke, Nellie Strong, James Liddy and Elise Gergely from the production of *The Student Prince* then playing at the Empire Theatre (*Columbia* 0705, 0729 & 02511).

West Australian Beryl Mills, who won the first Miss Australia contest in 1926, recorded a double-sided 'Miss Australia speaks to Australians' on *Columbia* 0601, in which she describes in wide-eyed terms her trip to America. In this she strikingly captures the degree to which Australia in the mid-1920s was still relatively unaffected by direct contact with American culture.

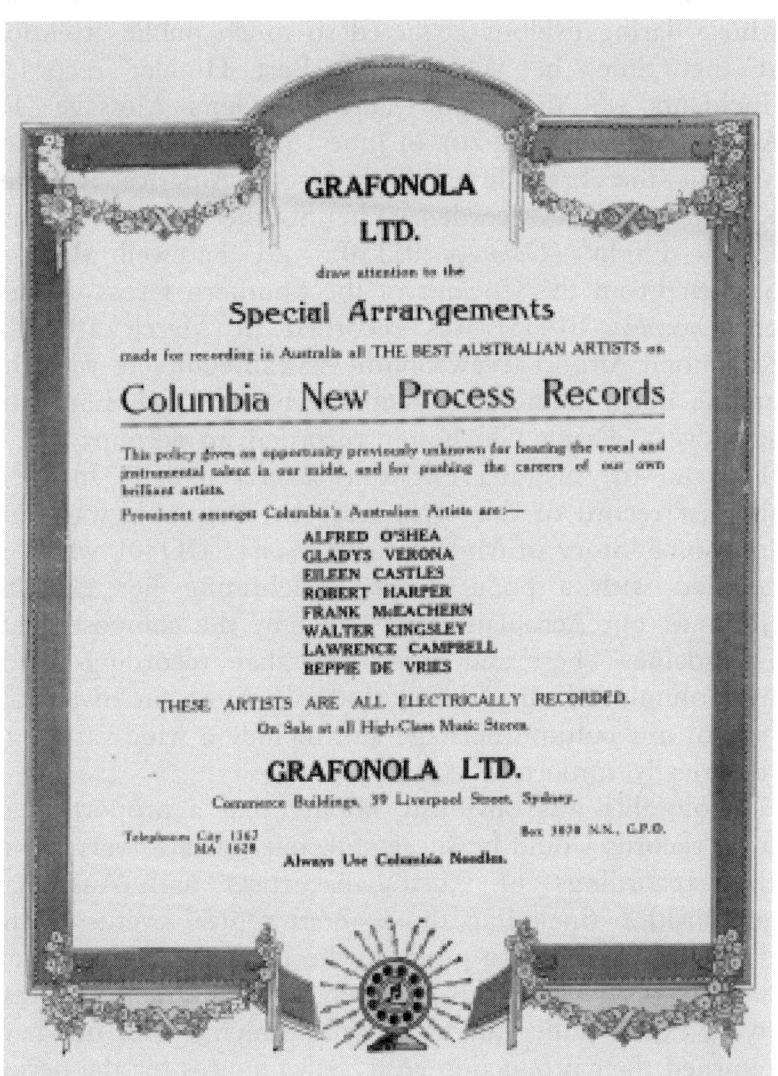

Columbia's promotion of Australian artists 1926. From the author's collection.

SOUND BEGINNINGS

Perhaps the recordings which capture the spirit of the age most graphically are the series of discs made by aviators whose daring exploits attracted so much public attention at that time. In March 1928 Bert Hinkler recorded 'Incidents of My Flight' and 'Hinkler's Message To Australia' (*Columbia* 0970); in June 1928, on his arrival after making the first direct flight from America, Charles Kingsford-Smith recorded 'The Southern Cross Trans-Pacific Flight' (*Columbia* 01150); and 'Farewell Message Spoken From the Cockpit of the Southern Cross' (issued on *Columbia* 01435) was recorded in March 1929 at Richmond Airport (New South Wales), complete with the engine noise of the aircraft in the background. Later the same year, Frank Chichester recorded an account of his 'England to Australia Flight' (*Columbia* 01839). In 1930 the last record of this type made by Columbia was Amy Johnson's 'Story of My Flight' (*Columbia* DO50), which is coupled with a popular song celebrating her exploits, 'Johnnie, our Aeroplane Girl', sung by the composer Jack Lumsdaine. These and other Australian recordings made by Columbia during this period constitute an invaluable part of our cultural heritage and include a wide variety of historically important items.

Columbia was obviously hoping that a proportion of local records would be successful, but was also very aware that recordings of Australian artists and Australian composition (including those about topical events of the day) could be used to promote the company. While a few local recordings did sell relatively well, the majority seem to have had rather moderate sales which would not have returned their production costs. Sales figures for the period July/August 1927 [Appendix 4] indicate a promising beginning for local production, but it is difficult to ascertain trends from only two months' figures. Unfortunately, sales figures for the following years are not available. However, William Donner, managing director of Columbia

Graphophone (Australia), stated in his evidence before the 1931 Tariff Board Inquiry that Australian recordings were approximately 13% of total sales. [47]

An early account of Columbia's local recording activities appeared in the Sydney *Sun* on 16 March 1927, describing the recording of 'Song of Sydney':

> One treads softly in this lofty, spacious chamber. Muffling felt deadens every footfall – fold on fold: green curtains sweep upwards to the roof. There is a sense of cloistered quiet. It is a locality apart from jarring noise, a place of melody – it is the recording studio of the Columbia Graphophone Co., at Homebush.
>
> Yesterday, in that great Australian studio, there was performed a piece of Australian music, the simultaneous recording of which may be of historic interest as the years lengthen. 'O! Sydney, I love you!', the Sun's tremendously popular £100 prize song – the Song of Sydney – was made imperishable.
>
> Placing Sydney's song on a Columbia record disclosed the modern methods now in use.
>
> Facing the members of the 2FC Studio Dance Band, led by Mr E. Pearse, and immediately in front of the vocalist, Mr L. Maurice, stood the magic disc – a radio microphone, familiar to all broadcasting enthusiasts. It was explained by the recording officer, Mr R.V. Southey, that modern recording was done electrically, and that the wide-mouthed trumpet, into which bands used to blare, was now a thing of the past.
>
> After preliminary practice work, the actual recording was carried out; the lilting joyous melody of 'O! Sydney, I love you' flooded the spacious studio, the sweet voice of the singer rising and falling in delightful cadence – and in the midst was the all-absorbing magic disc. The song ended, the last chords throbbed away – the musician's task was over – one's

eyes mechanically sought the magic disc. One saw, of course, a mere dumb, emotionless fabric of metal and electric wire, but beyond the small point of focus, the eye of fancy found that vast unknown audience for whose delighting the melody had just ebbed and flowed.

In thus recording the 'Song of Sydney,' the makers of the record will have literally broadcasted a flood of melody throughout the length and breadth of Australia – and further afield to foreign parts. Within a fortnight, the Columbia records of 'O! Sydney, I love you' will be ready.

Following the dispersal of the first issue of 'O! Sydney, I love you' within a few hours on Monday, the publishers, W.H. Paling and Co., placed a second edition in hand. This will be ready this afternoon, so those who were perhaps disappointed on Monday, will have an opportunity of securing copies. 'O! Sydney, I love you' will be sung at the Haymarket Theatre on Saturday next by Master Colin Crane, accompanied by the Haymarket Operatic Orchestra of 20. [131]

Shortly after local production of *Columbia* records began, the company's cheap label, *Regal*, also began to be produced using a G20000 catalogue series for 10in. records and a G30000 catalogue series for 12in. records. The *Regal* label was originally introduced in Britain by Columbia on 31 January 1914 as a means of competing with the cheaper record labels then entering the British market. This label had previously been imported into Australia by Columbia. The locally pressed *Regal* 10in. discs sold for 3/6 and 12in. discs for 5/- compared with the equivalent *Columbia* 10in. discs for 4/- and 12in. discs for 6/-.

The *Regal* label issued much the same mixture of standard repertoire, dance music, light classics, popular vocals, military bands and 'Hawaiian' groups as the dearer *Columbia* label. In some cases they were different selections

COLUMBIA

"O! SYDNEY I LOVE YOU"

Above: Making a recording of 'O! Sydney, I Love You' at the Columbia Graphophone studio, Homebush, March 1927. Left to right, the director of the orchestra Eric Pearse, Len Maurice, H.F. Cohen and Reg V. Southey.

Below: Recording the Australian Commonwealth Band at the Homebush studios, 1928. From the author's collection.

by the same performers (often disguised under pseudonyms). There was also the same range of sources for masters which included Australian, British, American and Continental recordings. A common practice was to issue similar selections by different artists on both *Columbia* and *Regal*. In other cases *Regal* featured performances not available on the *Columbia* label at all. The selection of material for each label seems to have been determined on the basis of class, with the more 'refined' material released on *Columbia* while less sophisticated repertoire appeared on *Regal*, but this distinction is not always readily apparent.

Some interesting Australian recordings were released on *Regal* in the 1920s including 'O! Sydney, I Love You', 'Sweet Hawaiian Sands', 'Dreams of Mine', 'My Home' and others. There were a few recordings by local dance bands, a range of locally-recorded instrumental performances on mouth-organ, steel guitar and piano-accordion, plus comedy routines like 'Father Fixes the Wireless' and in 1928 'Rupert Hazell Dreams He Is The Sheik'. In the latter sketch, when one of the characters is given a choice between death and 'living in Canberra forever', he exclaims loudly 'Not Canberra! Not Canberra!'. (Canberra was then mostly farming country. Parliament House was opened in May 1927.)

In April 1928, a further effort to compete with the most recent 'cheap' records selling at 2/6 or less (particularly the products of Clifford Industries) was made by reducing the price of *Regal* records from 3/6 to 3/-.

By early 1928 Columbia had begun providing a private recording service. A wide range of recordings was made, including amateur performances of all kinds, speeches, radio commercials, advertising records, political and religious messages and many other kinds of material. At first these records bore a generic *Columbia* label; in 1937 the name *Process Recording* appeared and continued to be used on most private recordings until 1959, after which they were described as *EMI Custom Service* records. Some discs used special labels at the request of the client. Both 10in. and 12in. discs were issued initially, and by the time 78rpm discs were phased out in the late 1950s more than 25,000 private records had been made by Columbia. However, their charges in the 1920s were quite high and only a few items had been made by the end of this period; the vast bulk date from the late 1930s onward.

A small item appeared in *Music in Australia* of 20 September 1928 announcing:

> For the next twelve months the advertising of the Columbia Company will be in the hands of Mr Leo Rogaly, managing director of Grafonola Limited. Mr Rogaly has had very wide and long experience in the talking machine world, and no one is better qualified than he to adequately handle the advertising and all problems connected with it. It is understood that the advertising appropriation of the Columbia Company will be more than twice the amount spent before. [90]

Figures for royalties paid to Australian artists from 1928 to 1930 [Appendix 6], show a steady decline, though production continued. They give a good indication of the falling record sales (for which no other figures are available) as the Depression began to bite.

During 1928 Columbia's engineer Ray Allsop made several short films using a sound-on-disc system in conjunction with his 'Raycophone' sound projection system, including a short featuring Cec Morrison's Orchestra, which must have been the first Australian dance band to make a sound film. In 1929 Columbia pressed the sound-on-disc component of a short film *Appeal against Entertainment Tax* with a commentary by Stuart Doyle, head of Union Theatres. Despite this pioneering involvement

SOUND BEGINNINGS

with the sound-on-disc technology, Columbia seems to have lost interest in catering for small-scale Australian productions and from 1930 its facilities were used only to press discs of soundtracks recorded in Hollywood. The Australian market was left to smaller players such as the Melbourne-based Vocalion and the Flexible Record Company.

In September 1929, Columbia recorded a series of speeches by the major political figures standing in the forthcoming Federal elections. Stanley Bruce spoke on 'The Issue of the Election' (*Columbia* 01673), Treasurer Earl Page on 'The Abolition of Duplication of Industrial Control' (*Columbia* 01674), Deputy Labor Leader E.G. Theodore on 'Industrial Arbitration in Australia' (*Columbia* 01675), and Labor leader W.M. Hughes on 'The Issues Before the People' (*Columbia* 01676). Perhaps not surprisingly, these records sold poorly and are very rare today. However they have great historical importance, and it is interesting to note that it was at the October 1929 election that Stanley Bruce lost his Victorian seat, becoming the first sitting Prime Minister to do so.

In 1930, the arrival of 'talking' pictures in Australia began to put theatre orchestras out of work. In January of that year two recordings were made by large groups of unemployed musicians. The *Australian Phonograph News* of 15 February 1930 carried an article on these recordings which seemed to reflect the view of the record company:

> In order to help the numerous local musicians who are unemployed owing to the introduction of the talkies, the Columbia Graphophone (Australasia), Ltd., decided to make two records and pay a substantial royalty to the Musicians' Fund. Arrangements were made to select good instrumentalists, who were conveyed in a number of cars, provided free by many people interested in the scheme, to Homebush. After preliminary tests, two orchestral numbers

COLUMBIA

*Packing and dispatch, Vocalion Factory, Richmond 1930.
From the author's collection.*

were recorded on the first day and two band selections on the following day. It speaks volumes for the efficiency of the Columbia Australian factory that the orchestral items were recorded on Tuesday, and the records placed on sale on the Friday, within three days.

Mr W.A. Donner, managing director of the Columbia Graphophone (Australasia), Ltd., had such a faith in the success of the records that several days before the recording session he handed over on behalf of the company a cheque for £100 as an advance against royalties to come.

A symphony orchestra had not previously been recorded in Australia, and the disc [*Columbia* 05055] is therefore, of historical importance. The 12-inch orchestral record consists of the *Hungarian March* from Berlioz's 'Damnation of Faust' (conducted by Albert Cazabon) and the charming *Coppelia* waltz, by Delibes (conductor, Fred Quintrell). The performance was very good indeed, and, in fact, much more satisfactory than at the Conservatorium orchestral concerts, for, instead of youthful students, the players were all men of long experience who had acquired artistic vision by playing under various conductors. Both Cazabon and Quintrell are infinitely better and more virile than Orchard, who, as even his friends admit, is a very poor conductor.

The standard of recording was exceptionally high, in fact, astonishing considering the circumstances, and the record compares very favourably with any recent European or American orchestral record.

The ten-inch band record [*Columbia* 01830] introduces Waldteufel's waltz, *Ever or never* and Williams' *Guard's patrol* the conductors being Horace Sheldon (Capitol Theatre) and Will Prior (State Theatre). The volume, clearness, resonance and performance leave nothing to be desired.

It is gratifying to hear from almost all dealers that the records are selling remarkably well and that the Musicians' Fund will considerably benefit. [113]

COLUMBIA

The generosity of Columbia in this case may have had something to do with the fact that, as the same publication reported, the company was doing good business pressing sound-on-disc records for imported films:

> Under Mr W.A. Donner's energetic leadership the Columbia Graphophone (A'asia), Ltd., has shown remarkable enterprise at the Homebush factory, where 'talkie' records are now being most satisfactorily pressed on the famous non-scratch Columbia surface.
>
> Two presses were designed under Mr Power's supervision, and were entirely made in Australia. Every bolt and even the armoured hose are of Australian manufacture. Each press weighs nearly two tons and the dye [sic] weighs 4cwt. For manufacturing records a 60lb. pressure is used. 'We are very proud of these two presses, which are a fine testimony to Australian enterprise and ability,' claims Mr Power with his genial smile.
>
> The 'talkie' records are 16-inch diameter, single-sided discs, and are beautifully finished off, highly polished, and with a perfect surface. Several rejected records were shown, which had a mere scratch on them. A 16-inch record has nearly twice the area of a 12-inch record, and as it is played at about 32 revolutions per minute (the standard phonograph record is played at 78), the disc plays nearly fifteen minutes.
>
> Mr Donner explained that the Columbia Company set itself to make perfect records and that the installation of the two new presses could supply the entire requirements for Australia and New Zealand. So far many 'talkie' records have been made for Metro-Goldwyn, First National, Paramount, and others. The reverse side of the record has the famous magic notes embossed on it with the inscription 'Columbia Records'.

In the *Australian Phonograph News* of September 1930 we read of 'New Columbia Maori records'; and the October

SOUND BEGINNINGS

1930 issue reports that 'the pre-view of Columbia's Rotorua film attracted an interested gathering and its future use in conjunction with the Columbia Maori recordings will help to popularise these numbers, and enable customers to visualise the fascinating environment in which they were actually recorded some months ago'. This appears to be an early example of a film being used to promote gramophone records.

Another item in the *Australian Phonograph News* of December 1930 states:

> There is not the slightest doubt that possession of a recording studio in Sydney has given the Columbia Company great prestige in being able to record many items of local and topical interest, and also by many people of note. This was also shown by the splendid series of Maori records, which were made early in this year when the recording outfit was taken over to New Zealand. This enterprise and alertness of the company have been exemplified in the record of the popular song '*Our Don Bradman*' which was recorded by Art Leonard some months ago, and proved a very good seller in Australia. No opportunity was lost by the company in England, and during the visit of the Australian Cricket Team, Don Bradman was asked to make a record, which is now released. In '*How it's done*' Don Bradman explains various aspects of cricket, and draws a comparison between cricket as played in England and Australia. He also speaks of many other topics of interest to cricketers, and expresses his view regarding the future of cricket. It is not generally known that in addition to being a cricketer Don Bradman is quite an accomplished amateur pianist, and on the reverse side of the record he is heard in two short items, '*The old fashioned locket*' and '*Our bungalow of dreams*', which he plays with a certain degree of brilliancy which is enhanced by the excellent recording (*Columbia* DO243). [108]

Australian recordings continued to be an important part of local sales, though comprising only a small proportion of the discs were released onto the market each month. Figures for total sales of Australian recordings for the period July 1929 to June 1931 [Appendix 7] show that, while not very large, they added significantly to Columbia's profits at a time when any additional business was desperately needed. The Depression was forcing sales of *Columbia* records during this period into steady decline, and the gradual falling off is clearly shown by the figures for the number of stampers produced between July 1929 and June 1931. [See Appendix 9]

The dramatic fall in record sales prompted Columbia to make a further reduction to the price of *Regal* records, and an item in the *Australian Phonograph News* of January 1931 notes that:

> ... the reduction in the price of Regal records to 2/6 has caused a stir amongst all dealers, and speculations are being made as to what the future will bring. Many dealers are inclined to think that if Regal put out the right titles without any delay, they will wipe out of existence the cheaper makes of records, which will be unable to stand up to the wonderful quality offered by the Columbia surface.

While the price reduction was forced on Columbia by the increasingly poor business environment, it certainly had the effect of making *Regal* by far the best selling label produced by Columbia. Once *Vocalion* had ceased production in October 1931 (partly due to the increased competition from *Regal*), Coles' Stores began retailing *Regal* records. Within a year they had forced all the other cheaper record makes out of the market. It was the *Regal*, almost single-handed, that enabled the company to survive.

In the early 1930s Columbia continued to promote record sales by releasing some topical material on *Regal*.

This ranged from 'Our Don Bradman' (G20744), to songs about Phar Lap, the Sydney Harbour Bridge (including 'Colonel Campbell and Mister Lang' on G21331); and even about the Depression – songs such as 'Banish the Budget Blues' by Art Leonard (G20758) which was released in late 1930; and 'Mister Depression (Will Soon Be Dead and Gone)' by Alec Regan (G21568), released in early 1933.

Another innovation was the introduction of a 'long playing' record. Initially this was simply a finer-grooved record with a slightly increased playing time; certainly not comparable to the long-playing microgroove record which began to be marketed in Australia in the 1950s. However, it is not generally known that the first 33⅓ rpm records sold in Australia were introduced by Columbia in June 1931. These records were not intended for general sale – few people would have had the necessary equipment to play them – but were produced for use in theatres as intermission music. The records were 12in. shellac pressings resembling 78rpm discs and were in a 'YOX' catalogue series, costing 8/- each.

On 31 August 1931, William Donner, managing director of Columbia Graphophone (Australia), provided revealing background on the operations of Columbia in Australia to a Tariff Board Inquiry:

> The Company was registered in March 1927, with a nominal capital of £100,000, divided into 100,000 shares of £1 each, all of which have been fully paid up. The objects of the Company were, inter alia, to take over from the Columbia Graphophone Co., Ltd., London, the assets and liabilities as of 1st November, 1926.
>
> It was decided by the London Company to commence manufacturing operations in Australia during 1925, with the result that the necessary buildings were purchased at a cost of £40,000, and the installation of plant and machinery –

including recording studio – involving an expenditure of 50,000, was put in hand during that year, the major portion of which was completed towards the latter part of 1926...

The plant we have operating in our factory embraces every branch and section of record manufacture, from the raw materials, including all matricing processes from the recording studio to the finished commercial record.

It has been the policy of the Columbia Company since it came to Australia to procure every possible manufacturing commodity within the Commonwealth, and where supplies of such material have been difficult to obtain we have encouraged local industries to produce them for us, rather than look elsewhere for our requirements...

The factory is equipped with the most modern copper deposition and nickel plating plant, together with a backing and mounting section, by which we manufacture all our stamping matrices from the imported mother, and, in addition, in the case of local recordings, i.e., the recording of Australian artists in our studio at Homebush – of which we do a very considerable amount – we process the master, mother and stamping matrices from the original recording wax...

In conclusion, I would submit that as the Company has invested capital to the extent of considerably over £100,000, and has a factory capable of handling all operations from the raw materials to the finished commercial record, thereby spending money within the country and giving employment to Australian workmen, it should be protected by an adequate tariff both as regards the importation of the biscuit and stamping matrices...

At the present time, owing to the merger which recently took place, the manufacturing of gramophone records is confined to our Company, and at the present time the Gramophone Co. Ltd., is closed, and the whole of the manufacture has been transferred to us...

The Chairman then asked: 'How many companies are actually making records in Australia at the moment?'

Mr Donner replied: 'There are the Columbia Company, the Gramophone Company and the Parlophone Co. conjointly, and the Brunswick Co. I don't think the Clifford Industries Co. is working now, as I understand they are in liquidation, but of this I am not certain. The Vocalion Company is also in liquidation... There was also the Flexible Record Company of Melbourne, but that also is in liquidation. I think that exhausts the lot...'

Sales figures for most of 1932 [Appendix 8] show the number of Columbia records sold during the whole of 1932 were less than sales for one month in 1927 [Appendix 4]. It is obvious that but for sales of Columbia's cheap *Regal* label the Columbia Company could not have survived. (This table also shows the comparable sales figures for *Parlophone* over the same period.)

The *Columbia* label did survive, but in 1931 Columbia Graphophone (Australia) was subsumed into a new corporate structure formed by a merger with Columbia's chief competitor, the Gramophone Company, manufacturer's of *His Master's Voice* records. This story is covered in Chapter 13.

Chapter 7

PARLOPHONE

The Parlophone Company Ltd. was established in Britain in 1923 and from the start its records were distributed in Australia by Best & Gee Pty. Ltd. of 103 York Street, Sydney. This company also acted as Parlophone's local agent. Parlophone's parent company was the Dutch firm of Carl Lindström AG and when Columbia Graphophone Co. Ltd. took a controlling interest in Lindström in October 1925, Parlophone became part of Columbia (International) Ltd.

Parlophone continued to maintain a separate identity and had a large degree of autonomy within the Columbia organisation. During 1926, the Australian *Parlophone* A2000 catalogue series was initiated, but at first the records were manufactured in Britain for export to Australia. The selections made for the Australian market differed little from those on the British *Parlophone* label, although some titles were never released in Britain. A few Australian compositions were also recorded in London for release in this series, such as 'Aussie Rose' by Jack Lumsdaine, or 'My Sweet Australian Wattle Girl' by Herschel Henlere. There were also some reissues of earlier recordings with

SOUND BEGINNINGS

A Parlophone label of 1928 with an Australian recording of a song about the animated cartoon character, Felix the Cat. From the author's collection.

local appeal, such as those by the Australian-born comedian Billy Williams.

Best & Gee continued to handle all Parlophone business in Australia until October 1926, when Parlophone sent Alan Wright out to act as their representative and to set up a branch office in Sydney. He had joined the Parlophone Company in 1925, and already had experience working in the company's factories in London, Paris and Berlin. Wright was instructed to arrange for local recordings to be made and for *Parlophone* records to be pressed by the new Columbia factory in Sydney. His responsibilities also included selecting artists and repertoire for the local recordings, acting as recording engineer, arranging advertising in the local press, and managing the Australian office. Best & Gee's role was reduced to that of sole distributors for Australia and New Zealand.

Parlophone originally had a recording studio at Burwood, Sydney (probably at the offices of Best & Gee), but this studio seems to have been in operation for only a few months in mid-1927. The masters made there apparently used the acoustic recording equipment which had been sent to New Zealand to record Maori songs at Rotorua during the tour by the Duke and Duchess of York in February 1927. These Maori recordings were issued in a special 'AR' series with a distinctive label which pictured a Maori chieftain and sold for 6/-. Regular *Parlophone* 10in. records were 4/-.

After a few months of acoustic recording, Parlophone decided to utilise the more modern electric recording facilities at the Columbia studio in Homebush. Alan Wright referred to this at the 1927 Tariff Board Inquiry: 'The Columbia Company and ourselves have both recording plants, but I usually use the Columbia recording plant.' [45] The Columbia factory definitely began filling Parlophone's pressing requirements from November 1926 onward, and by July 1927 Wright could state 'they are now supplying almost all of our orders in the Commonwealth from locally made stocks.' [33] Wright set out further details of Parlophone's working practices in correspondence with the Comptroller-General of Customs dated 11 July 1927:

> It is necessary to explain that this Company is at present working a Branch Office in Australia, and has entered into arrangements with the Columbia Graphophone Company, by which the 'mother' matrices are imported from abroad, and the Columbia Company then manufactures them for us. The object of this is to reduce the overhead charges of both firms, it being a reciprocal arrangement between the two Companies, for, as they are manufacturing for us here, so we, or our associated firms, in various other countries are manufacturing for 'Columbia'.
>
> Our actual staff employed is very small, comprising a representative, who is also a technical and recording expert, and in charge of all the Company's interests in Australia [i.e. himself], and his assistant. This means that the actual capital of the Company in Australia is very small, being limited to the cost of the recording machine and equipment, the value of the stocks of 'masters' recorded in Australia, and the imported 'mothers', giving a total of approximately £1,060. This will, of course, be a gradually increasing amount as more 'mothers' are imported and more recordings are made locally.
>
> Though we do not directly employ workmen in the final process of pressing our records, they are being pressed by the 'Columbia' Company, you will readily understand that our own Company is the means of adding considerably to the total amount of the 'Columbia' plant and of their wages account. They have, we understand, already included their output for us in their returns furnished to your Department, but for your information we append our monthly figures up

to the 30th June, 1927 [see Appendix 5]. From these it will be noted that whilst there was a natural increase right up to April last, the figures from then onward have remained stationary, and will, if the 'dumping' competition continues, most assuredly affect us by causing a decline instead of a gradual increase.

As already indicated we will be only too pleased to attend, and give evidence before the Tariff Board in Melbourne to save time, and thanking you in anticipation of your having our application dealt with as expeditiously as possible. [33]

Wright was obviously doing his best to give the impression that Parlophone was an independent entity, rather than a wholly-owned subsidiary. He had reason; Parlophone was a relatively small-scale operation and sales figures (by value) for the first eight months of local production [Appendix 5] show that Parlophone's sales were much smaller than those on the *Columbia* label, and this trend was to continue.

From the time *Parlophone* records began to be pressed in Australia each release included some local recordings. However, unlike Columbia, Parlophone did not attempt to offer a wide range of recorded repertoire but confined itself, with only a few exceptions, to popular vocal recordings. Among the exceptions were two records by the comedy team of Stiffy and Mo (comedian Roy Rene's first recordings); the contralto Jessie Shmith's only 1920s recording; a long series (1927-31) of records by Australian-resident Hawaiian performer David Kaili (mostly with his wife Queenie); some piano and organ solos, and a few records by dance bands and instrumental groups.

Parlophone made no special effort to enter the private recording field (it is likely that it was company policy not to compete with Columbia in this area), but Parlophone did produce three records for the XXIXth Eucharistic Congress held in Sydney in September 1928. These were two 12in. and one 10in. records with a special *Official Congress Record* label. An article entitled 'Papal Legate Makes a Record', published in *Music in Australia* at the time, refers to part of this series.

In April 1928 the first locally-pressed 12in. recordings were released in an A4000 series, and these records were priced at 6/-. Around the same time another higher priced 12in. 'AR' series was begun, which sold for 8/6. Most recordings in the 12in. series were pressed from imported masters, although the famous Italian opera singer, Fernando Autori, recorded two 12in. masters while visiting Sydney in August 1928 (*Parlophone* AR1006).

In late 1928, Parlophone began producing the *Kismet* label for sale in Woolworths stores for 3/-. The sources were the same as were used for the *Parlophone* catalogue; however most of the masters selected for release on *Kismet* never appeared on *Parlophone*. The label was possibly introduced on an experimental basis and discontinued before national distribution was arranged, because it has been found only in Sydney and Perth. For some reason it was never made available in Melbourne or Adelaide by Woolworths, but it may have been sold in other cities. *Kismet* was on sale for barely twelve months, and sales must have been poor, as it is among the rarest labels produced by a major company during the 1920s.

The years 1928 to 1930 appear to have been uneventful, as there are few press reports of Parlophone's activities during this period. However, an item in the *Australian Phonograph News* of May 1931 reports:

> From May 1, Best and Gee Ltd., are relinquishing the sole agency of the Parlophone Co. Ltd. for Australasia. It is not the intention of the Parlophone Co. Ltd., to appoint new sole agents, as the Company's branch office at Homebush will carry out distribution work throughout Australasia itself,

PARLOPHONE

through the present State agents. The Australasian Manager is Mr P.A. Wright. [105]

Clearly, the Depression was taking hold. A document tendered to the 1931 Tariff Board Inquiry regarding recording expenses states that 'the total amount involved in respect of local recordings from July 1st 1929 to June 30th 1931 is £1895.16.1d. This amount excludes any monies paid to Columbia for use of studio.' [35]

On 5 December 1932, W.A. Donner, managing director of Columbia Graphophone (Australia), wrote to Louis Sterling at Hayes in relation to the future of the *Parlophone* label:

> I have taken out the shipment figures of Columbia, Regal, and Parlophone records for the eleven months of this year, January to November [Appendix 8]... from which you will see we [*Columbia* and *Regal*] have sold 803,761 records against Parlophone's 128,354. Of our total 161,111 are actually Columbia sales, but what must be taken into account is that we reduced the Regal records to 2/6d., and made the line more interesting by transferring to it a considerable number of Columbia items... We were forced into this position because of conditions out here in an endeavour to get some kind of turnover which would give us a cost. Regal today is the biggest selling record, and because of it we are able to keep the factory going, and get down to a cost which at least is nothing like as bad as it would be if we were not carrying out this policy.
>
> My view of the matter is this; as we are losing a good deal of our Dark Blue [Columbia] sales because of our Regal policy, if we could strengthen our Columbia line with Parlophone matrices it might be considered a good move as we could possibly sell more Parlophone artists on Columbia than Parlophone are selling on their own label.

> ... Conditions are very difficult out here today. It would definitely make for economy although I appreciate it would mean submerging the Parlophone trade mark.
>
> An alternative proposal would be for us to take over Parlophone here and run the line. At the present time we are selling Parlophone records through our Wholesale Departments in New South Wales and Victoria. I recently fixed up with Mr Wright for Nathans to handle Parlophone in Auckland. Webley is willing to do it in the South Island [of New Zealand], and in South Australia our agents there are now handling it.
>
> Today when economy is so essential I mention this alternative suggestion because there is really no necessity for a separate staff, and it would help us in our endeavour to reduce our loss to a minimum if we handled it ourselves and got what profit we could out of Parlophone. [6]

From this, it is obvious that *Parlophone* was in a very precarious position. In the event, it seems that while *Parlophone* continued as a separate label, the level of autonomy it had previously enjoyed could no longer be sustained.

A letter of 7 February 1933 from Paul Offenbacher (director of the Carl Lindström Aktiengesellschaft, Berlin, which controlled the German branch of the Parlophone company) to Wright, provides a rare insight into the predicament of the record industry during the early 1930s:

> I have received your hand-written personal letter of November 9th and have been delaying my reply for a week or two, as I was expecting to be in London where the question of the Australian business will have to be gone into.
>
> Unfortunately, the losses have continued month by month and it is difficult to see how under these conditions we can continue the business. However, I shall not be able

PARLOPHONE

to be in England for another week or two and I do not wish to keep my answer to your letter waiting any longer.

I am glad that you have made the suggestion that on account of the bad times the business is going through, you should for the year 1933 not take the rise which was laid down in the contract. This step of yours, which I much appreciate, has saved me from the unpleasant task to ask you to agree to a reduction... I may be taking an undue pessimistic view, but it would be doing you a poor service if I did not point this position out to you in good time to enable you to carefully consider the situation from your own personal point of view.

If the Parlophone business comes to an end in Australia, would you wish me to suggest to Columbia that they should take you over in Australia? Would you be inclined to work under Mr Donner and do you think there are many chances for you with them? Of course, I cannot say whether Columbia would be in a position to take you over... No need to tell you that things in England are particularly bad at present, and no sign of improvement can be detected.

It is not at all impossible that Australia being one of the first places to start the Depression, it may be the first country to be out of it. You may prefer to stay out in Australia now that you have been there for so many years and know a good many people, and have no doubt got some useful connections. I wonder if there would be any possibility of doing something with the Parlophone business, as after all it would be a terrible thing to give it up after so much money has been poured into it in the hope of holding it through until better times. Perhaps you could find a firm of some standing and capital to take the whole business over...

Whatever happens, my advice for the present would be, if it is at all possible, to keep out of Europe. I do not know whether you still have a great dislike to Australia, but no doubt with time you have got over it. Everyone who is outside Europe under the present conditions, ought to be very glad, since the chances are so small that they cannot be worse anywhere...

... Today for economic and political reasons it is quite impossible to make any arrangements for the future and it is almost impossible to look forward for a month, and all we can do is to look from day to day. I am doubtful whether the Parlophone business in Australia can continue. As you know, Mr Donner has already suggested to Mr Sterling that he should be allowed to use Parlophone recordings on Columbia, as it would strengthen Columbia and reduce Columbia's loss... This would mean that in the same way as we are issuing Odeon records in England under the Parlophone label, Parlophone records in Australia might be issued as Columbia records, Parlophone series. I want you to clearly understand that the matter has not been discussed or considered so far, but we cannot continue losing money for ever and some step will have to be taken, and it is therefore quite probable that some such suggestion will arise.

In that case I do not quite know where your position would come in after your contract expires... It is difficult to say whether there would be a suitable job for you. Similar conditions unfortunately prevail in all other countries where either we have taken over the other E.M.I. firms or they have taken over us. Unless an economical miracle occurs – and I am not a believer in miracles – the position will not improve for a long time... [36]

Alan Wright retired as manager on 31 August 1933, following the completion of the merger of Parlophone with Columbia and HMV to form the EMI group. He then joined United Radio Distributors in Sydney as their sales manager, a position he held until January 1943 when the directors of the company decided to close down until after the War as they were experiencing difficulties in obtaining stock under wartime conditions.

PARLOPHONE

The *Parlophone* label continued a nominal independence, but after Alan Wright's departure it was run 'as a sort of branch of Columbia', as predicted by Offenbacher. The Australian *Parlophone* A2000 catalogue series reached the end of the A3000s in October 1934 (the last number used was actually A3993), before jumping to A6000 as the A4000 and A5000 blocks had already been allocated to other *Parlophone* series.

SOUND BEGINNINGS

From Sun News-Pictorial, *1 May 1928.*

Chapter 8

VOCALION

From its earliest days the Aeolian Company seems to have taken a particular interest in the Australian market. The Aeolian Co. Ltd. was established in Britain in 1920 and produced the *Aeolian Vocalion* label (later simply *Vocalion*). Like many other labels of the period, the *Vocalion* label and its lower-priced subsidiary label *Aco*, which was established in 1922, were quickly exported to Australia. *Vocalion* issued special releases for the Australian market, some of which featured the first recordings of Australian compositions. They also recorded an unusually large number of Australian performers in Britain during the early and mid-1920s.

This practice attracted the attention of the *Music Trader* which commented that 'the popularity of *Vocalion* records in Australia is probably due to the recording of some of her most famous artists of recent years. Well-known among these are Madame Evelyn Scotney, Horace Stevens, Malcolm McEachern, Alberto Zelman, John Amadio, Max Pirani, Frederick Collier, and the idol of the Australian musical comedy stage, Miss Gladys Moncrieff.' [65] Other Australian artists who appeared on *Vocalion* included John

Collinson, Kitty Reidy, Clara Serena, Albert Whelan, the Australian Newcastle Steel Works Band (who toured Britain twice during the 1920s) and the Australian Commonwealth Band.

In January 1925 the *Vocalion* label was acquired by the newly incorporated Vocalion Gramophone Co. Ltd. This company continued to record many of the Australian artists already appearing on *Vocalion*, and also produced further issues especially for the Australian market. In mid-1926 two new *Vocalion* series were established which seem to have been sold only in Australia. These were the 12in. S100 series priced at 6/-, and the 10in. T2000 series priced at 4/6. Although all recordings issued in these series were made in London, most featured Australian artists who had previously had records released in the regular British series.

The April 1926 issue of the *Music Trader* advised that:

> The recent announcement by the Aeolian Company that they intend to open a record pressing plant in Victoria, is another indication that overseas companies are showing appreciation for Australia as a market. Already the Brunswick and 'His Master's Voice' companies are making records in Australia, and I understand that it will not be long before the Columbia plant is operating. Thus, soon, we shall have four big companies producing records within the Commonwealth. So far, however, the only one of the overseas companies making phonograph cabinets in Australia is the Aeolian Company... [70]

Three months later, the same trade journal reported that 'information is to hand that the Vocalion Company of Hayes, England, have definitely decided to press records in Australia. We understand the very latest of plant is to be installed in a portion of the Aeolian Company's assembling factory at Richmond.' [180]

At the end of the year, the *Music Trader* carried an article, 'Melbourne's new industry':

> Convinced that Australia offers them remarkable opportunities, a number of firms have established factories for pressing records in the Commonwealth. For various reasons those companies have displayed a preference for Sydney and opened up there... As Melbourne citizens, [we rejoice] heartily at the decision to establish a record pressing works in this city, which has been reached by the Aeolian Co. (Aust.) Ltd. of Collins Street. The machinery, which is the very latest, is on its way and is expected to be here within a few days. Last January, Mr Gendle, the general manager of the London pressing house of the company, visited this continent, and he was impressed with the wonderful possibilities for this work in Australia. He travelled extensively in the Commonwealth, and eventually voted for Melbourne as the centre for the factory. A considerable number of employees will be required by the new undertaking. The pressing will be done by the new electrical recording process [sic]. Thousands of compositions will be on hand and a quick service will be guaranteed. [135]

Work began on a factory for pressing Vocalion records at 49-59 Coppin Street, Richmond, in January 1927. The *Music Trader* of 15 January 1927 reported that 'preparations for the pressing of Vocalion records in Australia by the latest processes are now in full swing. Mr C.H. Gendle, formerly general manager of the Aeolian Company in London, arrived in Melbourne by the Moldavia 11 January to take charge of this work. [76] On 20 April 1927 Charles Henry Gendle, manager of the Vocalion Gramophone Co. was appointed agent for the company in Victoria. [62]

A report in the British publication *Talking Machine World* on 15 April 1927 about 'the establishment in

Melbourne, Australia, of a factory for the electrical recording of musical and elocutionary performances and for the pressing of disc records is reported to be under consideration...' makes it sound as if the Melbourne factory was merely a proposal; in fact the first records came off the presses on 28 July 1927, according to the caption on a staff photograph taken that day.

The first locally-manufactured *Vocalion* records were issued in a XA18000 series (to distinguish them from the British *Vocalion* X9000 series) and about 80 records had been issued in this series by the time it was discontinued a year or so later. Vocalion also released an Australian *Aco* label at about the same time, as well as continuing to press selected releases in the various British series on both *Vocalion* and *Aco*, using the British catalogue numbers.

Other labels were also soon introduced. Some were uniquely Australian, such as the *Gaiety* label. The trade mark for *Gaiety* was registered on 15 August 1927, and the design for its record sleeve was registered on 14 September 1927. A letter signed R.E. Sanders of Craig Williamson Pty. Ltd. dated 26 October 1927, reads: 'Confirming our call of today, our Mr Brown has instructed us from Sydney to let you know that the business with reference to the 'Gaiety' records is now definitely off.' [15] This would seem to indicate that the *Gaiety* label was discontinued from that date, giving the label a lifespan of only about two months. There were only 24 issues released during that time, priced at 2/6.

Vocalion produced other labels under licence. These included *Polydor* (the export label of the *Deutsche Grammophon Gesellschaft*) and *Gennett* (a label produced by the Starr Piano Company of Richmond, Indiana). Both of these labels had previously been imported into Australia, and in the case of *Gennett* the Vocalion pressings are believed to be the only issues on this label produced outside

VOCALION

the United States. Local production of these labels was short-lived, however; both had been discontinued by 1928.

Initially, *Vocalion* and *Aco* records were distributed by the Aeolian Company which had outlets at 416-418 George Street, Sydney; and 252 Collins Street, Melbourne; as well as in Brisbane, Adelaide and Newcastle. But on 21 March 1928 an announcement was made in London that 'the Vocalion Gramophone Company is forming a new company, Vocalion Foreign, Limited, with a capital of £200,000, to acquire the Vocalion Company's Australian factory and business. The purchase price is £60,000.' [207] The *Vocalion* XA18000 series was still in production, and is notable for including the first recordings made by Vocalion in Australia, at their recording studio in the Sunshine Building, 654-664 Bourke Street, Melbourne, between May and July 1928.

In May 1928 Vocalion introduced the 8in. *Broadcast* record which sold for 2/-. This record was advertised in newspapers at the beginning of that month, with claims that it was 'undoubtedly a remarkable record... and so convinced are we of its qualities that it is introduced with all the confidence and enthusiasm due to such an excellent proposition.' [196]

An item in *Music in Australia* announced:

> Broadcast electrically recorded long playing records are now on the Australian market. Those who do not yet know Broadcast records will be interested to learn that they are by the Marconi Company's exclusive electrically recording process. The local agents claim that they are double sided and play as long, but in some cases longer, than ordinary 10" records and have good volume and clarity of tone. The New South Wales distributors, Norman L. Burnell & Co. (New South Wales) Ltd., 350 Kent Street, Sydney, state that Broadcast records are now obtainable at all leading music stores... [82]

Charles Gendle, Vocalion's Australian manager, speaking of the new 8in. *Broadcast* disc, said that:

> It has established itself in England against the cheap records selling there; it is a novelty in its appearance and excellence of volume... The position is that in England they have discontinued the production of 'Vocalion' and 'Aco' records in view of the success of the 'Broadcast'... I may say this has been the salvation of our company... They are recorded 100 lines to the inch as against 90 on the standard record. These are made by the Marconi Company's electrical process of recording which is peculiar to us. We get perfect reproduction right to the finish, irrespective of the variations in the surface speed past the needle. [61]

A few days later the *Argus* newspaper published an item about the Vocalion flotation:

> Particulars have been received in Melbourne of the terms of the flotation in London of Vocalion (Foreign) Ltd., with a capital of £200,000 divided into 400,00 ordinary shares of 10/- each. The issue just made was 240,000 ordinary shares. The prospectus states that the Company was to acquire from the Vocalion Gramophone Co. Ltd., the entire assets and stock of its Australian factory and the business at Melbourne as at December 31, 1927. It also took over the sale and exclusive right to manufacture and sell throughout the world, except in the United Kingdom, Irish Free State, Russia, and North America, records under the name of 'Broadcast' and 'Aco', and other records of a similar type to the 'Broadcast' now being manufactured by the Vocalion Gramophone Co. Certain other business rights have also been acquired by the new concern. The prospectus states that the Australian factory was commenced in January, 1927, and had been in production since November of that year. It was equipped with the latest type of machinery imported from Great

Britain and the United States for the manufacture of gramophone records. The present output of the factory was already fully contracted for, and plant additions to be installed would increase its capacity to 4,000,000 records a year.' [206]

On 5 June 1928 Vocalion (Foreign) Ltd. was registered under the Companies Act 1915 and replaced the former entity of Vocalion Gramophone Co. Ltd. [62] A few months after the changeover, the *Vocalion* label was discontinued, leaving the 8in. *Broadcast* label as the only record being marketed by the company. Early in 1928 some local recordings began to appear on *Broadcast*, vocals by Jack O'Hagan proving especially popular.

By June 1928, Vocalion was offering the services of its recording studio to the general public for the production of personal recordings. An advertisement in September 1928 advised:

> There are folk around the other side of the world who would welcome more than anything else a record of your voice.
>
> To hear the recorded voice of a far-distant son or daughter or close friend produces profound emotion, second only to a meeting in the flesh, infinitely more eloquent than letters, it is not hackneyed, not usual, not common, but brings the additional thrill of the totally unexpected.
>
> Your voice, your husband's voice, and your children's voices, can be recorded as faithfully as a prima donna's song. The process is extremely simple – you can speak as though you were casually chatting, or sing as though in your drawing-room. With the unapproachable accuracy of electrical recording, the exact tone, lilt, accent and 'warmth' of your living voice can be permanently preserved.
>
> From one recording, any number of records can be made. Come to the studio and get all particulars, and let us show you the way in which records are made (under the charge of an expert of high European standing), or write to us and we

will send a free post-free booklet, beautifully produced and illustrated, covering every aspect of 'personal recording'. Note: Students of singing should have their voices recorded at regular intervals. [187]

As each personal recording was numbered in a 'PR' series, it seems that less than 260 such recordings were made between 1928 and 1931. Only a fraction of these survives. Among the last was a two-part item titled 'Astor-isms' by the well-known radio announcer Renn Miller (recorded around July 1931). Unfortunately, no copy of the 'beautifully produced and illustrated' booklet mentioned in the advertisement has so far been found. If any reader has information about these recordings, I would be grateful to hear from them.

During 1929 Vocalion produced several new labels including *Broadcast De Luxe*, *Broadcast Twelve*, *Embassy*, *Arcadia*, and *Savoy*. These were 10in. records and were introduced in early 1929. *Broadcast Twelve* was registered as a trademark on 9 January 1929, priced at 3/6 and the catalogue consisted mainly of light classical and 'standard' repertoire. *Broadcast De Luxe* was used mainly for releases of popular material, and it probably cost 3/-.

The other three labels were pressed for various specific outlets. *Embassy* was a new trademark being used by Coles Stores for a wide variety of 'own brand' products, and was registered on 12 July 1929; the first records were released the next month. The *Arcadia* trademark was registered on 26 August 1929 by Picot & Rosenthal of 250 Pitt Street, Sydney and was probably sold through Edments Stores. No trademark registration has been traced for *Savoy*, nor is it known for what outlet they were produced. All these labels are believed to have sold for 2/6.

By mid-1929 Vocalion was increasingly active with local recording, and many of these appeared on the *Broadcast*, *Embassy*, *Arcadia* and *Savoy* labels. But despite this burst of

Advertisement for Vocalion private recording from The Listener In, *September 1926.*

renewed activity, Vocalion was already in financial difficulty. The British publication *Wireless and Gramophone Trader* of 2 November 1929 reported that 'the first six months of the year Vocalion (Foreign) Ltd. incurred a loss of £16,624, of which £11,191 was in its Australian operation.'

The parent company was apparently unwilling to continue funding a loss-making operation, and moves were made to sell off the holdings in Australia by setting up a wholly Australian-owned company. The *Argus* of 9 May 1930 carried an item headed 'Vocalion company sold':

> Mr M. Rosenthal, a Sydney business man, announced yesterday that a group of Australian and New Zealand investors had purchased the assets in Australasia, including the factory at Richmond (V.) and trade marks of Vocalion (Foreign) Ltd. for the sum of £125,000. The negotiations with the British company, from which the purchase was made, were conducted by telephone from Sydney, the conversation with London occupying 28 minutes 4 seconds. A new company would be formed to conduct the business of manufacturing and distributing phonograph records.
>
> Mr Rosenthal, who will be general manager of the new company, stated that in future no royalty would have to be paid to the English company, and that it would be possible to reduce materially the price of Vocalion records. The plant at the Richmond factory was capable of producing 4,000,000 records a year and would remain under the management of Mr C.H. Gendle, who was the technical expert. The new company would have the use of all Vocalion matrices for the purpose of producing the records. [209]

A similar story appeared in the *Sydney Morning Herald* the following day. It mentions that in addition the new company would have 'the services of the American Record Corporation' (which was a source of masters used by the previous company).

On 29 May 1930, the *Sydney Morning Herald* published a full-page advertisement carrying the 'Abridged Prospectus' of Vocalion (A'asia) Ltd. which included the statement that 'so far as the Directors are aware, this issue presents the first opportunity to the public of Australia and New Zealand to participate in the profits of an established gramophone record manufacturing company'. [64]

The same 'Abridged Prospectus' was published in *Smith's Weekly* on 7 June 1930 and probably in other publications. A section headed 'Estimated profits and returns to investors' makes the following claims:

> The sale of better class records, i.e., 1-inch and 12-inch records retailed at from 3/- to 6/6, amounts to approximately 10,000,000 annually in Australia and New Zealand. Popular, dance, and vocal records, with the demand continually increasing, are usually retailed at 4/- each. It is the intention of the Company to sell to the public a product equal in every respect to these records, embracing an extensive range of the very latest theme songs from talkie films, and the latest hits from musical shows, in both vocal and dance form, at the popular price of 2/6 each, and a range of 12-inch records, comprising world-famous and ever-popular light classical, operatic, and standard numbers by many famous artists, orchestras, and military bands (usually retailed at 6/6) for 4/-. It also intends to support the sale of these records by an extensive advertising campaign. On this basis the following estimated profits for the first year are considered conservative. It is anticipated that during the first two years £30,000 will have been spent in advertising and developing the sale of the Company's records, which, with the normal expansion of business to be reasonably expected under these circumstances during the second year's trading, fully justifies the Directors in estimating a considerable increase in profits for that year, and they therefore, consider it not unreasonable

to anticipate the following Dividends will be paid: 10 per cent. Dividend – first year: 20 per cent. Dividend – second year.

The 'Abridged Prospectus' gives the 'gross profits on sale of records, Vocalion portable gramophones, Vocalion radio combination, gramophone needles, and revenue from recording studio (after allowing for factory overhead costs, royalty and copyright charges)' as £65,000, less 'advertising and distributing costs, Directors' and Auditors' fees, rent legal expenses, office rent and all expenses generally connected with administration' debenture interest, and income tax to a total of £41,100. Leaving an 'estimated net profit' of £23,900. [64]

This prospectus was rightly greeted with some scepticism, and an item in the *Sydney Morning Herald* of 7 June 1930, headed 'An unexplicit prospectus', comments:

> The prospectus of Vocalion (Australasia) Ltd., a company which has been registered in Sydney, and which is making an issue of shares for public subscription, quotes, for a period of years, share values of gramophone company shares as listed on the London Stock Exchange. Quotations of three companies' shares for 1929 are stated as follows: Vocalion Gramophone Co. Ltd., ordinary 10/- shares, £3/16/3; The Gramophone Co. Ltd., ordinary £1 shares £16/5/-; Columbia Graphophone Co. Ltd., ordinary 10/- shares £18. The prospectus does not indicate what the range of the prices of these shares was during the year, nor what were more recent quotations, which would be information of interest to the investing public. The full range of prices of these shares during 1929, it might be pointed out, was as follows: Vocalion, highest £3/16/3, lowest 13/-; Gramophone, highest £18/12/6, lowest £3/15/7; [and] Columbia, highest £18/6/3, lowest £3/12/6. The 'Weekly Official Intelligence' of the London Stock Exchange gives the following highest

and lowest prices of the shares for the week ended April 23 last: Vocalion 11/9, 8/6; Gramophone £4/15/-, £4/11/3; Columbia £6/7/6, £6/3/9. [210]

Vocalion was certainly putting the most optimistic interpretation possible on 'estimated profits' by selectively quoting figures which gave a less than realistic impression of the value of holding record company shares.

However, despite this, in mid-1930 Vocalion (Foreign) was superseded by Vocalion (Australasia) Ltd., which was incorporated on the 4 June 1930. The new company represented a transfer to Australian ownership of the former British owned entity, and was set up with capital of £300,000 'divided into 50,000 8% Cumulative Participating Preference Shares [at] £1 each [for a total of] £50,000 (participating with ordinary shares up to and not including more than 10% in any one year), [and] 1,000,000 Ordinary Shares of 5/- each [for a total of] £250,000'. [59]

It was also noted that:

... one Debenture of £40,000 for a term of 10 years from 1st March, 1930, at 6½% per annum has been issued to Vocalion (Foreign) Limited, the Company's predecessors, as part consideration for the purchase of the Company's assets. The Company is under no obligation to provide a Sinking Fund for the redemption of these Debentures.

The net purchase price of the factory, including all machinery, stock, etc., was £125,000. This £125,000 was to be satisfied as follows: £40,000 Debentures, £45,000 Ordinary Shares, £40,000 cash, Total £125,000. Of the above £125,000 wherein it shows £40,000 to be paid in cash, the Vendors to the Company have agreed to apply for this £40,000 in shares, showing their faith in the future of the Company. It will thus be seen that the purchase of the factory and equipment by Vocalion (Australasia) Limited has been accomplished without any cash consideration. Under the

Contract of Sale, part of the consideration was that the Vendors have an option to purchase at par, £35,000 worth of shares at any time within two years from the date of incorporation of the Company, 4th June, 1930. [59]

The directors were Haliburton A. Sheppard, chairman of the Melbourne Stock Exchange, director of North Broken Hill Ltd. and other companies; Sir John Butters, former general manager, Government Hydro Electric Department, Hobart, former chairman, Tasmanian Committee, Commonwealth Advisory Council of Science & Industry, director of Associated Newspapers Ltd. and other companies; Joseph S. Emanuel, managing director, Reliance Loan Mortgage & Discount Corporation Ltd., Auckland, New Zealand; William V. Worth, director, Reliance Loan Mortgage & Discount Corporation Ltd., Auckland, New Zealand; and Maurice Rosenthal, managing director, Picot Rosenthal Pty. Ltd. of Sydney and Melbourne. A Vocalion information circular stated with confidence: 'It will be seen from the above list that the Directorate comprises men of outstanding ability, well known in Australia and New Zealand.' [59]

It should be noted that several of the directors had, or represented, significant financial interests in the new company. The information circular informs us that 'under an underwriting agreement between the Company and the Reliance Loan Mortgage & Discount Corporation Ltd., dated 12/9/1930 the latter Company has through itself or its nominees underwritten £9,809 of shares.' and also 'the purchase price of the whole shares of Picot Rosenthal Pty. Ltd. of Sydney and Melbourne (who had the distribution contract with Vocalion (Foreign) Ltd.) was £22,000.' [59]

The registered office of the company was 250 Pitt Street, Sydney; the head office and factory were at 49 Coppin Street, Richmond (Victoria) and the company had branches in Sydney, Adelaide and Brisbane. 'All the Branches are main distributing centres for the various dealers and wholesale houses as each Branch of the Company on account of its new and successful method of distribution, acts as a clearing house for the benefit of giving excellent service and co-operation to its dealers.' [59]

This seems, once again, to be putting the best gloss on the decision by Vocalion to effectively become its own distributor. The decision was undoubtedly driven by financial considerations. All the labels previously produced by Vocalion were quickly discontinued at the time the new company was set up and other changes made by the new management were not slow in coming. In July 1930 the *Vocalion* label was re-established with a new 10in. series beginning at 500. No 12in. discs were released during the life of the new company, despite the reference to them in the Abridged Prospectus.

An item in the 'Trade notes' section of the *Australian Phonograph News* of September 1930 reports: 'Mr C.L. Kempton, the Managing Director of Vocalion (Australasia) Ltd., has visited America four times during the last nine months, and finds that the depression there, at the present moment, is as bad as in any other part of the world, and record sales have naturally been considerably affected.' By December 1930 Maurice Rosenthal was managing director, according to *Australian Phonograph News*, which reported that he 'is shifting his headquarters to Melbourne, but will make frequent visits to Sydney.'

A new series of 7in. children's records on the *Vocalion Midget* label were released in late 1930. The trademark was registered on 20 December 1930. They sold for 9d each, but only about 16 issues are known and, judging by their rarity, sales seem to have been very low.

A Vocalion information circular of 12 January 1931 provides some additional information on its activities:

The Company's policy is to provide records and gramophones at prices attractive to the public and which, at the same time, provide the dealers with the usual trade discount, and the success met with the introduction of the Vocalion record to retail at 2/6d. each, measured up to the expectations of the Directors...

The growth of the Company's operations may be gauged from the fact that when the new Company commenced operations in March of 1930, the sales of records were just under 36,000 for the month. The succeeding six months were marked by a general dislocation of trade, due to the introduction of the new Vocalion record in replacement of the Broadcast, Savoy, Arcadia, and Embassy... At the same time this period marked the putting into operation of the Company's policy of establishing branches in the various States, thus making direct contact with its customers, in preference to functioning through wholesale distributors. The organization to this end having been completed by about the end of September, 1930, a marked increase in sales resulted and although December figures are not yet available, November sales amount to over 80,000 records and it seems safe to say that the monthly average of records sold should reach an average of 1,000,000 records per annum. [59]

This good news is supported by an item in the 'Trade notes' section of the *Australian Phonograph News* of December 1930: 'The Vocalion record factory is now working with full staff on two shifts, so they must be making a difference to the sales of the dearer records.'

But external forces had already set the pattern for a downward spiral. The sales for late 1930 were probably the high point for the company. The circular also provided details of the company's management at the beginning of 1931:

VOCALION

In an effort to diversify its operations, in about October 1929 Vocalion put the general management of the Company's affairs in the hands of Mr Maurice Rosenthal, who has had extensive experience in the distribution of gramophone records. Mr Rosenthal is responsible for the direct system of distribution which is proving so efficient and successful. The Managing Director is also developing the policy of the Company regarding the newly opened Commercial Sound division of Vocalion (Aust) Ltd.

The factory management is in the hands of Mr C.H. Gendle as Production Manager and Technical Expert, who was sent to Australia by the Vocalion Gramophone Company to establish and install the present plant which the Company is operating. His many years of experience cover every phase of the record manufacturing industry. Mr Gendle has held important positions with gramophone companies in England and is familiar with the industry as operated in Europe, America and Australasia.

The Pressroom Foreman is Mr C.C. Cordell, who was also transferred to Australia by the Vocalion Gramophone Company in England.

The Company has a complete Grinding Mills Unit in charge of Mr J.A. Philips, who was also transferred from Vocalion Gramophone Company of England.

Mr J.W. Quirk, who is in charge of the recording studio, was for many years leading operator in the Vocalion Gramophone Company's studios, prior to which he was with Messrs. Pathé Frères. Mr Quirk has recorded many of the world's greatest artists for a period of years, and is recognized as one of the world's foremost recording experts.

In connection with the studio, the Company is fortunate in having the services of Mr D.H. Clyde Box as Sound Engineer. He is an expert on the principles of electrical process recording, not only for ordinary gramophone

Above: The Vocalion factory in Richmond, Victoria. Photo courtesy of Mike Sutcliffe. Below: The pressing room of the factory, 1930. From the ScreenSound Australia collection.

records, but particularly in respect of disc recording for 'talkie' pictures and commercial sound. [59]

Vocalion upgraded its recording in September 1929 by importing the first cutting lathe for 33⅓ rpm discs available in Australia; and as a result was able to provide facilities for making sound-on-disc recordings, the sound component for the first Australian 'talking' pictures. [134] The studios were also equipped for making what appear to be an early form of radio transcription, suitable for broadcasting commercials, according to the circular:

> The plant is capable of the highest class of work as demonstrated by the synchronization done by the Company quite recently for the Commonwealth Government, in connection with their publicity 'talkie' film – *'This is Australia'*. There exists in Australia today a very substantial demand for talking pictures for educational, industrial, and commercial purposes apart altogether from the purely amusement aspect. For international advertising purposes alone, the field open to us in this department is very wide. With sufficient capital the Company would be able to still further equip its studio with what is known as a 'sound truck' equipped to record sound on film to make 'talkie' pictures of current and other events. There is an immense number of 'silent' films and this Company is in the unique position of being able to convert these into 'sound' pictures. The benefit to the smaller theatres of the big cities and to the many suburban theatres must be apparent inasmuch as the cost of these pictures would be very much less than the price ruling today for first class releases. In the field of commercial advertising the Company is in the position to make a complete programme for a half hour or hour's broadcast, featuring the different imports or manufactures of various commercial concerns. Under this system it enables the manufacturer or merchant, or in fact any other person who

has anything to sell, to conduct a national advertising campaign 'via' broadcast uniformly throughout the Commonwealth of Australia and New Zealand, upon the same day and at the same hour, and by well-known national artists. [59]

After the Vocalion studios were upgraded with new equipment in September 1929 the company produced sound-on-disc material for a number of 'talkie' film productions. Syd Guest, a Vocalion technician, had developed a synchronizer which linked the new disc recorder to a Prestwych camera, and this technology was first used for a series of short films featuring Colin Crane, Ivan Massounoff, June Mills and Prime Minister Scullin, which were screened privately at the South Yarra Regent Theatre on 29 October 1929; and then given public premiere at Hoyt's De Luxe Theatre on 2 November.

By January 1930 the system was sufficiently reliable to be used in the first Australian sound feature, *Fellers*, which was directed by Arthur Higgins and Austin Fay. This film retained some silent sequences (directed by Higgins) and the rest of the film was accompanied by music from a sound-on-disc source, with dialogue and song featured in the last reel (directed by Fay).

On 11 March 1930 a series of discs were also produced at Vocalion to accompany the MacDonagh sisters' talkie *The Cheaters*. Another use for the new process was to provide commentary by Norman McCance for the *Australian Talkies Newsreel* during mid-1930. [75].

Another film known to have been made using this equipment is mentioned in the *Australian Phonograph News* of December 1930:

> The first talkie to be produced by the Commonwealth Government, '*So this is Australia*', is being shown at the Prince Edward Theatre, Sydney, and has had a very

successful run in Melbourne. The entire sound dialogue was made by Vocalion (Australasia) Ltd. The quality has so impressed all who have seen it that Paramount have arranged a world distribution of the picture. Vocalion is establishing a most complete studio for sound production, and the company of which Mr Rosenthal is the Managing Director is to be congratulated on their eminent initial success. [189]

However, by the time these facilities had been installed the business climate in Australia was already very difficult. As conditions continued to deteriorate, there was less and less chance that business would make use of these services. Within two years the use of the sound-on-disc process had been rendered obsolete by the widespread use of optical soundtracks.

In fact, despite the introduction of new technology and the generally up-beat tone of the January 1931 information circular, Vocalion was once more in serious financial difficulty. The *Australian Phonograph News* of August 1931, reported that 'Vocalion Distributing Pty. Ltd., has taken over from July the distributing business of Vocalion (Aust) Ltd., which will henceforth carry on exclusively as a manufacturing concern. The branch addresses remain unaltered and all former branch staffs remain in the employ of Vocalion Distributing Pty. Ltd.' This seems to have been yet another restructure made in an attempt to keep the struggling business afloat.

One of the last known Vocalion personal recordings [PR231] is mentioned in a news item in the *Australian Phonograph News* of May 1931:

> The Australian National Travel Association, 435A Collins Street, Melbourne, has recorded for the first time in gramophone history the hearty laugh of the kookaburra. On the reverse side of the record is an interesting talk on Australia's amazing animals by Doctor Brooke Nicholls, the

well-known naturalist and travel lecturer. This novel record, which many purchasers are mailing overseas, was made in the studio of Vocalion Australia Limited, and the kookaburra was produced by Mrs Jury, of Healesville. Jack is seven years old, and will laugh at any time of the day or night by request. [174]

In fact, only the script of the 'interesting talk' is by Dr Nicholls: it is read by the Melbourne radio-announcer Renn Miller.

By the end of August 1931 the company was being sued for bankruptcy. The *Argus* of 25 August 1931 headed 'Company wound up' reported:

> Mr Justice Macfarlan, in the Practice Court yesterday, granted a petition for the winding up of Vocalion (Australasia) Limited, of Coppin Street, Richmond. The petition was presented by the Queen City Printers Pty. Ltd., of Cardigan Street, Carlton, for whom Mr D.M. Little (instructed by Messrs. Gillott, Moir and Ahern) appeared. The petition set out that the Company was incorporated on June 4, 1930, in New South Wales... The Vocalion (Australasia) Limited owed the petitioning company £1,574, and a demand for payment had not been complied with. The omission constituted an act of bankruptcy. Mr Justice Macfarlan granted the petition, and made the order asked for. Mr J. Wallace Ross was appointed liquidator. [212]

The September issue of the *Australian Phonograph News* reported that 'the trade is full of rumours concerning Vocalion (Aust) Ltd., whose board of directors was reported to have resigned in a body. Interstate deliveries were interrupted for a few weeks, but normal deliveries have again been resumed, and Vocalion Distributors Pty. Ltd. is still carrying on in every state and also in New Zealand. The trouble is due to an action being taken by Vocalion (Foreign) Ltd., the largest creditor of Vocalion (Aust.) Ltd.'

VOCALION

The following month the *Australian Phonograph News* carried an item headed 'The Vocalion debacle':

> The grand finale of Vocalion (Australasia) Ltd., was even worse than one could have expected, and resulted in an overwhelming debacle which engulfed the head office, all branches and executive officers. Twelve months ago when Vocalion records were booming without an opposition, being the only 2/6 discs on the market, several men connected with the phonograph business shook their heads and predicted that the Company would be bankrupt within six to ten months. The staggering cost of window displays in every large city and the system of selling records on consignment were leading to eventual disaster. At the beginning of this year things began to shape badly. The Vocalion Company was obviously short of funds; many accounts were not paid, and correspondence on this subject was simply ignored. With the entry of Regal and Panachord records into the 2/6 class, Vocalion began to rapidly lose support, and the final catastrophe was not far off.
>
> It is quite certain that the Melbourne factory has been definitely closed, and that Vocalion records are no longer manufactured. The debacle is complete and overwhelming.

Vocalion (Australasia) was finally struck off the Companies Register on 26 September 1934.

In early 1932 a new company, Moulded Products (A'asia) Pty. Ltd. was set up to make use of the facilities of the former Vocalion factory. This resulted from a merger between two small Melbourne businesses: the Australian Moulding Corporation, a company formed in 1927 to manufacture radio parts from phenolic resins; and Moulded Products Pty. Ltd., formed in 1931 to manufacture plastic household goods. On 4 May 1932 the new company had the patent attorney A.J. Callinan of 395 Collins Street, Melbourne, lodge a patent specification for 'An improved composition for the manufacture of phonograph records and the like...'. [32] The address given is 49 Coppin Street, Richmond, so it seems the company was already established in the old Vocalion factory.

In fact, Moulded Products must have been active several months before this, as they are known to have been making local recordings as early as March 1932 and they were pressing records even earlier. The main source of masters used by Moulded Products was the British Decca Record Co. Ltd. in London. Moulded Products must have had the rights to use the *Decca* trademark but no documentation has emerged to confirm this. However, it was certainly the first local company to produce an Australian *Decca* label. The British company had been established on 14 February 1929, but until 1932 they had no outlet in Australia for their recordings. This first Australian *Decca* label had no connection with the American *Decca* label, which was not formed until 1934, or the later Australian Decca label which was launched by EMI in February 1936. The Moulded Products Decca records sold for 2/6.

The patent specification referred to above claims that:

> ... this invention related to an improved composition for the manufacture of phonograph records... [and] one object of the invention is to provide a composition, which will provide requisite smoothness and hardness in the finished record and will also impart increased resonance thereto... The improved composition will be found to be particularly advantageous in use and phonograph records manufactured from it will be found to possess special strength, resonance and other desirable properties. [32]

Despite these claims, Moulded Products' records were generally of inferior quality, and produced some of the worst levels of surface noise of any record produced in Australia.

VOCALION

Moulded Products had their own recording studios at 664 Bourke Street in Melbourne, but they were used only to a very limited extent. The few local recordings issued commercially on the Australian *Decca* label all involved Jack O'Hagan in some capacity. His company, Jack O'Hagan Music Pty. Ltd., located at 239 Collins Street, Melbourne, was also wholesale distributor of *Decca* records for Victoria and Tasmania. Moreover, Jack O'Hagan Music was the local publishers of more than a dozen of the British compositions which appeared on the *Decca* label during 1932. Quite unusually, Jack O'Hagan's own composition 'Carry On' was recorded in London by Jack Hylton and his Orchestra (who were at that time recording for British *Decca*) on 4 November 1931, and this record was also released on Australian *Decca* M1076 during 1932. As O'Hagan was by this time a very successful local composer, it might be surmised that he had an investment in Moulded Products, but the details of his financial involvement are not known.

The commercial sound division of Moulded Products appears to have been the main user of the Bourke Street recording facilities, making a number of private recordings, advertising records, and discs made for use in cinemas. Details of only a fraction of these are known, but it seems that there were just over 70 recordings made by the commercial sound division during 1932 (compared with only about 15 titles recorded for commercial issue, of which only six were ever released). The last known private recording was master MPR73, a radio play entitled *The Trader* performed by the Aircast Players on 23 December 1932. It seems likely that a few more recordings were made by the commercial sound division in the following months.

One of the most unusual records was one of the first commercially-released recordings of Australian wildlife sounds. 'The History and Song of the Lyre Bird' was made for Herschells, sound picture producers of Melbourne. Part

Decca advertisement, 1932.

1 is a studio recording by Alfred L. Samuels detailing the physical features, habits and mimicry of the lyre bird, Part 2 is 'the first record of the lyre bird ever made in the native haunts of Australia's premier songster' (according to the sleeve) – a field recording made in Sherbrooke Forest (Victoria) under the supervision of Ray Littlejohns of the Royal Australasian Ornithologists Union. This recording was obviously associated with the documentary film *The Lyre Bird* premiered on 9 July 1931; but the disc was certainly available for public sale in its own right, although no details are known about its distribution or price.

The known lifespan of record production by Moulded Products was from early 1932 through until early 1933. All work at the factory ceased in early 1933 after a fire; and the operation was by then not profitable enough for the company to invest further capital in repairs. This ended a period of almost continuous record production at the Coppin Street factory, established by Vocalion in 1927. During 1934 the Dunlop Rubber Company, which had acquired a controlling interest in Moulded Products, moved the plant and personnel to their own plastics division in a North Fitzroy factory.

Dunlop disposed of its interests in 1936, and in 1939 Moulded Products became a public company. It continues to make plastic goods, but its move from Richmond effectively ended the first period of record industry activity in Melbourne.

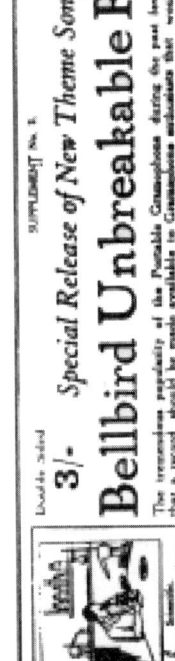

Bellbird Supplement, c. 1921.

Chapter 9

UNBREAKABLE RECORDS

Despite the failure of World Record (Australia) Pty. Ltd. in early 1926, the World Record factory in Brighton (Victoria) did not stand completely idle. Some of the former staff, most notably Frederick George Mitchell, continued to work at the site on attempts to develop the Pemberton Billing patents into a more marketable form of disc record. These activities eventually led to the formation of another short-lived venture.

William Manson, of the Gramophone Company, reported on recent activities by Mitchell in a letter to his London office on 31 January 1927:

> You will have noticed in our Minutes and in some of my letters references to the proposed flotation of the Mitchell Unbreakable Gramophone Record Company. Mitchell was the technical expert in the Pemberton-Billing's factory, and apparently purchased the concern and has recently endeavoured to float a company. I am enclosing herewith a cutting from the Melbourne *Herald* of Thursday, January

27th, from which you will see that Mitchell stands very little chance of fleecing the public in the way he intended [23]

The *Herald* article was part of a regular column called 'Investor's guide' and headed 'Unbreakable Gramophone Records – An impudent flotation':

> Should the State Parliament require additional information to be convinced of the necessity for proceeding with the long contemplated legislation to regulate the issue of prospectuses, ample evidence is supplied by the flotation of the Mitchell Unbreakable Gramophone Record Co. Ltd.
>
> It is the most striking recent example of a 'promoter's float'. Investors are invited to contribute £81,250 in cash, and £61,750 will be absorbed by vendors' and promotors' consideration and establishment charges. In addition £39,000 shares are to be allocated to vendors and promoters. The only tangible asset is property recently valued at £14,000.
>
> A few months back The Herald Investor's Department received details of a scheme for establishing a small company to exploit a process for manufacturing unbreakable gramophone records, the discovery of Mr F.G. Mitchell, who had been the technical expert engaged for Pemberton Billing's ill-conceived venture. As a basis for flotation, the syndicate contemplated paying £21,000 of shares, but no cash, for the rights to the process, and as promoter's consideration, and £14,000 more shares were to be allotted to acquire the factory, at North Brighton, that had been equipped for the Pemberton Billing enterprise.
>
> The proposition has since undergone a remarkable transformation. With the magic so frequently practised by the professional company promoter, the public is now asked to pay for the property asset and the patent rights (for Australasia only), £51,000 in cash, and £39,000 in shares. Taking property as £14,000, a process that quite recently

UNBREAKABLE RECORDS

was estimated to be worth £21,000 in shares, the value of which depended upon the success of the company, is now presented as being worth £37,000 in cash and £39,000 in shares. In addition, it is proposed to spend £10,750 on share-selling and other flotation activities, and provision is made for the inventor and promoters to collect not less than £250,000 in royalties over a period of 10 years.

This consideration is declared to be quite modest, because after paying 10 per cent. on £65,000 of preference capital, £101,850 profit is expected to be available for £104,000 of ordinary shares each year. Indeed, even larger profit ratios are expected, because it is not proposed to fully call up the shares.

The prospectus is made more remarkable by the inclusion of a so-called 'certificate' from a public accountant. This report states that the valuation of patent rights appears very moderate, that capital will be fully recouped when the first year's estimated profits are realised, and it further expatiates on the splendid asset the patent rights represent to the company. Very little value attaches to this type of certificate, which accountants' organisations, both in England and in the Commonwealth, are very wisely endeavouring to eliminate from prospectuses.

In endeavouring to ascertain the merits of Mr Mitchell's process for manufacturing unbreakable and flexible records, the investor will fail to obtain any conclusive evidence in the prospectus, because the optimism of the promoters is not supported by any independent expert report. No information is given as to where and when the patent rights to be acquired were granted, and no details are given of the process.

Perhaps the most extraordinary feature of the prospectus is the withdrawal of so large a cash consideration from a venture claimed to possess such phenomenal profit earning possibilities. The investor might well ask also why a comparatively new share-selling organisation is being entrusted with the placing of 130,000 shares, when an issue offering only a fraction of the return expected from these shares would be eagerly snapped up through usual subscription agencies. The reason, of course, is that, in addition to the cash consideration payable to the joint promoters and share-sellers they are also to receive up to 7 per cent. on shares placed. That is the nominal rate the effective commission charge, depending on the amount to which the shares are called, and the prospectus does not anticipate that they will be fully paid...

The scheme provides for the issue of 65,000 ordinaries and 65,000 preferences carrying 10 per cent. cumulative dividends. Called to the amounts stated above, cash contributions would amount to £81,250. Of that the vendors propose to take £51,000 and as share hawking and other charges are estimated at £10,750, only £19,500 will be available for working capital. This small residue is to provide the finance for trading, with its stock requirements and credits to the trade, represented by an annual turnover of £300,000.

The section of the prospectus that is of greatest interest to the Attorney-General's Department, and to the organisations that have been endeavouring to secure amendments of the Companies Acts, is the right reserved for the promoters to go to allotment when 1000 shares are subscribed, involving payments in cash totalling only £500. When that amount of scrip has been taken up, the promoters have the right to allot to themselves the £39,000 of shares, and levy on all incoming subscriptions to the extent of £51,000, covering the cash consideration for the patents and property. Should they so desire, the promoters will be in a position to sell any portion of their 39,000 fully-paids. The sale of vendors' and promoters' shares should, in such circumstances, be prohibited by law, and any share-hawker selling them be liable to imprisonment.

The public has had ample evidence in the past that such a basis of flotation is not in the best interests of investors, if only for the one reason, that until at least £56,000 odd of cash is provided by shares, the vendors' and promoters' consideration cannot be satisfied, and no working funds will be available.

In several respects the prospectus makes impudent claims. The introductory statement claims that the proposition is a sound investment, backed by a valuable freehold, and subsequently investors are informed that they will be secured by a substantial freehold property, machinery and plant. No valuation of these assets is supplied... But, then, the vendors and promoters, with their fully-paid gift shares, have become eligible to share in the tangible assets.

The actual position would be that the tangible cover for £48,750 of preference capital would be only £33,500, patents representing the balance, and also every penny of ordinary capital.

Mitchell Unbreakable Records are expected to be 'sold universally, and in millions, with no competition,' and the company is stated to be 'the only gramophone record company in Victoria.' Evidently the promoters are not aware that the Aeolian Company is at present engaged in establishing a factory in Melbourne, and they also discount the fact that three Sydney factories, His Master's Voice, Columbia and Brunswick companies, are well established in the Victorian trade.

The outstanding feature of this flotation is that no evidence whatever is given to indicate whether the Mitchell process of manufacturing unbreakable records has been proved a commercial success and until its trading possibilities are assured only a developmental syndicate, and not a big company funded with a £14,000 property and over £86,000 in flotation and goodwill charges can be justified.' [88]

Despite these well-founded reservations, Unbreakable Disc Records Ltd. was incorporated on 21 June 1927. The three directors named in the company papers are Robert Duncan, merchant of Adelaide, Robert Norman Finlayson, accountant of Adelaide and William Smith, wool merchant of Geelong. The registered office is given as Yorkshire House, 20 Queen Street, Melbourne, which was the office of the company's accountant, Alfred Berriman. [53]

The company prospectus describes its manufacturing resources as:

> ... a modern brick factory, with certain plant, machinery, fittings, and furniture, and adapted to the manufacture of phonograph records... The machinery installed is recent and includes... a complete manufacturing plant for records, a modern recording plant (with studio), and a complete printing plant to be used for labels, covers, etc. The property above described and machinery is being acquired on very favourable terms, owing to the fact that it is being purchased from a Company in liquidation [the former World Record company]... The existence of a factory and appropriate machinery at considerably less than half its cost price adds immense value to the patents, and means that capital need not remain idle for several months while the factory is built and machinery imported and installed.'

The prospectus continues:

> The Mitchell Unbreakable Record will be manufactured by a completely new but proved patent process. The process is not an adaptation of and has no connection with any other patent process previously exploited in Australia. The main features of the record are its extreme flexibility and the fact that it is practically unbreakable. The flexible nature of its texture lends itself to an unusually mellow tone. It is unaffected by needle scratches, and can be dropped, stamped

on, or otherwise ill-treated without noticeably affecting the quality of its tone. It is only about one-third of the weight of an ordinary record. For the above reasons it can easily be sent through the post in a cheap paper envelope without risk of damage. It is indifferent to heat and moisture and is cheaper to manufacture than the existing type of record. These qualities make the record of considerable value to manufacturer, retailer, and purchaser. The percentage of waste owing to breakages in the existing record manufacture is very high, and manufacturers write off hundreds of pounds a week from this cause alone. This waste will be saved. Another feature about this record is that very short treatment enables a title or selection to be eliminated and new title or selection to be stamped upon the record.

Mr Mitchell has spent many years patenting this record, and is agreeable to place his services at the Company's disposal. So far as title is concerned, the patent is held under Provisional Patent No. 2571/26. Complete specifications (due April 30th, 1927) have been filed... The whole of the Australasian rights of this patent will be taken over by the Company.

Mr Mitchell, the inventor, has had considerable technical and engineering experience, and has specialised in the production and manufacture of talking machine records.

Mr Mitchell came out specially to Australia as technical adviser to Mr Pemberton Billing and superintended the construction of the first talking machine factory built in Australia. He has spent some years and a great deal of money in perfecting, testing, and protecting his processes. The Company has secured his services on very favourable terms as factory manager, his remuneration depending largely on results, and the Company not being bound to keep him beyond one year if dissatisfied. The Company will also be entitled to the Australasian rights of all improvements made during his service with the Company. [55]

Included in the prospectus is a 'certificate' dated 9 June 1927 from Savery's Pianos of Adelaide, who claimed to be 'quite independent, and have not a pennyworth of interest in the record and received nothing for the test', which declares:

> We have examined the unbreakable records you lent us and have not only used them but greatly abused them, and after the tests can only exclaim in surprise at what they will stand without apparently showing any ill effects. Some of the treatment they have gone through was to soak them overnight in water, then dry them out in front of an electric radiator, scratch the surface with pins, walk on them as well as throw them against a wall. After that treatment they played the music equal to the ones we took care of, showing no effect from the previous treatment. In our opinion this record should be a ready seller, and above all will overcome the difficulty of storing and care necessary in handling record stocks. We wish you every success with the manufacturing of them, especially so as we understand it is an Australian invention. Signed O. Cyril Beale, Managing Director. [55]

Finally, the prospectus claims:

> ... a conservative view of the output of the factory is 40,000 records a week, or 2,000,000 a year, working only one shift a day. The consumption of records in Australia is over 14,000,000 per annum, and is rapidly increasing. On the most conservative basis the Company with an improved record should obtain 10 per cent. of this market, or, say, one and a half million records a year... Advertising expenses will sink to a minimum as soon as the records become known, say in six months. The average price of 1s. 6d. per record to the Company allows an ample margin for both distributors and retailers on standard prices... [55]

Many of these statements were, at best, optimistic. There was certainly no way the antiquated and inadequate pressing facilities available at the old World Record factory could ever produce anything like '40,000 records a week'. The small scale of the operations at the Bay Street factory and the obsolete presses, out-of-date even in 1925 when they were installed, had contributed significantly to the failure of the World Record venture only 18 months previously. It is difficult to understand how Unbreakable Disc Records could not have recognised that these factors would also undermine their confident predictions of success. Mitchell, with his long experience at World Record, must have known that these claims were highly exaggerated. The evidence leads to the conclusion that the directors' intentions were at best dubious and at worst fraudulent.

The Return of Allotment, filed on 10 October 1927, showed that almost all the shareholders in the new company were in South Australia. There were two shareholders with Sydney addresses and only one from Victoria – the same William Smith previously named as a director. Two share promoters (Malcolm Scott of Adelaide with 12,500 shares, and William Goldfinch of Melbourne with 1,000 shares) accounted for the bulk of the shares allotted, with another 4,000 being allotted to Frederick George Mitchell. [56]

According to a statutory report filed on 14 January 1928 the total cash from shares allotted was £7,110. After payments to the vendors for plant and patents of £4,000, part payment for the Brighton factory of £1,500, wages and materials costs of £330, 'sundry preliminary expenses' of £100/5/3, and 'brokerage on sale of shares' of £410, the 'balance to credit of company's bankers' was just £769/14/9. This still left an amount payable on the 'balance due for brokerage on sale of shares' of £545. [56]

Despite the odds, the company seems to have begun record production in May 1928. Two labels were produced, the principal one being *Aeroplane* which was inscribed 'Manufactured by Unbreakable Disc Records Ltd. under Mitchell patents 2571-26 at 225 Bay St., North Brighton, Victoria, Australia' and which sold for 2/6. The initial release consisted of eight records, and a further ten issues were to be 'available in June', after which there were no further releases. The second label was *Golden Tongue*, distributed by Craig Williamson Pty. Ltd. in Melbourne and these issues were recouplings of the same few recordings also released on *Aeroplane*. Unbreakable Disc Records released no further recordings after June 1928. Subsequently, *Golden Tongue* records were produced for Craig Williamsons as conventional shellac pressings by Clifford Industries in Sydney.

That Unbreakable Disc Records had ceased production after only two months of operations, is confirmed by documents filed under the Companies Act. Little advertising or promotion was done. In fact only a single advertising supplement, produced by Records Limited of Adelaide, has been found. Without the predicted huge sales income, and with so little working capital, it is hardly surprising that the whole operation collapsed so quickly. Both the *Aeroplane* and *Golden Tongue* labels are very rare today, indicating how few sales they had made. It is unfortunate that the first wholly Australian-owned company producing disc records should have had such a brief, inglorious history.

The only other evidence of activity by Unbreakable Disc Records in 1928 was their filing of a 'Notice Of Change in Situation of Registered Office' on 8 October, which advised that 'the registered office of the Company is now situated at 225 Bay Street, North Brighton'. [49] Nothing more was heard of the company until they filed a notice on 5 March 1930 advising that 'the Registered Office of the Company is now situated at 104 Queen Street, Melbourne'. As this was the address of the company's solicitors (Ford Aspinwall & DeGruchy) it would appear that legal action was being contemplated. [50]

The pace then quickens. A notice of a 'Special Resolution' was filed 'pursuant to Section 77 [of the] Companies Act 1928' stating that the company had passed a resolution to change its name to 'Record Holdings Limited'. [51] Another resolution passed and confirmed at further general meetings resolved the Company be wound up voluntarily under the provisions of the Companies Act 1928 and that 'F.A. Coghlan Esq. of National Bank Chambers, 271 Collins Street, Melbourne, Public Accountant, be hereby appointed Liquidator...' [54]

The liquidator's Statement of Account includes a profit and loss balance sheet showing that the company had ceased operations at the end of June 1928, but that in its brief period of operations it had accumulated losses of £6,833/3/3. The papers filed by the liquidator in September 1930 gave Frederick George Mitchell's address as 'London, England', so he had apparently already retreated to Britain by then. When the liquidator called the final general meeting of the company on 16 May 1932 nobody bothered to turn up.

However, this is not quite the end of the Unbreakable Disc Records story. By early 1930 work was already underway on the production of yet another 'unbreakable' record to be manufactured at the Bay Street, North Brighton factory. Despite the company's failure in 1928, Frederick George Mitchell had continued working on developing his process in conjunction with Thomas Rothwell (who had been factory manager) and Herbert Goody, the recording 'expert' brought out to Australia by Noel Pemberton Billing for World Record.

F.G. Mitchell lodged a patent application on 1 May 1929 for 'improvements in the manufacture of disc sound records'. An extension of the patent was lodged on 20 January 1930 by Rothwell and Goody. I have in my possession a test pressing made on 26 February 1930 inscribed 'Unbreakable Record Manufacturers Ltd.' which was apparently produced during the final stages of preparation for the launch of the new label, *Bellbird*. The first *Bellbird* records were released in March 1930, although no trademark registration has been traced. These show the legend 'Unbreakable' at the top of the label, but give no specific company or manufacturer's credit – just 'Manufactured in Australia'. The first *Bellbird* supplement described the records as 'bendable, dependable and light as a feather.' It also claimed they 'have taken Australia by storm'. The sole agents and distributors in New South Wales were Paling's who sold the records for 3/-.

By late 1930 there were already financial problems and production seems to have ceased for a few months. Thomas Rothwell and Herbert Goody made at least one further patent application, involving further improvements to disc record manufacture, in September 1930, and the company was renamed the Flexible Records Co. Ltd. with a capital of £10,000. When production of *Bellbird* records resumed around May 1931 the same label design was used but in a smaller format and the word 'Unbreakable' was replaced by 'Flexible'. There was still no manufacturer's credit, but it seems likely from the masters used at this time that *Bellbird* records were now being pressed at the Vocalion facility rather than on the antiquated presses at North Brighton.

Flexible Records also produced sound-on-disc soundtracks after their chief engineer, Herbert Goody, took out patents between September 1929 and January 1931. This system was used for a number of recordings, including 'Southward Ho With Mawson', 'Out of the Shadows' and the *Australian Sound Gazette* – a weekly newsreel featuring as announcer the young Charles Moses (1935-65), the future general manager of the ABC.

Despite these innovations, the revived *Bellbird* operation was also short-lived and the final issues appeared in June 1931. The July 1931 issue of the *Australian Phonograph News* reported: 'Bellbird records which started activities recently have decided to go into liquidation, but plans are already being made for future distribution on a different basis.' Whatever these 'plans' were, they appear to have come to nothing, as there were no further releases on the *Bellbird* label. Nor is anything known about subsequent operations at the North Brighton factory. Sadly, this building where Australia's first disc recordings were made, and which had such a colourful history during the 1920s and early 1930s, has been demolished.

Embassy record label, 1929.

Chapter 10

'DUMPING': THE 1927 TARIFF BOARD INQUIRY

The man who cuts prices of standard lines with the view to clearing slow-moving stock, or simply to increase sales, is a pirate who deserves no quarter. Price cutting always has been an evil with which it is difficult to deal. Distributors naturally refuse to supply a dealer if they know he is price-cutting, but unfortunately even though his supplies may be stopped, the price-cutter will often buy through a 'dummy.' It seemed generally impossible to stop the dealer from price-cutting. Like the burglar and the police, one is always using new dodges to outwit the other. [169]

During the mid-1920s Australia imported records from a wide range of countries [Appendix 1]. Cheap labels, obsolete stock of records sold at a reduced rate, or bulk purchases of records bought overseas at a discount price and imported into Australia, were a regular feature of the record business here as in most other countries.

Some of the cheap labels were perfectly legitimate business operations which simply specialised in the lower end of the market by producing a 'budget priced' product. Other cases, such as the 'price-cutter' mentioned above, involved dubious business practices. However, it is not true that all the records sold off cheaply could be described as 'dumping', as was to be alleged by the major record companies. In 1926 they asked the Commonwealth Government to impose a higher duty on imported gramophone records, a move which led to the 1927 Tariff Board Inquiry into the record industry.

During the period from 1925 to 1927 there was certainly a dramatic increase in demand for new records and in the number of record labels and outlets in Australia. As we have seen, this was due to a variety of factors, including the increasing popularity of dancing, an increase in the number of homes with gramophones, and the development of the 'new' (electrical) recording process which threw onto the market quantities of obsolete records made by the old mechanical recording process.

Some outlets purchased job lots from established importers; while others arranged through jobbers to import stocks of obsolete records which were available at cost price or less. As part of the deal the jobber would often arrange to have the records relabelled with the name of the new outlet; sometimes the record company selling this old stock insisted the records be relabelled to eliminate their trademark. There were also record manufacturers in America, Britain, Germany and Canada who produced record labels for export to Australia by special arrangement. These included *Aerona*, *Bon Marché*, *Grand Pree*, and *Vox Humana* all made in Britain; *The Hit* and *Lily of the Valley* made in Germany; *Beeda*, *Leonora*, and *Paling's* in Canada;

'DUMPING': THE 1927 TARIFF BOARD INQUIRY

and *Beeda*, *Bon Marché*, *Clarité* and *Dahlmont* all made in the United States. Most of these special labels were for sale in specific outlets such as *Dahlmont* for the Myer Emporium in Melbourne, or *Paling's*, the label for W. H. Paling, the Sydney music shop.

It is understandable that the major record companies in Australia were not only aware of, but also very sensitive to, the competition from the sudden influx of 'cheap' records selling for lower prices than those produced locally. However, the reality was that by early 1927 these locally-produced records were slowly but surely forcing inferior products, often obsolete stock, from the market. This was asserted by those opposing the application for increased duty on gramophone records put before the Tariff Board in 1927.

It is certainly true that some of the 'cheap' records complained of by the local manufacturers were intended to attract customers to stores which did not usually sell records, as Horace Newman pointed out at the Tariff Board Inquiry: 'A great many American records are sold simply because they are cheap. A woman goes into a shop to buy dishcloths or towels, and sees these records, and sees that they are cheap, and wastes her husband's money by buying them, although she really does not want them. That is how half these cheap American records are sold, because they are displayed in these places.' The Inquiry Chairman then suggested: 'Then for the sake of the husbands, they would be better kept out?' Horace Newman responded: 'Yes, certainly. Half of them would never be sold otherwise, and these people would never buy others in their place.' [45]

Setting aside their period flavour, these remarks convey how these outlets were seen to be damaging the market for records produced by companies manufacturing in Australia. Popular music records were of particular concern as they accounted for a significant proportion of sales. Most of the major companies had long since introduced 'budget' labels to meet this demand.

In order to protect their investments in Australia, the local record manufacturers gradually came to the view that the Government should be asked to look into the need to impose a duty on certain classes of imported records. The decision to ask for government intervention to prevent records being 'dumped' on the Australian market was initially taken by the irrepressible D. Davis & Company without any consultation with the other record manufacturers. On 31 August 1926, the secretary of the company wrote to the Comptroller-General of Customs, then located in Melbourne:

> Re Application for increased duty on phonograph records.
>
> As you are probably aware this Company were the pioneers of the phonograph record pressing industry in Australia, since which time the manufacturing of records has been taken up by other local manufacturers, and the requirements of Australian purchasers are now being well provided for. The greater proportion of the higher grade phonograph records are now made in the Commonwealth, but we find that the competition from overseas is hitting our industry very severely.
>
> We respectfully ask, therefore, that you will be good enough to submit this application to the Minister for Customs for reference to the Tariff Board for inquiry and, we trust, a favorable report with a view to having the duty increased on phonograph records to 45% *ad valorem*, which, if imposed, would enable us to work our factory to its maximum capacity.
>
> At such inquiry we would be only too pleased to submit any information required by the Board or, if it would be of service before then, we will be pleased to arrange just whatever is necessary at such time as we hear from your Department. We sincerely hope that the matter will be dealt

'DUMPING': THE 1927 TARIFF BOARD INQUIRY

with as soon as possible, say not later than October or November next. [16]

Following a reply from the tariff board (missing from the file in the National Archives of Australia), Herbert Davis wrote further on 12 November 1926:

> Referring to your letter of the 7th of September, I have to apologise for the delay in replying to the questions asked therein, but am setting out below the reason why your letter has not been replied to before this date.
> Being concerned by the number of phonograph records that were being unloaded by overseas firms into Australia, and noting the effect it was having on the production at our plant, my Board of Directors considered it necessary for me to visit the United States to endeavour to learn the reason. I left Sydney on the 26th of August and returned last Wednesday, the 3rd instant. On account of the trade bulletins mentioning the fact that I was in the United States, I was continuously besieged from the day of my arrival, by firms desirous of unloading surplus stocks of records for export to Australia.
> Quite recently a new system has been devised of recording records, known as the 'electrically recorded', whereas the ones made previously were the 'mechanically recorded'. It is estimated that there are approximately two hundred million mechanical recordings on the market in the United States today, which are practically unsaleable except at a very substantially cut price. I have correspondence in my possession, addressed to me, where companies have offered me any quantity of any brand of record which I might desire to purchase at 10 cents each. They also stated in their correspondence that they would have no difficulty in declaring to the Domestic value column for an Australian invoice in order to satisfy the Customs Department that the price was a genuine one, as the records have been and

are now being sold at that price in the United States. They are so anxious to get rid of the records that quantity is out of the question – they would sell either one hundred or a million at 10 cents each.

Traders in Australia are very concerned about these records. In the majority of cases, they are being imported by indent firms who have never previously been in the phonograph records business, and they are supplying them to drapers and department stores, who likewise have never previously been in this business, and who are now advertising and offering them to the public at ridiculously low prices of 1/3 and 1/6 each, whereas the lowest commercial price that an Australian-made record can be retailed at is 4/- each. The result is that the legitimate record business at the present time is in a very frenzied state. Production at our own factory has fallen off during the last five months appallingly, and whereas prior to May, we were able to keep three shifts continuously working, we are now having difficulty in finding sufficient work for two shifts.

Another thing that I desire to impress is the fact that the dumping into Australia of these 'mechanically recorded' records has not yet reached its full strength. In other words – very few indentors in Australia at the moment are cognizant of the fact that such cheap records can be purchased in the United States. The future for the industry in this country is therefore anything but bright, unless we can have the assistance of your Department in preventing these records from being dumped here.

I would say without exaggeration, that if a census taken of the number of firms in the phonograph and record retailing business operating in May, 1926 was compared with one taken today, it would be found that one third of the number had since been forced into bankruptcy or had been compelled to find other avenues of business...

As it will possibly be some considerable time before the increased duty, if recommended, could come into operation,

'DUMPING': THE 1927 TARIFF BOARD INQUIRY

I do not for the moment see how even that would save the Australian record-pressing industry from the present alarming situation. The Industries Preservation Act likewise does not appear to afford sufficient cover. However, I sincerely trust that your Department will determine some speedy and effective method of dealing with the critical position, even, may be, by prohibition. I cannot but feel that after providing so much capital, employing so many hands in the industry, and, with other companies, building it up to the stage where the Australian purchasing requirements are almost wholly catered for, the industry should be reasonably protected from the present 'dumping' and from subsequent foreign competition.

Another reason for us making application for a substantial protective tariff is that we have shortly to look forward to a very high basic wage being given to all labour in the State, besides being coupled with the facts that in the past nine months our working hours have been reduced to 44 per week and we are being forced to contend with a very distressing Workers Compensation Act during the past four months.

In all other British Dominions we understand there is a high protective tariff on phonograph records – Canada we believe is 40%, and India, South Africa and New Zealand 35%, whereas the protection here against foreign records is only 10%.

I expect to be able to leave for Melbourne next Sunday night the 14th instant, and I would very much appreciate it if you would afford me the opportunity of discussing this matter personally with you, at a convenient time. With your permission I will 'phone your secretary for an appointment on my arrival. [16]

A Department of Trade & Customs Minute Paper from June 1927 is headed 'Present position of request for increased duties on phonograph records':

SOUND BEGINNINGS

On the 12th November, 1926, the Managing Director, D. Davis & Co. Ltd., forwarded... an application for increased duties on phonograph records.

It was decided to circularize other Australian manufacturers of these goods and on the 7th February last letters were despatched to the Gramophone Co. Ltd., Erskineville, Sydney and the Columbia Graphophone Co. Ltd., Homebush, Sydney, requesting them to furnish their views on the subject, and if it was intended to support the request...

The Gramophone Co. Ltd. has intimated that its principals in England had definitely laid down that if the question of an increased duty were raised the local Company should not take any action until it had consulted the parent Company in England and received instructions as to the policy to adopt. No further letter has been received from the Gramophone Co., but it is pointed out that sufficient time has hardly yet elapsed for the Company to advise the English Company and receive full instructions as to how to proceed.

Mr H. A. Parker has replied to the request forwarded to the Columbia Graphophone Co. intimating that he feels quite sure that his Company's English principals would wish him to support the request for increased duties, but before taking any action he prefers to communicate with them and ascertain their opinion.

If replies are not to hand by the end of the current month, it is intended to communicate with the two firms in question and ask them if advice has yet been received from England.[41]

The other Australian manufacturers quickly joined Davis. On 11 July 1927 the Parlophone Company formally advised the Minister that they also wished to be a party to the inquiry, and the Vocalion Gramophone Company made a similar application on 25 July 1927. Their Australian manager, Charles Gendle, wrote: 'As instancing just what

'DUMPING': THE 1927 TARIFF BOARD INQUIRY

this competition means, such records as *Grey Gull*, *Domino*, *Banner*, *Oriole*, *Cameo* and *Tremont* are being bought in America for, we understand, 10 cents each (and in some cases even less). This figure... is... less than the cost of production abroad, and certainly much less than we can make them for here'. In a list of *Vocalion* record prices, he added a note: 'By far the more popular is that of 10in. Blue Label selling to the Public at 4/-. The other Australian manufacturing companies... maintain this price for that particular size record for popular numbers, but the imported article, especially from America, is offered to the public at prices ranging between 1/3d and 2/9d.' [60]

Since there was now considerable support among the record manufacturers for such an inquiry, a Department of Trade & Customs Minute Paper (1 August 1927) set out the background to the application for consideration by the Minister:

> In support of the request for increased duties it is stated that overseas dealers are able to purchase large quantities of cheap records the titles of which are more or less out of date in the exporting country, but are reasonably up-to-date in Australia. These records are sold for what they can bring and large retailers in Australia have recently interested themselves in the purchase of these records, and sell them as bargain lines in order to attract people into their stores. The action of these retailers, it is stated, is detrimental to the best interests of the Australian record manufacturing industry. The position has been further accentuated by a change from the mechanical to the electrical method of manufacture of records overseas, and larger quantities of obsolete records have thus been loaded on to the market.
>
> All the applicants emphasise the fact that they are now in a position to cater for the whole of Australia's requirements of these goods.

> The Gramophone Co. particularly desires that if an increased duty is imposed on phonograph records, that copy shells, and matrices or stampers, be exempted from such duty, as they are tools for the manufacture of records and not for sale to the public.
>
> The applicants have certainly built up a fine industry in Australia without practically any tariff protection. The rapid progress of the local companies is no doubt due to the action of the parent companies in refraining from directly competing with the Australian companies in the Australian market, although some of them jeopardize the local companies by jobbing their out-of-date records on to the overseas markets and these in turn are purchased by dealers and retailers and imported into the Commonwealth... [41]

The following day, a Minute Paper signed by Thomas W. Crawford for the Minister formally established the Tariff Board Inquiry into an increased duty on phonograph records (disc type only) imported into the Commonwealth of Australia. [41]

The battle lines were immediately drawn up between the Australian manufacturers of records and the importers and distributors. The company of Alfred A. & H.B. Newman, importers, of Sydney wrote to the chairman of the Tariff Board on 14 October 1927:

> With reference to application 'Request for increased duty on records, disc type, for phonographs'.
>
> We wish to oppose this application on behalf of the Crystalate Manufacturing Co. Ltd., 63 Farrington Road, London, England, for whom we are Australasian Agents, and we will therefore attend at your inquiry on Tuesday next, the 18th instant for the purpose of giving our evidence against the increase of Duty. [1]

A letter from Charles Gendle of Vocalion was included as evidence that local manufacture was competitive:

'DUMPING': THE 1927 TARIFF BOARD INQUIRY

Further to the conversation I had with you in Sydney, I have now gone more closely into the question of pressing and supplying 10 inch Imperial records, and find that to give you a product pressed with the same grade of material as we use for 'Vocalion' records, and incidentally the only grade operated in this factory, together with a standard quality label and envelope similar to that as brought back by me to Melbourne, our price to include royalty stamps... would be 1/5d. each. This quotation is, of course, based on the understanding that the Crystalate Co. would supply us with mother matrices at their own cost, from which we would make the necessary stampers for pressing the records. [1]

In a another letter to the Board dated 7 November 1927, Newman's added that 'we would also like to again point out that the *Imperial* record is in no way a job line, or specially made for export, or that the stocks exported are made at slack periods to keep the factory going. *Imperial* records are a standard cheap line in Britain, they are advertised, catalogues and lists are supplied freely...' [1]

Mr Kelson of Kelson & Company, Sydney, was more emotional:

We are the Agents of Artiphon Records of Berlin, Germany, and as such we hereby most respectively beg to file our protest against the introduction of a higher tariff on foreign gramophone records and beg to submit the following for your consideration.

An increase in duty, demanded by a combination of local manufacturers, is not destined to protect the labour of this country, but it is recommended only and solely for the purpose of confining the business in gramophone records in this country to 4 or 5 firms pressing here.

By excluding foreign competition it is not the working man who will benefit. Their wages will not be increased and even if their wages would be doubled, the income derived by the few who have evidently combined as a trust, would not materially be decreased.

The exclusion of foreign records would simply mean, that the workingman or the man with limited means is deprived of the enjoyment of good music at reasonable cost.

Can it be the office of the Government to support a movement which is dictated only by egotistical motives of a few? No, this cannot be.

The working class, which has come from all parts of the universe to settle in this wonderful country, have a right to demand that they are given what they are longing for, namely good edifying music, which keeps them at home with their families and away from the public houses. Is there anything else in the world which will have a better influence on a person's mind than music? There is not. Why do we sing hymns in the churches, why do we sing the National Anthem? Because it brings us together with our fellow men, it keeps us together and lets us cultivate the spirit of friendship, and it makes us realize that we are one great community, in which every one of us has duties to perform towards ourselves, our family and our country.

Good music has saved many a man, and has made many a man a law abiding and loyal citizen, and music is the only link which will keep us together and make us all brothers and co-workers for the welfare of our own and the coming generation, and for the welfare of the country in which we have made our home.

Should the poor man be deprived of this privilege, should he be forbidden to cultivate the taste for good music and thereby elevate himself and his family to a higher standard, only because 4 or 5 men want it?

Are these men doing everything possible to exclude foreign competition in order to insure work to the Australian labourer? No. They are doing it because they want to uphold

'DUMPING': THE 1927 TARIFF BOARD INQUIRY

the high prices for records, which they could give to the public at considerably lower prices if they would be willing to sacrifice a portion of their profits.

Why can a first class gramophone record be bought in America at 33 cents retail, which is equivalent to 1/3, where [the cost of] labour is much higher than here? There should be music for every purse as it is in [the] U.S.A., where records can even be bought at 10 cents in any of the Woolworth stores or similar houses.

There is absolutely no doubt that it is only the desire to maintain the high prices, which has asked for the increase in duty, and the undersigned is prepared to state on oath that he was actually told that if he agreed not to sell his records below 4/-, the consent of the copyright owners could be obtained.

The men who are wanting a higher duty are the same who own the copyrights or act as agents for the owners of same. These men are not only clamouring for a higher duty, but they also seek refuge behind the Copyright Act, which in letter may give them a right to prohibit the importation of records, but not in spirit.

If these men refuse to sell us the royalty stamps on our imported records, we feel that they are acting unfair to the public, especially if they do sell these stamps to others who make exactly the same records.

Music is a gift by God and the master composers belong to all of us and every man, woman and child has a right to hear what has been and will be cherished by all nations of the universe as long as the world exists. [31]

The Tariff Board Inquiry included three days of public hearings, held on 18 and 21 October 1927 in the Minister's Rooms at the Commonwealth Bank, Martin Place, Sydney; and on 10 November 1927 in the Board Room of the VCA Buildings, Flinders Street, Melbourne.

SOUND BEGINNINGS

The following individuals gave evidence to the Inquiry:

Herbert Afriat, director, Grand Pree Record Co., Sydney
Charles R. Barton, Barton & Co. Ltd., Sydney
Kenneth A. Besly, importer, Sydney
Herbert Davis, managing director, D. Davis & Co. Ltd., Sydney
Clarence Eutrope, managing director, W.H. Eutrope & Sons Pty. Ltd., Melbourne
W.M. Fowler, solicitor representing Anthony Horderns, Sydney
Arthur H. Franklin, director, Franklin's Pty. Ltd., Melbourne
Jack L. Goldhill, proprietor, The Music Box, Sydney
William Manson, manager, Australian Branch, Gramophone Co. Ltd., London
James Murphy, company secretary, D. Davis & Co. Ltd., Sydney
Morris H. Nathan, departmental manager, Norman L. Burnell & Co., Melbourne
Horace B. Newman, director, Alfred A. & H.B. Newman, Sydney
Sydney A. Parker, managing director, Columbia Graphophone (Aust.) Ltd., Sydney
Clarence Pinnock, director, Pinnock Sewing Machine Co. Ltd., Sydney
Sydney P. Power, factory manager, Columbia Graphophone (Aust.) Ltd., Sydney
Maurice Rosenthal, manager, Rosenthal & Salon, Sydney
Reginald E. Sanders, departmental manager, Craig Williamson & Co., Melbourne
Albert V. Thomas, manager, Music Department, Myer Emporium, Melbourne
Cyril D. Trevitt, managing director, Trevitt's Ltd., Sydney
Francis Wilson, president, Retail Music Traders' Protective Association of New South Wales
Philip A. Wright, public officer, Parlophone Co. Ltd., Sydney

'DUMPING': THE 1927 TARIFF BOARD INQUIRY

The following extracts from the transcript of the Inquiry hearings refer to all the important issues raised, and give the style and flavour of the proceedings. The hearings opened with a statement from Charles Barton of Barton & Co.:

> I should like to point out that it was my intention, if at all practicable, to have a joint resumé and schedule prepared of the data already submitted, and now to be supplemented by the various applicants. Seeing that much of the information is rather of a confidential nature between the respective parties, and that some of it has already been sent in to your Board in the first instance, coupled with the fact that the Vocalion Gramophone Co. Ltd., withdrew from further action almost at the last moment, I was precluded from doing as I intended...
>
> For your information, the first word I received as to the Vocalion Gramophone Co. Ltd. withdrawing was a telegram from Melbourne from their Australian Manager, Mr C.H. Gendle, intimating that in consequence of advice he had received from his English principals as to an alteration in their policy regarding the English market, which affects their Australian interests, he considered it incumbent upon his Australian company to withdraw their application... It is perhaps needless to add that Mr Gendle is in no way opposing the application. [45]

The first witness to testify was William Manson, who put the case for the Australian manufacturers:

> In making our application for a tariff on disc records, we desire to point out that the large and growing demand for these records induced the following companies, namely The Gramophone Company Ltd., The Columbia Company, and the Brunswick Company, to erect and equip factories in Australia for their manufacture... Capital amounting to hundreds of thousands of pounds has been invested in these

factories, and employment has been given to a very large number of workpeople, thus establishing an industry which is absolutely new to this country.

We desire also to specifically draw your attention to the fact that the establishment of our industry in Australia has not only provided a livelihood for those engaged directly in the manufacture of records, but it has been a considerable source of income to printers who supply the many millions of labels which are required and who print catalogues and other publicity matter for us in quantities which we venture to think you would find astounding. Bag makers also receive huge orders for the envelopes in which records are placed – box-makers are kept busy providing the large number of boxes in which records are packed – engineering firms are called upon very extensively for machinery – heavy supplies of coal have always to be held – many tons of copper manufactured in Australia are purchased annually, and in various other directions great benefit has accrued to the community as a result of our enterprise.

The factories which have been built are so large and completely equipped that they are in a position to supply the total quantity of records which is likely to be called for in Australia for some considerable time to come.

Unfortunately, just as our workers are acquiring a knowledge of their jobs and are approaching that state of efficiency which gives manufacturers reasonable hope of producing at a fair profit, our industry is threatened with, and indeed is suffering from, unfair competition from abroad, which may well cause serious hurt, and possibly may make it necessary either to close down the new factories or to greatly reduce the staffs employed in them.

The competition referred to comes from the large consignments of records which are being despatched from America and elsewhere, and which are sold at prices for which they could not possibly be produced here. The hours

'DUMPING': THE 1927 TARIFF BOARD INQUIRY

of work and general labour conditions in the United States as compared with those that obtain in Australia are all in favour of cheaper production in the former country while taxation is very much lower there, thus giving American manufacturers a great advantage over us. From a study of the official figures, we find that in the financial year ending June 30th, 1925, the taxation per head of population in New South Wales was £17/13/10 against £10/18/6 (approximately) in the United States of America. Since then, income tax in the United States of America has been considerably reduced, but taxation in New South Wales is much heavier. As a consequence, manufacturing and selling costs have been greatly affected, and very much to our detriment.

We have been informed also that some of the large factories in America in which cheap records are pressed have been known to make up more in stock than is wanted for their domestic requirements in order to get a lower manufacturing cost, and the extra profit made on the goods sold in their territory enables the makers to dump goods in other countries at prices equivalent to or below the actual cost of production.

All these points will show you how heavily the manufacturers in this country are handicapped and we, therefore, come to you to ask your kind assistance in getting such protection as will enable us to continue to carry on our industry in Australia, and to find employment for the very large number of workers who now depend upon us for a living. At the same time, we wish to assure you that in making our application, we are not inspired by any desire or intention to raise prices in the event of our being granted that measure of protection for which we have asked. We think it only fair to ourselves to remind you that when we established our factories in Australia we did not then ask for a tariff and we hoped it would not be necessary to do so,

> but being now faced with foreign competition of such a nature that our very existence is threatened, we ask for such help as will enable us to continue to give employment to Australian workers and will also give us a chance to obtain a reasonable reward for our enterprise.
>
> Representatives of those companies which have established record factories in Australia are present, and are ready to furnish any evidence which you may require. Some of the particulars which are likely to be called for are of a highly confidential nature and we are prepared to furnish such particulars, in writing, for your private study, if you desire us to do so.
>
> Representatives of the Dealers' Association are also present and are prepared to give their testimony as to the ruinous effect which the importation and marketing of cheap records is having on their business. [45]

Manson's evidence was followed by several other senior executives from the other record manufacturers, who confirmed his evidence. Francis Wilson, president of the Retail Music Traders' Protective Association of New South Wales, put forward another argument in favour of the application:

> My evidence is that owing to the irruption of these cheap records, particularly of recent years, the demand for the standard records has been so greatly decreased that it has affected the local production of gramophone records, and our figures go to show that this decrease is very real. It has affected our trade, and through our trade, the wholesalers, through them the manufacturers, and through the manufacturers, their employees. It has been most noticeable in the last six months, during which period there has been a bigger number of these things coming on the market. One firm which was represented here this afternoon did not

import these things themselves before, but dealt only in the standard records. They have now imported a record of which you have a sample before you. We understand that they are importing that record in great quantities running into 20,000 or so, that it is being sold at a cheap rate, a great deal below the record which we consider is the standard record...

Previous to that period we were not faced with very heavy competition in these things, because the one [cheap] record which practically held the market was the Grand Pree. I understand that this was an English record, and it held the market only through one house, and we did not feel the competition of that very much, but because of the success of that one, possibly, of the fact that records had become very popular, others saw the possibility of getting in with a cheap record, and got busy under the lower rate of prices. Certain people imported these records, which were hawked around the trade. The Banner record was offered to me at 3/- by the people who handled it at first, but I did not touch it, fearing that they would not be able to handle it, and that it would be thrown on the market later... We have had the Lincoln, the Grey Gull, and the Domino, all in comparatively recent years, and they have made the difference... My figures show that my sales have decreased by approximately 20% for the last six months, as compared with the corresponding period of 1926...

The decrease in sales of the type of record in regard to which we are seeking relief is greater than those figures would indicate, because I have increased my sales of better class records by giving recitals in the last six months, and by my own musical activities as a practising musician in my own district.

We formerly bought weekly an average of 45 to 50 records of fox trots and other popular stuff, whereas now the average is five or six, unless some particularly hot hit comes out. Last week my purchases of the novelties issued

SOUND BEGINNINGS

by the His Master's Voice people on Fridays were only one of each. Previously, I could buy at least three of those I was not sure of, and about a dozen of those I felt sure I could sell. My purchases of popular titles from the Brunswick people from April to September were 258 in 1926 and 210 in 1927, which corresponds with the 20% decrease mentioned above. [45]

The next important witness was the energetic Herbert Davis, managing director of D. Davis & Company which manufactured *Brunswick* records:

> I understand that your Board has had information that about 70% of the records now used in Australia are Australian-made, and that about 30% are imported. Whilst this is true as to the value, I believe that the quantity of records imported would be about equal to those manufactured here.
>
> I would like to mention here that the cheap records which are being sold in this country are sold practically at cost, and are being sold in what we in the trade know as 'illegitimate' stores.
>
> Our experience is that they are sold primarily by drapery stores, who advertise them, usually omitting to give the name of the record, but mention the price [which is] as low as 1/-, 1/3 and 1/6 in order to attract people to their stores.
>
> There are over 4,000 dealers on our books, and we are in constant touch with those 4,000 dealers, and from the knowledge gained from my travellers and from my own movements amongst the trade, I do not know of one single store of those 4,000 that is handling an imported cheap record, such as the drapery stores that I mentioned previously are carrying...
>
> There have, however, within the last six months or so been 'specialty stores' opened up in the various cities which sell nothing else but the cheap record, and which do not handle any of the records manufactured in Australia.

'DUMPING': THE 1927 TARIFF BOARD INQUIRY

There are several stores in this city which arrange with an indenter here to import for them a large parcel of records, usually every month. The titles do not concern them. They say 'Get me down 20,000 records a month at the best price.' usually they know what the best price is. It may be 6d. or 8d. or 10d. in England, or 10 cents up to 15 cents in America. These people have in many instances opened up specialty stores to sell these records...

We have information which we believe to be from a reliable source that several people are at this present time forming into a company with a substantial capital for the purpose of making a large purchase overseas... I understand that this large quantity is to come from America. We understand that it is their intention when these records are landed into Australia to open specialty stores such as I speak of and sell these records for about 1/- each.

That is a matter which is causing us a great deal of concern. We believe the information we have received to be authentic, and we understand that the quantities they intend to import are very large. We know that they have very substantial capital... and if they bring these large quantities of records here at the present rate of duty, it will be a serious matter to the Australian manufacturers. We have been afforded a very small measure of relief within the last month by the action of the Customs Department in imposing a dumping duty, but it really does not afford us the relief that we want...

I believe my company is the one most seriously hit by the importation of cheap records, as unlike The Gramophone and Columbia companies, we established our factory here for the prime reason of being able to supply the demand for the popular titles as soon as the demand manifested itself. The cheap record which is being imported of titles which have outlived their popularity in America, and which are just beginning to enjoy popularity here, have defeated the purpose for which we opened our factory. After making such a heavy investment, it places us in a very embarrassing position.

We believe that if the imported records that are being sold were sold at the same price at which we are compelled to sell our record, they would have little chance of success against us, as we have already lived down the prejudice which certain Australians have against goods manufactured in their own country, and as a matter of fact, our records of popular titles were those generally preferred by the public until the advent of the cheaper record. I refer particularly in this instance to popular titles which I think you know as jazz titles. It is quite clear, therefore, that the only reason the cheap record sells against our record is on account of the fact that they are half the price of the ones we are offering...

[You may believe] that the cheap record must be manufactured by some almost unknown firm in America. This, however, is not the case, as several of the makes which come here are made by the Plaza Music Company of New York, who will make up a record under any title which may be asked for, and further, if they are unable to make it up at the low price of 10 cents or thereabouts, they are agreeable generally to re-label any record which they have available with the music requested by the overseas purchaser. The Plaza Music Company is a company with a very large capital, and I have used it only as an example. There are several other large companies in the United States which adopt the same principle...

In conclusion I say that so far as I can see, the profit from the cheap record does not go to any party but the company who retails it here. The sufferers are:-

(1) Thousands of legitimate music traders throughout the Commonwealth;
(2) The manufacturer of phonograph records in Australia;

'DUMPING': THE 1927 TARIFF BOARD INQUIRY

(3) The owner of the copyright in Australia;
(4) All the people depending for their livelihood on the business of the manufacturers and publishers as well as contributing industries to the manufacture of phonograph records.

A further disheartening aspect is that we are seeing the dealers with whom we have been associated, many for 10 and 20 years, being slowly forced out of business by drapery firms who are handling cheap records only for the purpose of drawing the public to their stores to sell them goods on which they make a larger profit. [45]

At this point in the proceedings W.M. Fowler, a solicitor representing one of the department stores Herbert Davis referred to, intervened: 'It will perhaps save the Board's time while on the subject of the re-labelling of cheap records, if I hand these examples in now.' Davis was forced to respond as the records handed in were in fact Australian-made *Brunswick* records which had been sold off as a job lot, re-labelled as *Simolian* records, and sold cheaply in exactly the way Davis had just been complaining about. He responded:

I expected that the matter would be brought up, but it is a very trifling one. In the early stages of manufacture here, we were offered 1/- each for those records, which were a lot of overstock records, by the firm of Rosenthal & Salon, who sold them again to Mick Simmons. They were Brunswick records made in Australia, and we overmade the stock. We made a very serious mistake in selling them. I should like you to ask some of these gentlemen if they have seen a Brunswick record which has been relabelled in the last two years. I think every manufacturer will make a mistake, or is liable to make such a mistake as we made then. I assure you that we lost, not only thousands of pounds, but tens of

> thousands of pounds worth of business on account of the mistake we made then through selling our obsolete records for re-labelling purposes at a lower price than 4/- each. We got 11d. or 1/- each for them, and we accepted that price sooner than break them up, as we had no means then of using the material again, and the record would have been of no value whatever. Now that we have a machine and can grind old records down again, an obsolete record is worth 3d. to us, but at that time those records were not worth a farthing.
>
> INQUIRY CHAIRMAN: You descended to the practice of your competitors?
>
> HERBERT DAVIS: No, at that time I do not think there were any cheap records coming in here... To the best of my memory, that sale was made at our stocktaking period in December, 1925. [45]

After hearing from the record manufacturers and dealers, the inquiry called representatives of the record importers. Herbert Afriat of the Grand Pree Record Company was the first to give evidence:

> The sitting of the Tariff Board to consider the increase of duties on phonograph records was a complete surprise to us, and until we saw the report in the press on the 19th inst. we were unaware of there being any intention of any such application.
>
> We have on the water, landing in four weeks and five weeks time, large quantities of records, and have entered into contracts for further large supplies to leave England in December, January and February, and had we been aware of there being any such application, we would certainly have refrained from contracting such liabilities until we had heard the finding of the Board.

The record we sell is known as the Grand Pree record. It is retailed at 1/9, costs 1/3 to land, and is sold in England under the name of Vox Humana at 1/9 each, retail.*

The vast inroads made into the phonograph trade by wireless innovations will account for any depreciation of trade in records, and this applies all over the world today.

I have never heard of the Music Traders' Protective Association, and have never been approached either directly or indirectly to join them.

The statement in the press attributed to Mr Murphy that for the years 1925/26, £438,000 value of records were imported would be more interesting when the Board will find that about 80% of these were consigned to the His Master's Voice, Columbia and Vocalion companies, that the average landed cost of these 10 inch records was 1/2d. each, and yet the public were charged 4/- and 4/6d. each, in some cases 6/6d. each, and of which the retailer got 1/3d. profit. I have reason to know the landed cost of these records. At the end of 1924, or the start of 1925, I landed a consignment of Perfect records, from America, that cost 22 cents F.O.B. When they arrived here the Customs authorities held them until they compared the prices with English Columbias and H.M.V., and I saw the original declarations.

The His Master's Voice, Columbia and Brunswick will not supply any person with records unless they enter into an agreement not to sell under their fixed price. In the case of His Master's Voice, they will not supply anybody unless they purchase a certain amount of machines and records in the first case. I think the amount of £80. I myself have been refused records, needles and phonographs from this Company. I believe that this arrangement also applies to the Columbia and Brunswick companies. When His Master's

---

* This last statement is incorrect as the Vox Humana label was sold only in Australia. The English equivalent to the Grand Pree was on the Pathé Actuelle label.

Voice have accumulations of obsolete numbers, they absolutely refuse to sell at any concession, and either scrap them or when they were importing, returned them to England. This last statement I cannot vouch for, but when I applied to them to purchase these numbers some three years ago, that was the reply I got.

A factory could be equipped today to press requirements for N.S.W. for £3,000 without the cost of the building. It is hardly likely that the firms interested in this application would have stopped importing records at a cost of 1/2d that retailed at 4/- and 4/6d. each, unless they were certain that they were going to make them cheaper.

I no longer import American records, as the cheap record sent from there is a very low quality 'dough' and the life of it very restricted, about 14 to 23 times plating being its average life. It does not interfere with the trade of the Grand Pree record to any extent.

The crux of the position is the way the records are distributed to the public. I do not supply the trade at all, but sell direct to the public, and the difference the public gain, and the firms making this application should do the same. I believe the cost to the Parlophone Company for their 10in. records is 1/3d each, yet their retail price is 4/-.

I should like to refer to a statement made by Mr Davis... He stated distinctly that the English records were obsolete quantities of records that were not able to be sold in England on account of the numbers being out of date. Every record that I import I purchase from a sample which is sent out to me every month. They send me out a copy of every release every month... If I like them and want them, I order them. If I do not like them, I do not buy them... so that it would be impossible for Mr Davis's statement to pass unchallenged. We never, by any chance, import a record from England from obsolete stock. Until we get our samples out here, we do not know what we are going to buy... I try the records over and cable the order – it takes about four weeks before we can get the sample – and when they get my order they supply me. I may say that in many cases or most cases I may have the doubling altered. For instance, if a record has *'Blue skies'* on one side and 'Yes, we have no bananas' on the other, I do not want that, and I will have 'Blue skies' doubled with 'In a little Spanish town'.* The records are made according to my specifications and are therefore not obsolete unsaleable stock as Mr Davis stated... I am the biggest importer of English records here, and if you want to see any of our invoices they are open for your inspection confidentially. We gave up importing the American records three or four months ago, as we found they would not last. [45]

The hearings of the Inquiry then moved to Melbourne where Herbert Afriat asked to give further evidence:

Before giving my further evidence, I would like to draw your attention to the trade paper known as the *Sound Wave* issued in England. The date of this number is September, 1927. The Board would be led to think from the complaints made by the applicants that only in Australia is there a record sold at 1/6d, 1/9d and 2/- against their sacred 4/- and 4/6d. record, but this paper shows that the same thing applies in England... My point is that the cheap record is widely on the British market... exactly the same as it is here, so that this condition is not peculiar to Australia...

In reference to the proposed duty – this in our case will be particularly unfair if any duty was imposed upon records actually on the water... We employ 3 salesmen in Sydney all receiving £5/5/- each per week, 1 in Brisbane receiving £5 per week, 2 in Melbourne receiving £5 per week. We employ 1 girl in Brisbane receiving £3 per week, 2 junior girls in

---

* This is definitely not correct, as there is not a single known case where the Grand Pree issue made in Britain is a different coupling to the equivalent *Pathé Actuelle* release.

Sydney receiving £1/17/6 each per week, 1 lad in Melbourne receiving £1/10/- per week, besides numerous packers, carters, etc. Our payment for catalogues alone is £10 per week. In the event of a tariff being imposed, especially on those records now on the water that are to arrive shortly for the Christmas trade, every one of these employees will have to be dispensed with as we have not sufficient stock to carry on...

We registered the name Grand Pree on the 14th June, 1923. This was a name created by ourselves, was unknown in Australia or any other part of the world, and in putting this record on the market we did not rely upon any established trademark or name to create a demand, but just put this record on the market in a modest way and relied wholly and solely on its merit. At this particular time no records were being made in Australia, and the wealthy corporations now making this application resented our intrusion into the field that they had had to themselves for a very lengthy period. Their records cost them a trifle under ours to import and yet the public had to pay as high a price then as they do today.

So far no mention has been made of the records that they sell at 6/6d, 10/6d, 12/6d and even higher prices. The cost of manufacture is no higher. The difference being only 3d between the cost of a 10in. and 12in. record, and the actual cost of the matrix is no higher for a celebrity artist than it is for a popular record.

The figures paid to the performers or artists has not been disclosed, but it can not be anything like the difference in the prices charged by the manufacturers here for the celebrity artists and the prices charged in other parts of the world. Although a lot of evidence has been given (which is disputed by the importers) of the prices that records have been offered at in America, I have heard no reliable evidence whatever of any stale or obsolete English records being offered for sale either here or in England...

'DUMPING': THE 1927 TARIFF BOARD INQUIRY

Some 3 years back we had an enquiry made for obsolete Winner records (this is an English record made by the Edison Bell people in London), and the only records offered were 10,000 at 1/- each, assorted numbers, no guarantee as to quantities of each, so needless to say we turned these down...

You will notice in our catalogue that we start with the No. 17000 and every new number of a consecutive number. Our latest catalogue number is 18629 showing that we have published 1629 new titles since 1923 when we first started...*
I would like the applicants to explain something that I cannot understand. What do they mean by a cheap record? Do they mean cheap when they compare it with a His Master's Voice record that sells for 4/- here and 3/- in England, and that has caused the Company making it to five-fold their capital of originally one million pounds in a few years at the expense of the public, and that puts them in a position to say: 'We will keep out all opposition, and if you want to hear a record you must pay 4/- for it at least, or go and listen to the Salvation Army Band for nothing.' Or to the trader that buys from them and who is loaded with stock that he cannot sell and is debarred from making any reduction at all in his selling price under any circumstances whatever?

If he did, the powerful corporation which set him up will ban him from getting supplies, the same as they did to me, and as all other suppliers would be cut off if this duty were imposed, so far as we're concerned he could go without.

I speak strongly because I'm fighting for my commercial existence. The company says to the trader: 'The price of His Master's Voice or Columbia or Brunswick records is 4/-. If

---

* That is actually a total misrepresentation of the facts, with the apparent intention of impressing the Board with the size of the Grand Pree catalogue. In fact, the 17000 series is devoted to 12in. records, and there were only 13 issues in this series before the catalogue jumped to 18000, which was for 10in. records – this gives a total of 652 issues – a vastly less impressive total.

you sell them at 3/9, we will not give you any further stocks and we will not allow you to distribute our records. No matter how slow they are, you must not sell them under that price.' We people are supplying the public with a cheap record just as is being done in England. We are charging the public here for the same record as the Imperial is selling in England for 1/6d retail and the lowest price which it is sold here is 2/-. Yet the companies say to us: 'You must not sell those records. We are going to apply for a big protective duty on them, and we will make that record cost you 2/6d before it gets here. Then with that 2/6d record which has not got the names of famous performers on it you can try to compete with ours at 4/-. [45]

Horace Newman, of the firm Alfred A. & H.B. Newman gave further evidence:

We as agents for the Crystalate Manufacturing Co. Ltd., of England, beg to oppose the imposition of a protective duty against disc phonograph records imported from England and elsewhere... The Crystalate Manufacturing Co. Ltd. are the owners and manufacturers of Imperial phonograph records, a popular standard and well advertised record.

I have brought with me our catalogues to show that it is a standard English line, not dumped or jobbed, but sold under that name in England at a fixed price...

We contend that the Australian made record is selling to the public at too high a price, and owing to the peculiar fluctuations in demand for phonograph records, the Australian manufacturer is so well situated to supply the demand that in our opinion competition from overseas has little, if any, effect on the demand for the local product. We have a quotation from an Australian manufacturer wherein he offers to press our Imperial record. This quotation is for equal quality material to what they use in their own record which retails at 4/- each...

'DUMPING': THE 1927 TARIFF BOARD INQUIRY

We have not carried the negotiations any further with this firm on the price they quoted, as the directors of our Company are of the opinion that a much better price than this can be quoted for pressing... in Australia, since the cost of labour from their knowledge of the wages paid here for the varied classes of work entailed in the manufacture of these records should average not more than 25% over the English wages, and taking into consideration the higher cost of material used here and other considerations, the total cost of the finished article made here should not be more than 50% higher than such cost of the English made article.

Further, the prices of the principal materials used, for example, shellac, have lately been on the downward trend.

Even at the price quoted, there is, of course, a good profit, so that we submit that if a factory is prepared to manufacture at this price for another firm, it can turn out an article with its own brand to sell retail much cheaper than 4/-, possibly as cheap as 2/6d.

The 10 inch 4/- record is by far the biggest seller here of locally pressed records, but there are one or two other brands at 3/6d, but this lower priced line does not seem to be pushed.

Incidentally, one item in the cost of a record, that is, the royalty which is based on the retail selling price, becomes less as the price is reduced...

A witness for the application mentioned the high taxation in Australia, but we need hardly mention to the Board that taxation in England is even higher.

In support of our contention that the local manufacturer has already an enormous advantage, we would point out that the bulk of the cheap records sold are dances, fox trots, etc., which have a very short run in the public favour, and very often the demand for even a good fox trot will not last more than a few weeks.

The factories here get the matrices out, or make them in Australia, and are able to supply the demand immediately. Whereas, the importer has to wait three months until he can get his supplies, by which time the local demand has often passed. Furthermore, the local factory has little risk of bad stock. It can press the records as and when the orders are taken from the distributors and retailers.

At the end of each month, we receive from London a list of the following month's releases, many of which are already being advertised from the Australian factories, but the earliest we can get our stocks will be eight to ten weeks later or 12 to 14 weeks after the advices are posted from England. Therefore, by pressing locally, they are able to overcome the almost unavoidable risk of bad stock, which importers must face, and they are able to supply the demand exactly as it arises. The risk of bad stock is very great, as once a record of the dance, fox trot or comic song type passes out of the public favour, it is worth very little indeed...

We submit that this accumulation of bad stock was one of the main reasons for factories starting in Australia, as the provision in their profits against bad stock must have been very big. In support of this contention, we mention the fact that about 12 months ago many thousands of well known records were sold in George Street, Sydney, by Gibson's Bazaar (now out of business) at 1/11d and less, although the normal selling prices ranged up to 7/6d each. Those were nearly all Vocalion records.

The demand for records of every description has been steadily increasing this last few years, mostly because of the popularity of dancing which created the sale of dance records, and also because of the big reductions in the prices of talking machines.

The demand for records caused many additional retail phonograph shops to open, and the big stores and other distributors who had hitherto not handled such lines took a hand in this trade, so that there are now more people handling records than before. The trade is, therefore, more distributed and naturally some of the smaller dealers find business not as easy as hitherto.

'DUMPING': THE 1927 TARIFF BOARD INQUIRY

The remark made here today about the big concerns using these lines as advertising is constantly made whenever the big stores attempt to sell anything cheap. As indent agents of 20 years standing, we find that directly the big stores produce cheap lines they are always accused of using them as advertising lines, but I think you will find that the big stores have to make a profit in every department, and it is only at odd times that they have cut out lines for advertising...

With the cheapening of talking machines, which were then bought by that portion of the community who could not afford more expensive phonographs, came the enormous demand for cheap records, and we submit that those in the community who wish recreation of this kind at a moderate price are entitled to get it.

In our opinion, the only effect of the present application, if granted, will be that those who desire to purchase a reasonably priced record will be unable to do so.

The figures for the importation of records during 1926/27, show a falling off from the previous year, part of which reduction is due to the fact that the big companies are now manufacturing here and not importing, and partly because the demand has gone off during the past 12 months, possibly due to the competition of wireless, but most likely owing to the present day fickleness of the public, which rushes a new craze and then gets tired of it. This is probably happening at present, but now that the boom is over, the industry will settle and stabilize itself.

As further evidence that the local factories are capturing the home market we draw your attention to the following comparative figures:

Importation of records into New South Wales

1925/26: £279,913 = Average per quarter: £68,477
1926/27: £130,469 = Average per quarter: £32,617
1927: Quarter ending 30th September: £12,582

Therefore, the last quarter is 2½ times less than the average quarter of the previous year, and only one fifth of the average quarter of the year 1925/26.

Even with the tariff operating at present, the local pressers are doing the whole of the business in the higher price records of a good standard of music, and as regards the hits, so aptly termed 'sloppy', their ability to produce these in quantities at the peak of their popularity has had the effect of crippling the sales of the imported English record, and should any duty, however small, be imposed on the importation of English records, it would mean that such would cease to be on the market place here, and the public would be forced to pay absurdly high prices for a popular article of fleeting interest, or forgo the privilege of deriving light recreation and amusement at comparatively small expense which the communities of other countries in the world enjoy.

It must be remembered as regards English records, while the capital employed is in that country, in the same way as the capital of the companies applying for the increased duty, and while the labour in the manufacture is not Australian, the distribution and profits of the same are still in the hands of Australian citizens. [45]

Tempers were rising in the 'no' camp. The next witness was Kenneth Besly, 'an importer of *Banner* records':

In opposing this application to increase the tariff on phonograph records, I beg to submit that the manufacturers of records in Australia are not in need of any further protection, as they already enjoy approximately 70% of the total business in this country. This very satisfactory state of affairs has been achieved on a tariff of 10%, and if such a result can be attained in the early stages of manufacture, it is only reasonable to assume that as time elapses, and the employees, by reason of their experience become more

'DUMPING': THE 1927 TARIFF BOARD INQUIRY

proficient, the overhead will be reduced and the manufacturer will secure an even larger percentage than he now enjoys.

I further wish to point out, that if any increase of tariff is secured as a result of this application, it will debar a large section of the public from the enjoyment of popular music, at a price within their means.

I also wish to submit that this application made to the Tariff Board is designed to totally prohibit the importation of phonograph records, regardless of the price at which they sell. Should the Board so desire, I am in a position to produce evidence that attempts have been made to prohibit the importation of phonograph records through channels other than that of a tariff.

With reference to the decline in importations from the United States in 1927, I submit that it is a decline in quantity as well as in value, and that in the case of Banner records, the price has increased during the past 12 months. The amount of this decline is shown to be £13,000. I myself am of the opinion that the total importation of cheap records from the United States did not total that figure during the whole year of 1927.

The record business generally has slumped during the past 12 months as has the whole gramophone business, including the manufacture and sale of machines, which would naturally mean a decline in the sale of records, as compared with the year 1926, which was regarded as an exceptionally good year.

I further wish to submit that from my own knowledge, the conditions under which Americans are employed in America, are equal, if not superior, to the conditions under which Australians are employed in Australia.

Under the circumstances, as the cheap American records cannot be said to be competitive, I suggest that the tariff should be reduced, and not increased. In contrast to the assurances given by the applicants, I will definitely undertake that, if the tariff is decreased, the price of Banner records to the purchasing public will be proportionately decreased...

As regards the fixing of prices, I should like to mention that owing to a quantity of records purchased by D. Davis, records which were slightly damaged, from the insurance company and thrown on the market at a ridiculous price, I was unable to continue supplying the regular trade, because of the fact that my records were on sale at a lower price than that fixed by me. The records I refer to were a shipment which arrived slightly worn, which were covered by insurance. I claimed my rights under the insurance policy, and the insurance company sold those records to D. Davis & Co. This was two years ago or thereabouts. Mr Davis came up to my office to take delivery in company with the insurance surveyor, and offered me his cheque. I pointed out to him that if he did this, he would materially affect my business. I pointed out to him that I was covered by insurance, but that as he bought these records without my knowledge and the insurance company was determined to give delivery, I was prepared to give him a profit of one penny a record on each record and destroy them in his presence, rather than have them put upon the market to the detriment of the trade generally. He refused my offer...

Another point I want to emphasise is that the Banner record is not sold at a cheaper price in Australia, either wholesale or retail, than in America. As a matter of fact, the price for Banner records in America is 25 cents, similar to another record made by the same Company. [45]

Besly was followed by Reginald Sanders:

I am Departmental Manager of the Music Department of Messrs. Craig Williamson & Co. Pty. Ltd. We have recently opened this department, in the last six months, and we find that the demand in Melbourne is definitely for two different types of records. The buyers of His Master's Voice, Columbia and the better makes of records are quite distinct from the buyer of the cheap record selling at about 2/-. One of the main things with which we are concerned is getting the maximum of product. We have the money and it does not matter whether we hold £100,000 worth of His Master's Voice records or £10 worth of them, the profit remains exactly the same. In England the dealer buys direct from His Master's Voice Co., but here we have to purchase through a second man. In England in 1919 His Master's Voice records were 4/-, and were afterwards 3/6d and then 3/-. The present system means that there are two profits made on that particular record. One is the profit that the distributor makes, and the other is the profit from the distributor to the retailer. In this I am referring to Australia. We have made inquiries from London for the importation of records direct, whereby we cut out the middleman. At the same time we have definitely made inquiries in Australia for an Australian manufactured record, and I can give the Board evidence so far as the Australian manufactured record is concerned... [to] show that we can buy in Australia a record cheaper than it can be manufactured in England...

The only difficulty about that Australian made record was that... anything that was to be manufactured for us was to be manufactured on the condition that it was not to be sold by us at less than 3/-. They did not mind us having a profit provided that we undertook not to sell it below a certain price. That record was to be made in Australia. We are most of us concerned in getting popular titles on the market, and that is where the importation of records from abroad has fallen short such a great deal. It is definitely known that the American Gennett record, the English Beltona, the German Polydor, and the English Vocalion are being manufactured here or will be manufactured here in Australia. Recently, we have received from the copyright owners a document to the effect that we cannot import any records unless we undertake not to sell them below 2/6d. That is the position, that unless we give them an undertaking not to sell below that price they will not give us the copyright stamps. That is so far as America is concerned, and so far as England is concerned the same arrangement will be made to apply to English imported records in September of next year. In buying cheap records, our best purchases have been made in Australia. In these cases we have taken advantage of somebody else's misfortune and have been able to make job purchases here on the spot, either from Sydney, or elsewhere. I am speaking particularly with regard to a number of Duophone records, of which the company went into liquidation, and also a number of Perfect records bought from Sydney, of a 1925 importation. Those are the cheap lines that we have handled to date, but we have gone well into the matter of records and I am in a position to say that it is cheaper to get our records manufactured in Australia than it is to import them...

It is hardly necessary to put the import duty on because it simply means that your big holders will keep the prices of their records up. They have certain conditions regarding distribution and retailing, but in England you get a bigger margin of profit. There you can buy a record for 1/3d and sell it for 2/6d, whereas here you get a record and get only one third off. They also make the condition here that certain retail prices must be maintained. The most important advantage in importing is that you can run your own retail price...

Directly an increased duty is put on there is no chance of a reduction. You have the importer locked out and you have the control of the record business in Australia...

Next Albert Thomas, the manager of the Music Department at the Myer Emporium in Bourke Street, Melbourne, gave his evidence. He confirmed Sanders' experience of two classes of record and an alleged cartel to keep up the price of records. This concluded the evidence presented at the Inquiry's public hearings.

On 17 November 1927, after the Inquiry had closed, Charles Gendle gave an interview to explain why Vocalion had withdrawn its submission:

> Our company are manufacturers of gramophone records, the chief products of which are the Vocalion and the Aco [labels]; these records are in the same selling category as those of our competitors – the Gramophone Company, Columbia and Brunswick. The Vocalion 10-inch record retails at 4/- and the Aco at 3/6d. In this factory we have also undertaken to manufacture records for other firms who can offer the business to us at a profitable price and we have not been against those firms selling a record at less than ours. It would have a different name of course, there are one or two records on this market which we manufacture in our English factory and they are exported to Australia.
>
> Obviously in establishing our factory here first of all we have the interests of our own product in view. We established our factory to assist our distributors, the Aeolian Company, in dealing with the situation that has arisen which makes the importation of records difficult, not only because of price but because they could not anticipate the requirements of popular numbers – dance numbers in particular... We did not do so as soon as our competitors... The result was when we established our factory we found that our business had gone down considerably and dealers had taken the line of least resistance and were handling other makes of records with the result that there was not enough business to keep going in the production of 'Vocalion' records. The other section of our business was to make a cheap record. We were in the position to manufacture a fairly cheap record if so desired. The application by other manufacturers was to stop the cheap record in this market, and I could not see how I

could very well endeavour to stop the sale of cheap records in this market and yet on the other hand manufacture them myself...

Our English factory has within the last six months introduced a new record that is called 'The Broadcast', it is 8 inches diameter and has a playing capacity the same as a 10 inch record... This record was launched on the market, and has met with considerable success so that the output has now reached a quarter of a million per week and our [English] factory is working day and night.

My people asked me what I could do with this record in Australia and I entered into arrangements for its introduction here; we wished to have it for the Christmas market, but owing to the rush in England we have had to defer the thing until next March. In the meantime I am putting in presses to permit of the local manufacture of this record here...

The question is how soon increased duties might be imposed – if it became necessary during 1928 for our firm in England to help us out with supplies...

It may be that our output here would be adequate, on the other hand this record may receive as great a popularity in Australia as in England, in that case our output here would be insufficient. Having created the demand we would have to be in a position to satisfy it... [61]

With commendable speed the *Report and Recommendation of the Tariff Board Inquiry on Gramophone Records* was published on 28 November 1927. It summarised the current situation:

> The industry in Australia was commenced and immense expenditure incurred in good faith under conditions which at the time appeared to offer such advantages that development would be possible without the aid of a protective tariff, and no assistance under the tariff was made by those engaging in the industry. Selling prices for the local

product were fixed at rates to suit the manufacturers and distributors.

However, the progress of industry has apparently brought about a sudden change in the situation. Inventions and new methods of manufacture have resulted in reduced costs of production in the overseas countries, with the result that the local manufacturers are now faced with conditions not anticipated and which they are not at present able to meet.

The import figures convey at first glance a totally wrong impression. In reading them there must be remembered the dates on which Australian output commenced. One company started in Australia in October, 1924 [Brunswick], one in January, 1926 [His Master's Voice], one in June, 1926 [Columbia], one in November, 1926 [Parlophone], and the latest one a few months ago [Vocalion]. Obviously the diminution of imports in 1926-27 is consequent on the commencement of Australian production, and obviously also such commencement is so recent that the statistical figures give no indication of the rise or fall of the proportion which the Australian production bears to the total consumption.

The Board is satisfied from the evidence of the applicants – and also that of the opponents – that imports of records made by firms other than those now manufacturing in Australia have recently increased. No great importance is ascribed by the Board to the alleged 10 cent record from U.S.A., but there is undoubted evidence of large quantities of records coming from U.S.A. and the United Kingdom – such records retailing in Australia at prices of 1s 3d, 1s 6d to 2s and 2s 6d. (and prices between those figures).

There appeared to the Tariff Board to be no doubt but that the influx of these cheap imported records has had a detrimental effect on the local industry and will have an even more disastrous effect unless some action be taken to place the local manufacturers in a better position to meet the situation.

SOUND BEGINNINGS

The industry in Australia, although controlled by overseas interests, is performing an economic service to the community in that it provides an avenue of employment for a large number of workers both directly and indirectly. The establishment of the industry was the means of attracting to Australia a considerable amount of capital invested by overseas manufacturing concerns, and was in keeping with the Commonwealth Government's expressed policy of encouraging manufacturers in the United Kingdom and other countries to start branch factories in Australia. In the opinion of the Tariff Board it is highly desirable that the industry be given the fullest opportunity to develop.

Reasonably protected from unfair overseas competition, the industry would be enabled to increase its output, and the result should tend towards reducing costs of production with a consequent reduction of the prices charged to customers.

A further advantage – and an important one – derived from the existence of the industry in Australia is that it has made it possible for Australian artists to be recorded, to the mutual advantage of the artists and of the Australian public.

After a careful review of the evidence the Tariff Board is satisfied that the applicants have established a case for protection under the Customs Tariff, and this being so the question arises as to the extent to which such protection should be granted...

In its efforts to arrive at what may be regarded as a reasonable measure of protection, the Board has considered several factors which in its opinion call for consideration, namely:

1. The prospect of local manufacturers further reducing costs of production of the records at present being made.
2. The prospects of new processes of methods of manufacture being introduced involving the production of a cheaper type of record.

'DUMPING': THE 1927 TARIFF BOARD INQUIRY

3. The possibility of reducing the margin which at present exists between the price at which the records are sold by the manufacturers and the prices at which they are retailed to the public.

In regard to the first-mentioned factor the Board is satisfied that the conditions under which the local industry is operating make for higher costs of production than obtain in overseas countries producing and exporting records to Australia. This state of affairs is not peculiar to the industry now under notice, but has been found to apply to other industries investigated by the Tariff Board. While this is admitted, however, the Board is of the opinion that a reduction in the present cost of production should be looked for. Already in the case of some of the more recently-established factories which have been operating but a few months costs have shown considerable reductions, and with the increased efficiency on the part of employees which must come with longer experience, it is only reasonable to anticipate and expect that further reductions will be brought about.

So far as the production of a cheaper type of record is concerned, information available to the Tariff Board indicates that already a large manufacturing concern in the United Kingdom has by means of a new method of manufacture and recording, produced a record of good quality and efficient service at a cost considerably lower than was previously possible. Notwithstanding that witnesses who appeared before the Board on behalf of the applicants held out little or no hope of the production in Australia of a record to sell at lower prices than those now being charged for the local product, the Board, as the result of information tendered to it in confidence, feels justified in anticipating that in the not too distant future the manufacture of a cheaper type of record will eventuate in Australia, and such records will be available to the purchasing public at prices considerably lower than those at which the locally made records can be obtained at present

As to the margin between the local manufacturer's selling prices and retail prices fixed by such manufacturers, information tendered to the Board shows that the manufacturers sell to distributors who, in turn, sell to the retailers. Figures submitted in confidence disclose a very wide difference between the prices at which the manufacturers sell and the prices which are paid by the actual users. It is, of course, recognised that in a business such as that under review the distribution charges must necessarily be high. Users of records are not confined to the more populous centres, but are located throughout the vast areas of Australia. To cater for the requirements of these users involves an extensive distributing organisation and the holding of stocks by a large number of distributors and thousands of retailers...

The Tariff Board does not suggest that there is not scope for reducing the existing distribution costs. As a matter of fact it considers that some reduction in this direction should be possible and practicable.

The Board is not prepared to recommend the granting of the full extent sought by the applicants. In all the circumstances it is considered by the Board that the position would be well met by the provision of the following rates in respect of disc type records exceeding 6 inches in diameter:

British Preferential Tariff 9d.
Intermediate Tariff 1/-
General Tariff 1/3

It is not considered necessary to provide alternative *ad valorem* rates as the fixed rates specified will, in the opinion of the Board, afford the necessary protection against the class of record the importation of which is likely to detrimentally affect the local product. Not only will the

'DUMPING': THE 1927 TARIFF BOARD INQUIRY

duties recommended protect the local industry in respect of the records now being made, but they will also assist in the establishment in Australia of the manufacture of the cheaper type of record already referred to. [98]

'High protection imposed – Purchaser disregarded' thundered the Melbourne *Argus* of 10 December 1927, reporting on the Board's decision:

> Judging from the report of the Tariff Board on gramophone and like records, the externally controlled companies now producing locally made records were crying out before they were hurt. It should be understood that record making in Australia mainly consists of making copies of pieces already 'recorded' in England, on the Continent, or in the U.S. The matrices or originals are sent out to branch or locally established factories, and copies are produced or 'pressed' wholesale for distribution by selling agencies. Necessarily, attractive music can only be 'recorded' in musical centres where great artists are to be found. So a duty on records is a duty on discs pressed abroad...
>
> At the time [the record companies] decided to establish factories to reproduce records in Australia no demand was made for tariff protection, it then being hoped, according to the manager of the Australian branch of the Gramophone Company, that none would be necessary. But since then, he added (and this is the gist of the whole case put to the Tariff Board for a high protective duty), Australian factories have been faced with foreign competition of such a swamping or dumping nature that their very existence is threatened. [117]

In the event, the recommendations of the Tariff Board Inquiry were acted on by the Government who passed the appropriate legislation in the Customs Tariff Act 1928 of 15 December 1927 which was gazetted on 31 March 1928.

SOUND BEGINNINGS

In January 1928 the *Australasian Phonograph Monthly & Music Trade Review* published the final article reporting on the result of the Inquiry from the industry's perspective:

> We believe the amended tariff on phonograph (disc) records will give renewed confidence to those manufacturers who have erected factories in Australia. The protection which it is proposed to give will justify them in developing and increasing their works, and the many trades which have profited by the establishment of the record industry will be assured of a steady and increasing demand for their products. It is perhaps not generally realised the large sums involved in the purchase of record labels, catalogues, and the various items of printed matter which are essential to the carrying on of the record business, but when to this is added heavy purchases of record envelopes, boxes, both cardboard and wooden, many tons of Australian made copper, big supplies of coal and the buying and upkeep of machinery, it will be apparent that the establishment of record factories in Australia has been a distinct boon to the community.
>
> The Tariff Board made most exhaustive enquiries into the whole position and the tariff which has been announced shows conclusively that the Board saw very clearly what enormous difficulties beset our young industry owing chiefly to the importation of records in huge quantities which, in many instances, are invoiced at prices lower than the actual cost of production. This, if persisted in without let or hindrance, would undoubtedly have eventually forced manufacturers to close their works, or at least to greatly reduce their staffs, and the many hundreds of employees who are at present earning a comfortable living would have to join the ranks of the unemployed. It may be that the increase in the tariff will be an inducement for some of the foreign manufacturers to erect works in Australia, and if so, it will be all to the good of the community. [193]

The quantity of records being imported dropped dramatically within a very short time as a result of the imposition of increased duties and almost all record imports ceased by early 1928. There were a few exceptions (*Edison Diamond Discs*, for example) and any overseas pressing not in the catalogues of the local manufacturers could still be imported on special request if the increased duty was paid. As the *Australian Phonograph News* of 15 April 1930 remarked:

> A few years ago, in the days of old recording, there were several makes of records in Australia. Today the 'Big Three' are left supreme in the field, stronger and better than ever: Brunswick, Columbia (and Regal), His Master's Voice (and Zonophone). What has become of Edison, Aeolian Vocalion, Polydor, Edison Bell, Lincoln? They are all but memories.

In fact, several local manufacturers went bankrupt in the early 1930s, and the 'Big Three' was reduced to two when Brunswick (Australia) collapsed in late 1931. At almost the same time the two remaining companies were forced to amalgamate, giving the new EMI a virtual monopoly of the Australian market until the end of World War II. Although from that time the number of multinational companies controlling the local music industry increased, the lack of competition from imported records was to be an overriding feature of the Australian record market from 1928 until legislation was finally passed in 1998 to allow for parallel import of compact discs.

Phonograph advertisement from the 1920s.

Chapter 11

PHONOGRAPH V. WIRELESS

A major issue in continuous debate during the 1920s was the effect the new radio stations might have on the sale of records. In the early 1920s when broadcasting was in its infancy this was not such a lively issue, as the limited number and usually poor quality of broadcast programs was not a serious challenge. However, as the number of broadcasters increased and the quality of their transmissions improved, what had seemed a minor concern began to develop into a major issue. Public interest at this time in anything relating to radio was high, and numerous articles appeared in both the popular press and the specialist journals relating both to radio and the record industry.

Typical of the discussion generated was an article in the *Australasian Phonograph Monthly* of July 1925, titled 'Phonograph v. wireless – Should there be rivalry?':

> At first glance, it might appear as if there would be strong rivalry between the phonograph and the wireless receiving

SOUND BEGINNINGS

set. The purpose of each seems to be the same, namely, the transmission to the individual, in their own home, of selections from the world of music and letters.

Actually, in the application of these two great discoveries to the pleasure or the occupation of the individual, there is no rivalry. One complements and supplements the other. Each takes its special part in a new field of human activity, in the development of which the imaginative mind can see no end.

This new field is the creation of systems of making records by sound. Up to this stage in our civilisation – from the crude scratching on the rock to the finest modern typography – all records have been made through one organ only, the eye. Now we are developing a system of record through another organ, the ear.

It may be argued that the new system is the better one. The message through the eye requires two distinct processes. The meaning is converted into a series of symbols, and the reader, seeing the printed page, converts the symbols back again to their meaning. There are no such changes in the phonograph. The meaning is expressed in sound, as it was in the very beginning of human intercourse, and from the record, at any time, it is reproduced in sound. Philosophers, centuries hence, may say that the almost simultaneous discovery of the phonograph and wireless telephony definitely marked a new era in human progress.

It is easy to carry much further the comparison between printing and sound-reproduction as systems of record. The phonograph record is like a book. The finest things in the world of literature and music are stored up in books, to be reproduced again, through the medium of the eye and the faculty of reading, at any time – today, next year, next century. Similarly, anything which can be expressed in sound may be stored up in phonograph records, which also may be reproduced today, or a hundred years hence.

PHONOGRAPH V. WIRELESS

A library of books is regarded as part of the necessary equipment of a cultured home. The time is coming – is, indeed, already here – when a library of phonograph records is just as necessary. Many people, in fact, already have such libraries, of considerable dimensions. They can be built up, by gradual, pleasurable accumulation, just as easily as can libraries of books.

The wireless service is quite different from the phonographic record proposition. In the field of sound-reproduction it occupies much the same position as the daily newspaper does in the field of literature. One buys a book because one wants a certain subject, treated in a certain way, and because one usually wants to store it away for record. One buys a phonograph record for almost precisely the same reasons. One buys a newspaper, almost always, because one wishes to know what is happening. It is a purveyor of current news, and it has a life of only a few hours. One obtains a wireless service for the same reasons – to know what is going on, to receive a certain amount of entertainment, to feel oneself in touch with the events of the passing hour.

One receives, by wireless, various musical selections, just as one receives in the daily newspaper short stories and extracts from the classics. But persons of good taste do not neglect to buy books because the daily newspapers, according to their whim – and the necessities of filling space – hand out extracts from books. Neither will cultured people fail to buy high-class and classical records for their phonographs because the wireless broadcasters 'pad' out their programmes with vocal and instrumental music.

With a wireless receiving set one takes what is provided, and there is no appeal. With a phonograph, one takes what one wants, and can alter it and change it as one wishes. Therein is the fundamental difference between the phonograph and the wireless, and therein is the basis of the argument that there should be no great rivalry between the two. [160]

SOUND BEGINNINGS

The early experience of the record industry had given no great cause for concern:

> ... radio, contrary to general expectations, has not interfered with the established music trade in any material way... In Australia, Victoria particularly, radio as a musical entertainment has not met with any marked favour, and this can reasonably be attributed to the programmes, the great static interference experienced, and the varied wave lengths. The latter is a fault that bothers even the most enthusiastic, for, as yet, to our knowledge, no set has thoroughly accomplished selectivity, but recent experiments, we learn, have done much in the way of improvement in this regard. [171]

However, another writer addressed the fears that radio would mean the end of records, much as it was later predicted that television, or more recently computers, would lead to the demise of books:

> Not many years ago, when the telegraph first appeared, it did a great business. Then the telephone came along and at once the cry went up... that in a few years the telegraph would be obliterated. As people could talk together, they certainly would not waste... time to telegraph and send long messages when the spoken word was so much cheaper. The prophets, however, were wrong as usual, and the telegraph business today, despite the telephone, is thousands of times larger and does more business than it did before the advent of the telephone. It is just another case of one utility aiding and enlarging another...
>
> Great was the shout that went up... from all phonograph manufacturers and dealers, and their gloom was matched only by their short-sightedness. Many articles appeared in the leading journals, particularly those devoted to the phonograph interests, depicting dark and dull days for the trade.

It is interesting to note that available statistics now show that there are more phonographs used at present than before the advent of radio, and that more records are being sold than at any time during the history of the phonograph. [172]

A few months later an article in a trade journal picked up on the American experience, and proposed that instead of fearing competition the record industry should embrace 'Broadcasting [as] an Ally to Selling Records':

> Though radio in its present state does not affect seriously business, most members of the trade are reluctant to offer an opinion regarding the effect when broadcasting conditions have been improved. Radio must necessarily pass through the probationary stages in Australia as in other countries. It must not be overlooked, however, that sooner or later wireless must come into its own. Instead of regarding it as an enemy or rival, there is no reason why it should not be regarded as a valuable ally... [83]

This was endorsed by H.E. Metcalf in *Radio in Australia and New Zealand*:

> There is no need for argument about the influence of radio on the music dealer. Though it may first have threatened to cripple the phonograph industry, recent adjustments have shown that the radio trade and the phonograph business go hand in hand, the one complementary to the other, and both mutually beneficial.
> Many music dealers have come into the radio business and doubtless many of them still feel a little uncomfortable about the new line of business which seems to involve them in the complicated technicalities of radio.
> No music dealer ever sold many player pianos or phonographs on the basis of the mechanism of the instrument. Customers did not enquire as to whether the

SOUND BEGINNINGS

player had rubber tubing for its air ducts or composition tubing. Nor was there very much discussion as to the inside of the phonograph. Both instruments were sold for their values as musical instruments, as ornaments of the home, and assets to family life.

The same is precisely true of radio, though the fact has been obscured by the initial phases through which the radio trade passed. Radio at first attracted the public as a mechanical curiosity. The pleasures of set-building and distance-getting over-shadowed the importance of radio as an asset to the home. Naturally the first to be attracted were men and boys of a mechanical turn of mind. Their mothers, wives and sisters had nothing to say about it.

Within the past year, the condition has obviously changed, but the mechanical side of radio is still so much discussed that many music dealers attach more importance to it than they need. They feel as though their salesmen should be 'radio experts,' though they well know that, in any merchandising, the expert can never beat the salesman at his own game of selling.

At the same time, music dealers often overlook their own assets, scarcely realising the enormous advantages they possess in having a business already organised to make the most of radio as a home-adjunct.

Music dealers accustomed to handling phonograph trade have, to begin with, ideal stores equipped with listening booths. Radio is now almost a 'fifty-fifty proposition,' attracting customers of both sexes, and music dealers are already versed in the care of feminine trade. They know how to sell the idea, sell the goods, close the sale, and get the money. Things the 'radio expert' may know nothing about.

Music dealers also have an advantage, in that they are accustomed to selling on terms. They know about house to house canvassing, creating new prospects, following up sales,

PHONOGRAPH V. WIRELESS

and giving service. They are accustomed to using advertising and dealers' helps, getting business by mail or telephone. And best of all their phonograph business has brought them in touch with innumerable customers, who are only waiting to be sold radio sets of the right kind, as will be now shown as briefly as possible.

First, let us recall some of the peculiar advantages of the phonograph in pre-radio days. It was a fool-proof machine. It could be used for years and gave no trouble. It was a handsome piece of furniture. And above all it supplied music for all purposes, for all occasions, day or night. It had no static, and never faded during a party. These advantages it had, and still possessed. They are still best assets, together with the fact that they keep bringing customers back to the store for more records.

Radio has taken nothing away from the phonograph, but has added much peculiar to itself. Added to music, it brings religious services, radio drama, fun-nights, news, household hints, an adventurous contact with the world outside the home that bids fair to change our whole social structure since it has, for one thing, robbed the lonely farm of its terrors of isolation. Also it brings the customers back for tubes, batteries, and other necessary accessories.

Obviously the radio and the phonograph are Siamese twins that are, or ought to be, inseparable. It remained only to combine them into a single piece of furniture.

In thousands of homes today, there are phonograph cabinets fairly yawning to receive radio sets of appropriate design, ready to swallow them, batteries and all. Thousands of people owning phonographs in small sized apartments are wondering just where they could put the radio if they had one.

Music dealers and phonograph dealers of established reputation, already have access to these homes, into which they have been selling records for years. They already have the customer's confidence and good will; there is nothing to do but to go after the business... [136]

After the initial rush of public interest however, there seems to have been a backlash against radio. An article in the Melbourne *Herald* on 27 January 1927 discussed the issues:

> From criticism recently published it seems that wireless must be progressing too rapidly, for of all the new arts it receives the greatest criticism. We read recently of Sir Thomas Beecham's strictures on broadcasting, and now we hear somewhat doleful prophecies from no less a critic than Thomas A. Edison, the famous inventor.
>
> Mr Edison is quoted as saying that broadcast wireless is a commercial failure. Sets are too complicated for the lay public who do not understand them. Service eats up all the profits, and business men are turning to other trades. Good music cannot be extracted from a wireless receiver, and that is why people are turning back to the phonograph. A rather dismal picture of radio, surely; but the wireless press in America responded heartily to the criticism, and as the radio turnover last year in America was estimated to exceed £100,000,000, nearly £30,000,000 better than 1926, there is a strong rebuttal of the charge of failure.
>
> It is interesting from our own point of view to read the defence against these charges. We are passing through exactly the same phases as America has experienced. Perhaps our receivers are behind the latest American types, which have been considerably simplified in operation, but a modern wireless set surely makes no more demands on the intelligence than does the modern motor car.
>
> Broadcasting, at the most, is five years old. We didn't know much about any of the modern inventions in the first few years of their creation. The motor car, for example, provided much humor for the comic journals of the period. The telephone for many years was a crude device, when

viewed in retrospect... We are not yet educated to radio, but to the rising generation wireless will be just another adjunct to the myriad pleasures of the twentieth century.

Perhaps the most harmful part of this criticism hurled at radio is the accusation that broadcasting is not truly musical. Musicians are critical, naturally, for music is their trade; but cold science depends neither on the ear nor eye in its appraisement of quality. If the sound waves from an actual instrument are photographed electrically – and that is very simple – an indisputable record of every little shade and tonal nuance is created. If the sound from the same instrument be picked up and broadcast, the broadcast reproduction being photographed in its turn, we have a means of comparison which – expert musicians notwithstanding – admits no dispute.

Now, when it is found that the photograph of the actual sound and that of the broadcast reproduction do not differ substantially, one can only conclude that a little bias has dictated the unmerited criticism... [220]

Throughout the mid-1920s the effect of radio on the record trade was debated back and forth. Gradually there was a shift in the record industry toward the view that radio was a threat, but even as late as 1928 a newspaper report quoted John A. Sabine, sales manager for Europe of the Columbia Graphophone Company, as saying that there were bright prospects before manufacturers of phonograph records in Australia. He believed that the records produced in Australia were equal to those manufactured in England and America and that phonograph manufacturers who had at first feared the developments of wireless, had found it had popularised the phonograph to a remarkable extent. [157]

As predicted, within a few years most of the technical problems that had bedevilled early radio broadcasts had been resolved. Radio receivers rapidly became more sophisticated; they became easier to assemble, as had gramophones some years earlier, and more readily affordable. By the late 1920s a wide range of radio sets were available to suit every budget, including combined radio-phonographs in stylish cabinets available on terms. An advertisement for the *Airmaster Dynamic Phono-Radio* claimed that:

> ... in a flash it gives you your favorite radio programme – or a selected recording, and how fascinating it is to change over from one to the other, merely by touching a simple switch. Radio and phonograph combined in one artistic cabinet make possible a complete and varied entertainment... All the best features of the most expensive combinations are included. The powerful dynamic speakers deliver ample and easily controlled volume which may be adjusted to the acoustics of a small home or a large ballroom. Here indeed is a quality instrument from start to finish, yet priced for the man of average means at only £60 complete and installed. A free trial in your home may be arranged without obligation. Then, if you are pleased, you may retain possession of the instrument for a small initial payment – the balance on easy terms. The temporary shortage of stocks caused by the phenomenal demand has now been overcome. Immediate delivery guaranteed. [197]

By the early 1930s the increased range and quality of radio broadcasts was arousing concern that music programs produced were having an adverse effect on record sales. Two additional factors now came into play.

One was the dramatic increase in the number of broadcast music programs reliant on the use of gramophone records. This was partly due to the gradual decline in the number of studio orchestras or small instrumental groups previously maintained by the radio stations. Such groups were used primarily for music programs, but they were also used to accompany guest artists and often provided backing and 'effects' for station announcements, advertisements and drama presentations. To cut overheads, radio stations had begun to make greater use of records, including sound effects recordings which had become available in Australia by 1930. Some stations continued to have their own orchestras, but used them only for special broadcasts. In many cases the orchestras were disbanded altogether, or reduced to one or two 'house' musicians – perhaps only a pianist.

The other factor was, of course, the dramatic downturn in business conditions during the late 1920s, which became far worse in the early 1930s. The decline in record sales is demonstrated by the figures for stampers (the metal parts used to make records) produced by Columbia Graphophone (Australia) between July 1929 and June 1931 [Appendix 9]. By the early 1930s the record companies were struggling to survive, and they took a much more serious view of anything they perceived as impacting negatively on their interests.

The *Australian Phonograph News* of 30 October 1930 reported that:

> ... efforts are [being] made to restrict, or rather limit, the broadcasting of records. No one can deny that the broadcasting of a new hit number immediately brings it under the notice of thousands of listeners. Many may desire to purchase the record, but after hearing it being repeated five or six times daily, the desire will promptly wane, and at the end of the week the listener can no longer bear to hear it without extreme impatience. The limiting of records, however, should be greatly commended, and will help everyone concerned. Negotiations are proceeding to that effect at the present moment, and it is hoped that they will be crowned with a successful result.

It was almost a year before any action was taken. The continued decline of record sales finally forced the record companies to protect themselves. On 22 October 1931 the *Sydney Morning Herald* reported:

> It was ascertained tonight that several of the largest phonograph record distributing companies in Australia intend to endeavour greatly to restrict the broadcasting of phonograph records. The companies will probably give notice in the next few days that their records must not in future be broadcast without permission. The decision, it is understood, arises from the belief that the recent rapid increase in the use of phonograph records in wireless programmes is destroying the market for records. The decision will react seriously on the B class stations, whose programmes are made up largely of gramophone records. [154]

The next day came further details:

> Inquiries made... yesterday show that the principal talking-machine and record manufacturing companies in Australia... have determined that, within a week or two, they will take definite steps to control the broadcasting of their records.
> Mr John Ritchie, general manager in Australia and New Zealand of His Master's Voice productions, whose statement was endorsed by Mr W.A. Donner, managing director of Columbia Graphophone (Australia), Ltd., said that during the past few years His Master's Voice, Columbia, and Parlophone records had been used by the broadcasting companies in Australia and New Zealand without restriction. The consequence was that the talking-machine industry had been badly hit. Not only had the companies found it necessary to economise generally, but they had also been forced to dispense with the services of many of their employees. The industry was now firmly established in Australia, and had so many ramifications that it was difficult

PHONOGRAPH V. WIRELESS

to say how many people... had been adversely affected by broadcasting. The action decided on was purely self-defensive. When it became effective work would probably be found for many of those who had lost their positions.

The view taken by music publishers and others, whose interests are closely allied with the talking-machine trade, is that the broadcasting stations themselves are largely responsible for what has happened. Money, it is stated, has been lavishly expended in the building of suitable premises, and the installation of the necessary equipment, which is costly. The trade, however, is at a low ebb, owing to indiscriminate broadcasting of music which the companies pay many thousands of pounds annually to have recorded. One company pays a heavy four-figure sum annually for the recording rights of the Philadelphia Orchestra. It also pays heavily for similar rights with regard to other orchestras. Artists, too, receive big fees, some of which run into four figures. The talking-machine companies disburse these sums in order that they may benefit themselves by offering recordings of the best music to the public. The public, however, will not buy so long as they can get the items over the air, practically free. The consequence is that recording companies find themselves paying heavily for something which, at present, yields them nothing commensurate with their outlay.

There are two classes of broadcasting stations. The A class stations derive their revenue from the licensing fees. The B class stations... depend wholly on advertising for their income. The A class station programmes include items by their own orchestras and specially engaged artists and speakers, whereas B class stations offer music provided mostly by mechanical means.

Mr Oswald Anderson, manager of 2UW, stated yesterday that the history of broadcasting had been full of such incidents as the proposed control. The broadcasters, however, had the whole world to choose from, and their experience had been that as soon as one avenue was closed to them, another avenue was opened up.

Mr C.V. Stevenson, manager of the Radio House Broadcasting Station, said that any restrictions such as those proposed would have a far-reaching and serious effect, particularly on B class broadcasting stations. The control would not apply to certain makes of records, but the range of these was limited.

A conference of broadcasters will open in Melbourne on Thursday, when it is expected the proposed control will be discussed... [85]

The attempt by the record manufacturers to control the use of their records on radio may have had some effect. But they certainly did not stop their use entirely. The letters column of the popular radio journal *Listener In* was positively cluttered with readers' complaints (and occasionally praise) about the broadcasting of records. In June 1932, 'Stop Mona' of Glen Iris, wrote under the heading 'A record that should be broken':

> Does it ever occur to the managers of broadcasting stations (particularly B class) that any one record played over and over again can, if one listens to it, produce a chronic state of nerves? There is one station which offends greatly in this respect, *Oh Mona*' (or something like that is the name of the record).* It seems ages since it was first played, 'and since then no other'. It has affected me to such an extent that as soon as I hear the beastly thing announced I dash to switch the set off. As B class stations depend on the number of listeners more so than A class, it would seem bad business to produce programmes which cause listeners to cease listening or else find another station. [175]

---

* The song was actually called 'Oh Mo'nah'.

PHONOGRAPH V. WIRELESS

The next month a listener from Warrnambool complained:

> I would like to draw your attention to the epidemic of fox trots sent over the air from all stations at all hours. These cold nights, when I am able to, I like to settle down before a nice fire with my pipe going and my feet on the mantelshelf to enjoy some music from the air, but I have to be continually jumping up and rushing to the receiver to switch off fox trots. These atrocities, when combined with that imbecile style of singing imported from America, are simply unbearable as musical selections to sit and listen to. Of course they are all right for dancing for which the main requisite is good rhythm and any sort of tune, syncopated or otherwise; but why inflict them at all times, especially when we are trying to enjoy our dinners or sitting at home yearning for some good music? Why cannot fox trots be confined to special dance programmes? These could be given day and night from any one station. Those who wanted to dance would know where to tune in, and those who did not would be able to escape these frightful freaks perpetrated in the name of music. [124]

Another letter from 'Musician' pleads:

> I should like to submit some observations regarding programmes for criticism by my fellow readers. Personally, I exist chiefly on 'red hot' dance music, though I can also appreciate, particularly on Sunday, some classical pianoforte numbers during pensive moments. The latter class of music is fairly abundant, but the former (jazz), though well patronised by the B's, is rather neglected by the A classes... I think that youthful readers will agree with me that more dance records could be 'put over' by the Commission... [163]

Whatever the effectiveness of the record company's ban they soon realised it was not as much in their interests as they had thought. 'Ban removed from B stations' announced the *Wireless Weekly* on 7 July 1933:

> In November, 1931, the gramophone companies, which control the copyrights of almost all records available in Australia, put special labels on all new recordings prohibiting them from being broadcast under any circumstances. The ban did not affect A stations, which had an agreement with the monopoly, but it hit the B stations very hard.
>
> As we go to press this ban on B class broadcasts of new recordings is being lifted. The gramophone companies have arranged a contract to be accepted by all members of the B class federation; the Victorian contracts have been finalised, and it is expected that the New South Wales contracts will be signed to operate from July 1.
>
> The contracts provide that each B class station shall pay to the gramophone company a fixed sum every year for the right to broadcast its recordings. The amount is fixed on a graduated scale, and although the parties did not disclose the precise figures it is believed that one station in Queensland is to pay £150, one in Melbourne £175, and another in Sydney £250, while, of course, stations of less power, and country stations, will pay less.
>
> In addition to the annual payments the B class stations will each give half an hour a week's special advertising to the records of the gramophone companies (mainly H.M.V. and Columbia records), and have agreed to announce the make of each record as it is played. There are also certain restrictions on the number of times one recording may be played; especially on the number of times new recordings may be played within a given period. The contracts are to run just about a year.
>
> The broadcasters believe that the half-hour of special advertising will be the most valuable to the gramophone monopoly; the monopoly grimly hopes so. The idea is that

PHONOGRAPH V. WIRELESS

every week each station will put over half an hour of new recordings, dwelling on the names of the great artists who have recorded them, putting due emphasis on the maker's name, saying where they are to be had, how to order them by number, and how much each.

As Mr Oswald Anderson says: 'For the first time the broadcasters intend to show the gramophone people how broadcasting can help them to sell records. In fact, it is my contention that broadcasting has always helped the sale of records. In October, 1932, after the ban on broadcasts of records had operated for a year, the sales of recordings had dropped even lower than before the ban. I am sure that the new broadcasting policy, of deliberately selling records, will increase their sales.'

And so a critical period in the history of B class broadcasting closes. Some of the more powerful of the B class stations had gone to the lengths of importing new records from England and the Continent; 2CH, 2UW, 2GB, 5AD – these among others, imported some thousands of new recordings, many of which never would otherwise have been heard here, since they would not be suitable for general distribution in this country. But the smaller stations suffered considerably from the ban, and, indeed, all the B class stations, although some of them claim the new contract as a victory, seem rather glad than otherwise to sign up.

The new arrangements were made, not by the tribunal which was proposed by the recent Royal Commission on Copyrights to adjudicate these matters, but at meetings voluntarily induced between the federation and the gramophone monopoly.

These contracts, of course, do not affect the Australian Broadcasting Commission, whose agreement with the gramophone companies was to expire at the end of June. Negotiations were being conducted with the Commission as we went to press. While it is not improbable that the

Commission and the gramophone company will find a suitable arrangement, it is not likely that this arrangement will please the B stations, whose opinion is probably best summarised in the statement of Mr Oswald Anderson: 'I am not inclined to criticise the Commission's policy, except in one matter, the playing of gramophone records. According to the report of the Copyright Commission, 2FC broadcast 59 per cent mechanical music in July, 1932, 61 per cent mechanical music in August, 1932, and 58 per cent mechanical music in September, 1932. The A stations cost the public over £500,000 a year, and yet more than half of their programmes is made up of recordings. The above figures are for the station which uses the least recordings; what the figures are for 2BL or 4QG or 6WF I leave to your imagination. The B class stations regard broadcasts of recordings as their special prerogative; they are, indeed, our bread and butter, and we believe that the A stations would do much better to subsidise performances by Australian artists than to exploit the performances of foreign artists, which is our province. [178]

Within a few years, radio stations were no longer so dependent on locally-produced gramophone records. They began to use many more imported recordings, including pre-recorded program material. By the mid-1930s the wider availability of lacquer discs, which began to be used in Australia about 1934, enabled the production of 'instantaneous' recordings without huge investments for record pressing plants. This development contributed to the rise of many Australian recording studios producing a wide range of documentaries, serialised radio dramas, and other kinds of recordings largely aimed at the rapidly developing radio market.

An article in the *Listener In* of 25 August 1934, 'Records! – Radio's valuable ally' reported on one of the first of these studios: 'A new service is at last available to Melbourne radio artists and advertisers... "Featuradio" as the enterprising company is known, is a by-product one might say of virile broadcasting. Its functions are long-awaited necessities to a radio-minded public...'. [181] Some of the staff at Featuradio had formerly worked for Moulded Products until that company's brief foray into the record business came to an end in early 1933. In this sense, Featuradio can be seen as a continuation of the Melbourne-based record industry which extended as far back as Pemberton Billing's over-ambitious World Record operation of 1924-25.

The relationship between the record industry and radio in Australia in the 1930s, including the role of production companies which supplied the most popular radio serials and documentaries of the period, deserves a separate investigation. The few details provided here cover only the earliest days, when there was not only very little cooperation between the two, but frequently a high level of suspicion and resentment. In retrospect, this can now be seen to have been largely due to mutual incomprehension. One can only surmise what might have happened if Pemberton Billing's short-lived experiment in 1925-26 of combining the appeal of radio with promoting record sales on his radio station 3PB had developed further. This venture certainly had the potential to become the prototype for what developed into a symbiotic relationship a decade later. Unfortunately this potential was not recognised at the time, and the story of the development of the intertwining of radio and recording, so taken for granted today, belongs to the years after the decade covered by this book.

SOUND BEGINNINGS

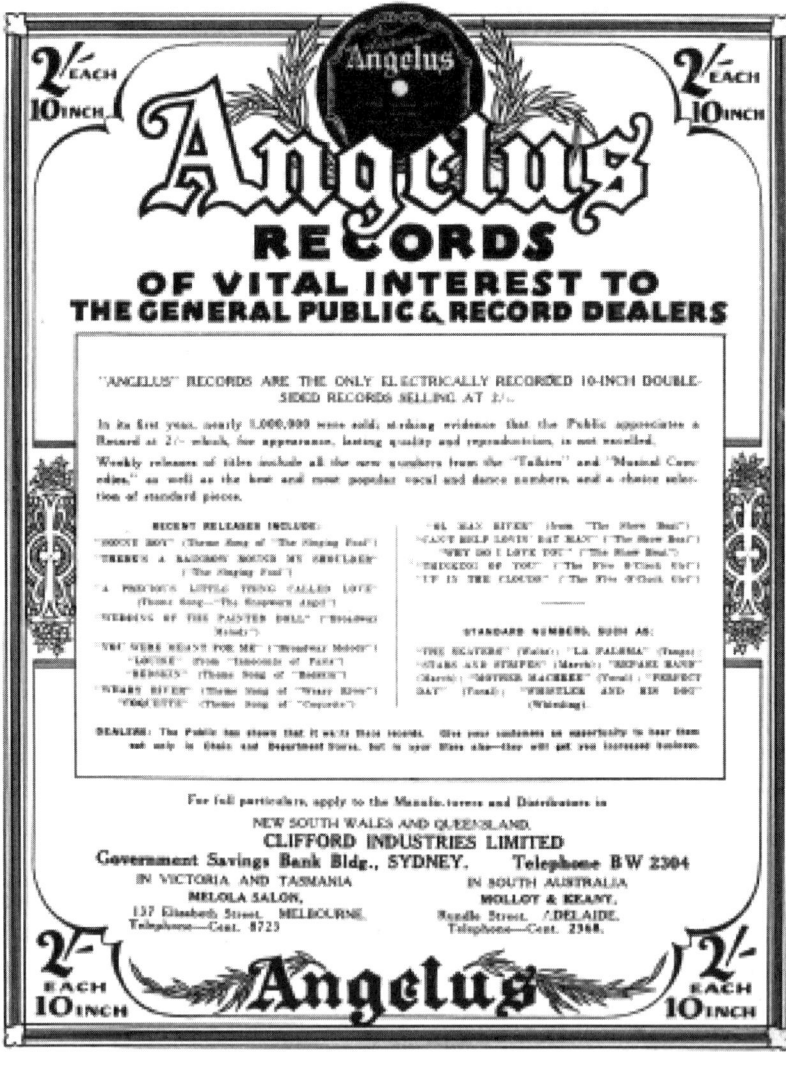

Angelus advertisement from Music in Australia, *August 1929.*

Chapter 12

CLIFFORD INDUSTRIES

Clifford Industries Ltd. was only the second fully Australian-owned record company to be established after local production of disc records began in 1924. It was set up in 1928 by the brothers Herbert and Jack Davis, sons of David Davis, the founder of the company with the *Brunswick* franchise in Australia throughout the 1920s. At almost exactly the same time the first Australian-owned record company, Unbreakable Disc Records, was ceasing production.

Clifford Industries Ltd. was registered on 21 July 1928, with £20,000 capital raised by issuing 20,000 £1 shares. The registered office was given at the time as 8 Junction Street, East Sydney, the address of the company's record-pressing plant in Woolloomooloo, but by November it had moved to Suite 704, Government Savings Bank Building, Castlereagh Street, Sydney.

Clifford Industries' aim seems to have been to produce cheap record lines for chain stores that wanted their own label. So they created a series of nominally independent 'labels' with fictitious manufacturer's credits and pseudonymous artist credits, from masters sourced from a variety of American and British companies which otherwise had no outlet in Australia.

These initially included the Cameo Record Corporation of New York, and Gennett Records of Indiana. As some of these early sources became unavailable because of mergers or bankruptcy, the company found additional sources from the American Record Corporation, the Grey Gull Record Company, the Crown Record Company, the New York Recording Laboratories – all American companies – and the Crystalate Gramophone Record Manufacturing Company in Britain. There was no discernible pattern in the way these masters were used. Sometimes two completely different versions of the same tune were released, on the same issue of the same label, but pressed from masters from two different sources. Probably this was because the original master was damaged; however the manufacturers knew that the purchasers were only interested in having a recording of the latest 'hit' song, and cared little about who performed it. This use of overseas masters continued from 1928 to 1932, both during the life of Clifford Industries and its reincarnation as the Klippel Record Company.

The first labels they produced in 1928 were *Electron*, *Paramount*, *Golden Tongue*, *Grand Pree*, *Melotone*, *Regent* and *Sterling*, and some of these continued into 1929. However, none of these labels were for general sale, and were almost certainly only available from a single retailer. *Golden Tongue* was produced for Craig Williamson stores and later for Marcus Clark. There is no manufacturing credit on the label, but Marcus Clark registered the trademark on 3 February 1928. As this label was not available until later in 1928, the earlier trademark registration date is probably because this was also the name for portable gramophones and record needles marketed by these stores. Like the majority of these labels, *Golden Tongue* probably sold for 2/-.

Paramount (no relation to the famous American label of the same name) is credited to 'Scott Henderson & Co., Sydney, Aust.' and was produced for the Scott Henderson record store at 9–13 Young Street, Sydney; Maurice Rosenthal registered the trademark on 1 June 1928. This label was produced from mid-1928 to early 1929 and was initially priced at 2/6, but later reduced to 2/-.

Electron was credited to a non-existent Electron Record Company and it was registered on 3 August 1928, also by Maurice Rosenthal. This label was made for Coles chain stores and so probably had Australia wide distribution. It was produced from August 1928 until around mid-1929 when Coles registered its 'own-brand' trademark, *Embassy*. This was (and still is) used on a wide variety of its goods, including records, so the *Electron* trademark was no longer needed.

Grand Pree was credited to the non–existent Grand Pree Record Company, but in this case the trademark was a long-standing brand first registered on 14 June 1923 by the Perpetual Trading Association which had been distributing records imported from Britain on this label since before 1923. With the introduction of a duty on imported records after 1927 the company required a locally-made product and turned to Clifford Industries to produce one. Despite the long life of the imported *Grand Pree* label, the locally-produced pressings seem not to have sold well as they are now quite rare. After 46 issues the locally-pressed label was discontinued.

Melotone was credited to an equally mythical Melotone Record Co. and had no connection with the later *Melotone* label produced by the American Brunswick Company in 1931. The Australian label was made for Foy & Gibson department stores. Most unusually, Clifford Industries did not apply for trademark registration until 22 January 1931, which was long after this label had been discontinued. (Chapter 4, 'Brunswick', reveals a possible explanation for this.)

The *Regent* label was probably sold by Selfridges but showed no manufacturer's credit, and there appears to have been no application for a trademark registration. *Sterling* was yet another label credited to a nominal company, Sterling Records, and for which there was no trademark registration, but Farmer's Stores were the probable distributors.

In November 1928 the *Angelus* label appeared. The trademark application of 13 August 1929 correctly assigns ownership to Clifford Industries, despite the attribution to the non-existent Angelus Record Company on the labels. *Angelus* was the first label produced by this company not intended for a specific outlet. It was probably simply a means of promoting sales as it utilised masters which in many cases had already been released on custom labels. As a result, *Angelus* had a much longer lifespan than any other Clifford Industries label (1928-31), and was apparently marketed widely. A broader range of music was also released on *Angelus* and in 1930 a special 1000 series was introduced devoted to light classical music; this was in addition to the usual popular music, novelties and standards in the main 3000 series. *Angelus* records usually sold for 2/-, but some stockists seem to have sold them at lower prices, perhaps discounting obsolete stock.

Angelus was also the only Clifford label to be advertised. There seems to have been a concerted attempt to promote the label when it was first released, and advertisements in August 1929 claim that in the 'first year, nearly 1,000,000 were sold; striking evidence that the public appreciates a record at 2/- which for appearance, lasting quality and reproduction, is not excelled'. This is rather overstating the truth as *Angelus* pressings were clearly inferior to the more expensive labels, despite being 'the only electrically recorded 10-inch double-sided records selling at 2/-'. The advertisements added: 'Dealers: The public has shown that it wants these records. Give your customers an opportunity to hear them not only in chain and department stores, but in your store also – they will get you increased business.' *Angelus* records were distributed in New South Wales and Queensland by Clifford Industries, by Melola Salon (Melbourne) in Victoria and Tasmania and by Molloy & Keany in Adelaide for South Australia.

Sometime in early 1929 a *Starr* label, priced at 2/6, was produced for Coles stores. It was probably marketed in the period between the old *Electron* label, introduced in 1928, and the *Embassy* label of the following year. Clifford Industries did not register the *Starr* trademark until 13 August 1929, but the label was probably produced before that date. It seems to have been discontinued after 53 issues when Coles introduced its *Embassy* label.

By 1929 Clifford Industries had given up crediting fictitious companies on its custom pressings, replacing them with a simple 'Made in Australia'. A further series of 'own-brand' labels for various stores were produced in 1929. These included *Gracelon* for Grace Brothers, *Plaza* (outlet unknown), *Embassy* for Coles and *Worth* for Woolworth's. *Gracelon* and *Worth* sold for 2/-, and *Plaza* was probably sold for the same price. Clifford Industries applied for the *Worth* trademark on 13 August 1929, but there is no trace of applications for the other labels.

Strangely the *Clifford* label, the only one correctly credited to Clifford Industries, was not produced until the beginning of 1930 and discontinued in early 1931 – a few months before the end of the *Angelus* label. As the *Clifford* label was not registered it was probably considered that the original Clifford Industries registration in 1928 would suffice. One of the few published references to this company's operations is a brief item in the *Australian Phonograph News* of September 1930: 'There is an increasing demand for the "Clifford" record, on which many popular hits are available.' Interestingly, the *Clifford* releases used the same couplings as *Angelus*, the only distinguishing features being a slightly different catalogue number and a different label design. However, they seem to have been marketed at the premium price of 2/6 (compared with 2/- for *Angelus*), and with worsening economic conditions during 1930 it is hardly surprising that the *Clifford* label lasted barely more than a year.

The *Orpheus* label, dating from late 1930, was the last custom label produced by Clifford Industries. It must be the rarest and most obscure of all the many labels produced by this company.

By early 1931 Clifford Industries was in financial difficulties and on 5 August 1931 an extraordinary general meeting of shareholders was convened. At this meeting:

> ... the following Extraordinary Resolution was duly passed: That as the Company cannot, by reason of its liabilities, continue in business, it is hereby resolved that the Company be wound up voluntarily, and that Mr Walter William Vick, of Deane, Vick & Co., Public Accountants 160 Castlereagh Street, Sydney, is hereby appointed Liquidator for such purpose. It was further resolved that the remuneration of the Liquidator be £5 per centum of the amount realised by him for the assets of the Company. [4]

The *Australasian Phonograph News* of September 1931 carried a notice advising that:

> An advertisement in the 'Sydney Morning Herald' invites tenders for the purchase of the assets of Clifford Industries Ltd., consisting of machines and tools of the complete record pressing plant valued at £6658/2/8, office furniture... and various other items. All creditors of the Clifford Industries Ltd., (in liquidation) are required to send particulars of their claims to Walter William Vick of 160 Castlereagh Street, on or before August 24th, 1931.

A month before this the *Sydney Morning Herald* announced the formation of the Klippel Record Co. Ltd, and the October 1931 issue of the *Australian Phonograph News* reported that:

> Clifford Industries Ltd., whose plant was valued at £6,658/ 2/8 according to the tender published in the 'Sydney Morning Herald' last month was sold to Messrs. Klippel. The name of the new company is Klippel Record Co. Ltd. (capital £5,000) record manufacturers and music publishers; and the first directors are A. Klippel, S. Klippel and C.R. Deane. The purchase price, so we hear, was £750. Messrs. Klippel are cousins of Messrs. Bert and Jack Davies [sic]. Mr Benjamin will still act as manager.

It is interesting to note that two of the three directors of the new company were relatives of the owners of Clifford Industries, and C.R. Deane is presumably the senior partner of Deane, Vick & Co. who were appointed liquidators of the former company. Klippel was also the legal surname of David Davis. It would appear that the previous management simply continued operations in another guise.

The Klippel Record Company was located at 222 Clarence Street, Sydney, and the new company soon discontinued all the labels produced by Clifford Industries; and introduced the *Lyric* label which continued the catalogue series formerly used by *Angelus*. The *Lyric* label appeared about October 1931, selling at 1/6, and continued to be produced until mid-1932.

The *Summit* label was also introduced late in 1931 and advertised as being 'obtainable from Woolworth's Stores', but they may not have been the sole distributors. The original price was 1/9, but by late 1932 the price had actually increased to 2/-. Although electric recording had been long established by 1932, *Summit* emphasised the fact that:

> Summit records are electrically recorded. The electrical process of recording is the latest development in the phonograph record industry. It is used by the moving picture industry in the production of 'Talkies,' and by the radio industry in broadcasts from 'electrical transcription records,' because absolute realism of tone is necessary. This same realism of tone is essential for the fullest enjoyment of your phonograph records and is available to you on all Summit records.

However, this seems to be no more than an attempt to gain credibility with a market increasingly turning to the 'talkies' and radio as sources of cheap entertainment.

Around the same time the company introduced two labels specialising in children's records. These were 6in. discs on the *Baby Summit* and *Nursery Rhyme Record* labels. The *Baby Summit* discs sold for 9d and were listed in the *Summit* supplements. *Nursery Rhyme Records* were advertised with *Lyric* records and sold for 6d each. It is a measure of the appallingly low level of sales at this time that even at these prices *Baby Summit* and *Nursery Rhyme Records* are among the rarest Australian 78rpm labels. However, *Lyric* had been discontinued well before the end of 1932. The *Summit* label appears to have continued until at least late 1932.

Although all the Klippel labels had Australia-wide distribution, by 1932 record sales had declined to such a point that the operation was no longer viable. Amid the general economic gloom, the demise of the Klippel Record Company seems to have passed unnoticed. Even the trade press had by now been forced to cease publication, so we have no details of exactly when or how the end came.

Despite the official resolution in August 1931 that Clifford Industries 'be wound up voluntarily' the company was still in existence in late 1934, even though its assets had been sold to Klippel Records. A letterhead on a personal reference for one of its staff dated 21 November 1934 claims the company were 'Manufacturers-Importers-Publishers' and gave the address as 7th Floor, The Block, 426-428 George Street, Sydney. The letter stated that 'the bearer... has been employed by this company from February 1931 to November 1934... [and that] he leaves our employ owing to the Company's cessation of manufacturing operations...'. It is signed by W.J. Benjamin, no doubt the same person who was manager of the record pressing plant for both Klippel and Clifford Industries. By 1934 Clifford Industries was certainly no longer in the record business, but the final winding-up of the company did not take place until 22 December 1937.

Jim Davidson's Palais Royal Orchestra which recorded for EMI's new Regal-Zonophone label in 1933.

Chapter 13

THE DEPRESSION AND THE FORMATION OF EMI

By early 1928 unemployment in Australia was already a serious problem. An article in the *Sydney Morning Herald* of 27 March 1928 noted that 'since the war the percentage of unemployment in Great Britain and Australia had been higher than normal. It had gone up to 8 per cent, and even higher. It is now about 7 per cent. According to official figures, the number of unemployed at present is about 14,000...' [202]

While the situation deteriorated steadily throughout the late 1920s and into 1930 many commentators continued to predict that the worst was over. An example of this optimism appeared in the *Australian Phonograph News* of December 1930:

> Opinion in the gramophone trade is freely expressed that bedrock has been reached in the depression, and soon things will again be on the upgrade. The present dullness seems

apparently due as much to a spirit of over-caution as to actual tightness of money. Many people whose incomes are never affected by business conditions seem to use hard times as an excuse for not spending as usual and for withholding payment of accounts for an unreasonable period. It is the general spread of this policy that acts as a stranglehold on retail business especially, and makes things much worse than they otherwise need be. If a salaried man takes up the parrot-cry of 'hard times' or 'bad times' and refrains from buying his record or two a week, the effect is soon felt, and a brake is put upon the wheels of commerce.

But instead the spiral continued downward. The confident expectation that 'things could not get worse' (and must therefore soon get better) was proven to be misplaced. Comments about 'poor business conditions' evolved into talk of the 'Depression'.

In evidence before a Tariff Board Inquiry on 31 August 1931 William Donner, the managing director of Columbia Graphophone, stated that currently four million gramophone records were being produced annually, and that 'a little over two years ago 12,000,000 would have been a more reasonable figure... the Depression is certainly responsible for a falling-off because of the falling-off of the spending power of people who can buy records...' [47]

The massive slump in trade undoubtedly had a devastating impact on the record industry not only in Australia. In 1931 the parent firms of Columbia Graphophone (producers of the *Columbia*, *Regal*, and *Parlophone* labels) and the Gramophone Co. (producers of *His Master's Voice* and *Zonophone* labels) were forced to consider a merger of both companies with Marconiphone, taking with them their worldwide subsidiaries.

The first local news of the proposed merger appeared in the *Sydney Morning Herald* datelined London, 10 March:

Subject to approval of the shareholders, the Gramophone Company and the Columbia Graphophone Company have agreed to amalgamate, forming a new company, acquiring the capital of both existing companies on the basis of an exchange of shares. Each company before the merger will pay a 3/- dividend on ordinary shares and the Gramophone Company will distribute a bonus. [66]

A notice in the April edition of *Australian Phonograph News* declared:

> Cabled advice in the press on March 20 announced a proposed merger of the Columbia Co. Ltd. and the Gramophone Co. Ltd. There was pronounced activity on the London Exchange, and the closing price of Columbia's was 58/9, and the Gramophone Co.'s 53/9. It is believed that the merger will result in such considerable economies that shares may rise to 100/-. [93]

A letter sent by a B. Mittell in head office to John Ritchie of the Gramophone Company on 31 December 1931, discussed the proposed merger:

> I am sending to you and to Mr [William] Donner an unsigned draft of the agreement which is being discussed between the E.M.I. Group and A.W.A. [Amalgamated Wireless (Australasia) Ltd.] and the American Radio...
>
> At the time of writing we have not had the final comments of the A.W.A. but our own Board has given approval of the scheme which, after a great deal of consideration, seems to be best in all the circumstances.
>
> Mr A. Clark and Mr [Louis] Sterling have had well in their minds the fact that as a result of your factory unification the H.M.V. and Columbia businesses are likely to show considerably improved results when trade picks up and when you have effected the control of the broadcasting of records.

They have also had before them your telegram of October 12th in which you indicate confidence in going ahead independently of A.W.A.

I think it must be obvious to you that it was with great reluctance that the decision was reached to take a step which involves our losing control of our businesses in Australasia. The matter was discussed both here and in America and the prevailing view has been broadly that in view of new developments coming up from time to time in the future, it will be better for all these parties to join together and support the new unified Company which will represent their interests in the electrical entertainment field. The various interests, of course, are quite substantial and therefore they cannot all have as big a share as they would like. Probably, however, the agreed division is reasonable.

You will see that the agreement forms a new Company which will take over the assets of ourselves and the A.W.A. in the entertainment field, that the new Company gets a share of A.W.A.'s licensing revenue and that it is licensed exclusively by the Americans and by us and, up to a point exclusively, by A.W.A., until 1981. This long duration is, of course, very important to us who are selling out our business, and that is one of the features which causes us to be reasonably satisfied with the terms which are embodied in the agreement.

I hope, when sending you further news, to draw your attention to points which must be taken great care of in the process of handing over. With the present letter my object is to draw your attention to a point which Mr Sterling is anxious that you should have well in mind. On page 84 and 85 you will see that whatever assets are there listed to be turned over to the new Company, shall be substantially as shown in the auditors' report on the position at 31st December 1930...

THE DEPRESSION AND THE FORMATION OF EMI

> The intention is, and I hope the agreement expresses it, that the total E.M.I. stock at the time of handing over shall be substantially the same value as given in the auditors' report.
>
> The date of handing over will be uncertain; the draft had March 1st 1932 as a probable date but it is now changed so as to be not later than 1st July 1932.
>
> You will, of course, understand that this is merely for your information and not for discussion with A.W.A. or with Hoffnungs or with anyone else... [23]

Previously it would have been unthinkable that the two biggest rivals in the Australian record industry would ever consider such a merger. That this amalgamation did go ahead is telling proof of just how serious the economic situation had become. A great deal of rationalisation was now required. By December 1932 the Gramophone Company head office was announcing:

> We now confirm cable sent to you on the 3rd inst. as per attached copy, under the joint signatures of the Columbia Co. and ourselves, informing you of the discontinuance in this country after the end of the current month of both the Regal and Zonophone records and their substitution, as from the 1st January 1933 by a new record to be issued under the combined Regal-Zonophone label.
>
> We also confirm receipt of your cable in reply dated 5th inst. as per copy herewith, from which we note that, as we anticipated, you advocate postponing the issue of the new combined record until after Messrs. Hoffnung's contract has expired (on the 24th April, 1933) which will mean that your first supplement of the new record will be dated May 1933.
>
> Further we note your recommendation that the record should be distributed by the Columbia organisation through both sets of jobbers who are now operating Columbia and

'His Master's Voice' business respectively. The Management have agreed to both proposals.

With regard to Victor titles – none of these are to be used for new issues under the combined label, but it has been agreed by the Executive that any Victor titles now in the Zonophone repertoire may be repressed under the combined label when stocks of the existing labels are exhausted.

In general any Regal or Zonophone record which it is desired to continue will be made available to the trade under the combined label after the exhaustion of stocks of the respective labels, and the intention is that such re-pressings shall carry the existing Regal or Zonophone coupling No. as the case may be... [23]

The combined *Regal-Zonophone* label was duly introduced in Australia in May 1933. This was one of the first indications to the wider public that the merger had taken place.

Chapter 14

THE END OF THE BEGINNING

By late 1933 the newly amalgamated EMI was the only record company still active in Australia. All the other Australian record manufacturers of the 1920s and 1930s, including the relatively large-scale operations of Brunswick and Vocalion, had been wound up. After such an energetic beginning, within only a few years the Australian recording industry was decimated. It was to be another two decades before the diversity and level of activity of the local industry in the mid-1920s would be regained.

While EMI dominated the local record market in the 1930s, there was significant new activity in the area of producing transcriptions for radio. With the growing popularity of radio there was a rapid increase in the need for what were then known as 'electrical transcription discs'. These radio transcriptions were originally mostly 12in. discs, but later 16in. discs became the norm, and the 78rpm speed gradually gave way to 33⅓ rpm. These transcriptions included pre-recorded radio programs of all kinds, music programs made specifically for radio, advertising recordings, public announcements, station identifications, jingles and promotional records. Almost all were made for radio, although some contained advertisements for theatres or cinemas.

Very little of this transcription material was intended for general distribution, but some companies also produced custom recordings for individual clients. As we have seen, companies such as Vocalion, Flexible Record Co. and Moulded Products had made some tentative beginnings in developing this field, but the use of special radio recordings was not widespread in Australia until the mid-1930s, by which time those pioneering companies had succumbed to the Depression.

In the early 1930s the first instantaneous discs were developed. A recording could now be made directly onto a blank disc in the studio; it did not require record presses and could be played immediately. Those first used in Australia were aluminium blanks which were soft enough for the cutting head to etch the recording directly onto the disc. Blanks were available in some department stories as early as 1931 and for a small fee members of the public could record personal messages on 5in. or 6in. discs which could be posted in a cardboard envelope without fear of breakage. Aluminium disc recorders were also on sale to the public. Larger discs were sometimes used in radio stations during the 1930s, but the sound quality was not really suitable for airplay.

In 1934 the arrival of lacquer discs marked the most significant breakthrough in instantaneous recordings. These usually had a metal base, but sometimes card or even glass was used, and they were mostly available as 10in. and 12in. discs. They were given a thin veneer of lacquer (or more rarely gelatine or some other coating) into which a groove could be easily cut, and this produced good quality playback sound provided they were only played a few times.

THE END OF THE BEGINNING

Since many recordings made for radio were used only briefly, this type of disc quickly became ubiquitous. A whole new generation of specialist recording companies came into existence to meet the increasing demand for transcription and 'instantaneous' recordings. Companies operating in Australia by the end of the 1930s included:

> The *Advertiser* Broadcasting Network in Adelaide.
> Amalgamated Wireless (Australasia) Ltd. (AWA), Sydney.
> Australian Radio Transcriptions Pty. Ltd., Sydney.
> Australian Record Co. Pty. Ltd., Sydney.
> Chas E. Blanks Pty. Ltd., Sydney.
> British Australian Programmes Pty. Ltd. (BAP), Sydney.
> Broadcast Services, Brisbane.
> Columbia Graphophone (Australia) Pty. Ltd., Sydney.
> Country Broadcasting Services Ltd., Sydney.
> Jack Davey Productions Pty. Ltd., Sydney.
> Du Maurier Productions Pty. Ltd., Sydney.
> Featuradio Sound Productions Pty. Ltd., Melbourne.
> Federal Transcriptions & Television Pty. Ltd., Sydney.
> Fidel-a-Tone Sound Productions, Melbourne.
> International Sound Recordings, Sydney.
> Legionnaire Sound Productions Pty. Ltd., Melbourne.
> Macquarie Broadcasting Services Pty. Ltd., Sydney.
> Radio Theatre Guild, Sydney.
> Sound Recording Studios Pty. Ltd., Sydney.
> Trans-Radio Advertising & Program Service, Sydney.
> Victorian Broadcasting Network, Melbourne.
> VOA Sound Productions, Sydney.

The story told in this book effectively ends with the demise of the last of the original independent record companies in 1933. In the subsequent years a new period of intense recording activity was initiated in conjunction with the 'golden age' of Australian radio drama. But that's another story.

After 1945 a significant number of new record companies were established but they operated under the restrictions on imports introduced after the 1927 Tariff Board Inquiry. As a result, during the 1980s concern arose that a small number of multinationals were effectively imposing their own terms and conditions on a significant sector of the Australian entertainment industry. The Government responded with an inquiry by the Government Prices Surveillance Authority into the prices of sound recordings. This enquiry was almost a mirror image of the Tariff Board inquiry held 63 years earlier.

In both cases the established local manufacturers argued strongly that any form of genuine competition from imported records was not in the national interest. In both cases the self-interest of the local record industry was cloaked in claims that a lack of protection by the Government would result in large job losses. And in both cases the economic uncertainty prevailing at the time was used as a powerful influence to encourage Government support of the local industry.

The inquiry's report of nearly 200 pages, published in 1990, recommended measures to break the control of the cartels, but a strong lobby group, coordinated by ARIA (the peak record industry body), was effective in quashing any action to challenge the status quo. By 1997 the record industry was still aggressively defending itself against any requirement that its prices be brought into line with those prevailing in most of the rest of the world. In commenting on the lack of any progress on this issue, the journalist Alan Ramsey in the *Sydney Morning Herald* on 11 October 1997 referred to the 'unconscionable profits to the Big Six, five of them subsidiaries of Japanese, American and European conglomerates'. [173]

The blow came at last on 12 July 1998 when, by the narrowest of margins, the Senate of the Federal Government voted to lift restrictions on CD imports. After this decision the Minister for Communications and the Arts, Richard Alston, and the Attorney-General, Daryl Williams, stated:

> The Government's reforms will break the monopoly on imports of CDs now enjoyed by a select few foreign-owned multinational record companies, which have used their market dominance to keep Australian CD prices artificially high...
>
> These multinational companies have, for far too long, gouged record profits from the pockets of Australian consumers...

This decision clears the way for the first significant importations of records since 1927. As such it represents the advent of what will almost certainly be the most momentous changes in the structure of the local record industry since it was first established.

The Australian record industry has been highly successful in maintaining an almost unchanged position of privilege locally, and history shows that essentially their arguments have remained much the same since the first record factories were established here in the 1920s. One of the claims made in opposing overseas competition was that this would remove incentives to produce records by Australian artists. This study has established that the percentage of Australian recordings sold here over 60 years ago was only 13%. An article 'Politics calls tune for compact discs' by Lincoln Wright in the *Canberra Times* on 15 July 1998, examining the effect of the two Copyright Amendment Bills on parallel importing of CDs, reported that 'only 16% of sales in 1995-96... were of Australian artists'. [184] So it seems that over 60 years local record companies have succeeded in expanding the market for records by Australian artists by only 3%; that there has been little real benefit for Australian artists; and that these changes in the regulation of the lucrative Australian music industry represent the first major shift in the dynamics of the record business for generations. As such, it opens a new chapter in the fascinating history of an innovative industry which, as this volume has documented, had sound, but in most cases much too short-lived, beginnings.

APPENDICES

STATISTICAL APPENDICES

Following are some interesting figures extracted from various official documents encountered during the research for this book. Exact figures are difficult to find for the early record industry, and those included in these appendices are collected here for easy reference, and are also referred to at appropriate points in the text.

APPENDIX 1

IMPORTS OF GRAMOPHONE RECORDS INTO THE COMMONWEALTH FOR THE YEAR 1926/27

Country of Origin	Value (£)
Commonwealth	1,246
United Kingdom	167,663
Canada	1,546
India	303
British Malaya	1
Argentina	5
Australia	2
Belgium	1
China	83
Czechoslovakia	104
France	35
Germany	5,934
Greece	1
Italy	75
Japan	108
Netherlands	1
Switzerland	3
Syria	1
U.S.A.	43,945

APPENDIX 2

BRUNSWICK RECORDS – FACTORY OUTPUT FROM COMMENCEMENT OF MANUFACTURE IN AUSTRALIA (from figures supplied on 18 October 1927)

1 October to 31 December 1924	114,938
1 January to 31 December 1925	946,791
1 January to 31 December 1926	1,618,986
1 January to 30 June 1927	600,482

APPENDIX 3

THE GRAMOPHONE COMPANY LTD., SYDNEY – NET SALES (1 Oct 1926–30 Sept 1927)

	Australia	New Zealand
1926		
October	142,053	29,149
November	161,159	17,077
December	107,005	29,041
1927		
January	99,758	28,548
February	155,146	37,452
March	168,252	42,612
April	155,674	23,567
May	219,047	41930
June	157,237	37,840
July	137,134	34,457
August	193,797	35,083
September	199,722	43,950
TOTAL	1,895,984	400,706

APPENDIX 4

COLUMBIA GRAPHOPHONE (AUSTRALIA) LTD. RECORD PRODUCTION & SALES FOR JULY & AUGUST 1927

	10in.	12in.
July 1927		
Records manufactured	116,809	16,034
Records sold	87,663	17,295
August 1927		
Records manufactured	187,897	15,855
Records sold	138,890	19,329

APPENDIX 5

PARLOPHONE RECORD SALES NOVEMBER 1926–JUNE 1927

	Ex-Factory	Price to retailers
1926		
November	£392	£560
December	£991	£1,416
1927		
January	£761	£1,093
February	£606	£866
March	£1,734	£2,481
April	£2,425	£3,439
May	£2,543	£3,633
June	£2,490	£3,614

APPENDIX 6

COLUMBIA GRAPHOPHONE (AUSTRALIA) LTD – STATEMENT OF ROYALTIES PAID TO AUSTRALIAN ARTISTS FOR THE THREE YEARS ENDED 31 DECEMBER 1930

1928

Quarter ended March	£1,022.3.6
Quarter ended June	£895.9.6
Quarter ended September	£768.0.6
Quarter ended December	£380.13.6

1929

Quarter ended March	£368.2.0
Quarter ended June	£262.3.11
Quarter ended September	£318.1.4
Quarter ended December	£309.19.6

1930

Quarter ended March	£388.10.4
Quarter ended June	£443.12.2
Quarter ended September	£442.1.3
Quarter ended December	£186.14

APPENDIX 7

COLUMBIA GRAPHOPHONE (AUSTRALIA) LTD – SALES OF AUSTRALIAN RECORDINGS FROM 1 JULY 1929–30 JUNE 1931

Series	Sales
10in. dark blue [popular]	257,850
12in. dark blue [popular]	4,129

10in. light blue [classical]	204
W' red [children's]	9,661
10in. Regal [cheap label]	164,404
TOTAL	436,248

APPENDIX 8

COLUMBIA RECORD UNIT SALES FOR THE 11 MONTHS ENDED 30 NOV 1932

	Columbia	Regal	Parlophone	Total
January	17,421	57,448	14,593	89,462
February	15,951	58,104	13,276	87,331
March	15,267	56,217	10,447	81,931
April	13,871	58,118	13,966	85,955
May	15,662	58,045	12,580	86,287
June	14,914	58,223	10,166	83,303
July	13,954	57,518	11,337	82,849
August	13,667	64,759	11,133	89,559
September	14,357	75,991	10,649	100,997
October	12,735	51,936	9,282	73,953
November	13,312	46,292	10,925	70,529
TOTAL	161,111	642,650	128,354	803,761

APPENDIX 9

COLUMBIA GRAPHOPHONE (AUSTRALIA) LTD – STAMPERS MANUFACTURED FOR TWO YEARS ENDED 30 JUNE 1931

Month	8in.	10in.	12in.	16in.	Total
1929					
July	-	739	207	-	946
August	-	682	238	-	920
September	-	539	172	19	730
October	-	540	89	58	687
November	-	454	171	80	705
December	-	450	266	14	730
1930					
January	-	621	182	74	877
February	-	515	133	169	817
March	-	403	79	83	565
April	-	291	90	58	439
May	-	429	98	74	601
June	-	410	142	17	569
July	-	341	105	57	503
August	-	246	57	29	332
September	-	301	121	23	445

October	-	326	93	21	440
November	9	265	56	42	372
December	14	239	132	51	436
1931					
January	-	230	116	36	382
February	6	276	164	59	505
March	-	321	41	32	394
April	-	236	140	13	389
May	-	270	145	-	415
June	1	203	44	-	

APPENDIX 10

RECORD LABELS AVAILABLE IN AUSTRALIA BEFORE 1934

The following is a comprehensive list of all the cylinder and disc record labels available in Australia before 1934, either by general distribution in a variety of outlets, or through special labels made for specific stores. Many other labels were brought into the country but were never sold here.

The list provides some general background on each label, plus details of distributors or outlets and selling price where known. However, often only scant details are available and many labels were on sale only briefly, leaving little evidence of their existence.

ACO

A budget-priced label produced in Britain by the Aeolian Company between 1922 and 1927. These records were routinely imported into Australia and distributed through the established outlets of the Aeolian Company in Sydney, Melbourne, Brisbane, Adelaide and Newcastle. The 10in. G15000 series was priced at 3/6; the 12in. G30000 series cost 4/-. After Vocalion began record production in Australia in 1927 they produced a short-lived Australian *Aco* 10in. GA20000 series. Some issues from the British catalogue were also pressed locally.

ACTUELLE

A British-made record produced by Pathé Frères between 1921 and 1928. *Actuelle* recordings were sold in Australia on the *Grand Pree* label made in Britain by Pathé Frères for the Grand Pree Record Company.

AEOLIAN VOCALION

A British-made record imported into Australia by the Aeolian Company during the early 1920s. The name of this label was changed to *Vocalion* in 1923 [see Chapter 8].

AERONA

A disc advertised as 'the cheapest double-sided, seven inch record in the world' and made in Britain by the Crystalate Manufacturing Company for sale solely in Australia. They were distributed from October 1926 by Salkeld & Wallace of Sydney, the trademark having been registered in Britain in April 1926.

AEROPLANE

A flexible record produced in Melbourne by Unbreakable Disc Records in mid-1928 [see Chapter 9].

AMBEROL

A new form of cylinder record produced in America by Thomas A. Edison Inc. it had a longer playing-time (4 minutes) than earlier Edison cylinders and was also more durable. *Amberol* cylinders were exported widely and were available in Australia by 1909. Their importation was partly responsible for the failure of local cylinder companies unable to compete against this superior and cheaper product. In 1912 Edison introduced an improved version called *Blue Amberol*, named from the colour of the dye used in their production. These cylinders proved very popular and sold well until Edison cylinder records were discontinued in 1929. *Amberol* records were distributed in Australia by the regular Edison outlets and sold for 4/-.

AMFONOLA

A label pasted over the *Regal* name on obsolete stock of American *Regal* records sold in Melbourne about 1925. In Australia the *Regal* name was the property of the Columbia Graphophone Company, but the American *Regal* records were produced by the Plaza Music Company of New York and could not be sold here without being relabelled.

ANGELUS

The chief label produced by Clifford Industries in Sydney. The series began at 3000 in November 1928, and there were over 350 issues until the label was discontinued in 1931. A short-lived 1000 series devoted to light classics and similar material was released in 1930-31 [see Chapter 12].

APEX

A Canadian-made label produced by the Compo Company of Quebec. It was imported into Australia during 1924-25 and distributed by Suttons which was based in Sydney with branches in Melbourne, Ballarat, Bendigo, Geelong and Adelaide. The records sold for 3/6.

ARCADIA

A label produced in Melbourne by Vocalion Foreign for a chain store, probably Edments, during 1929-30 [see Chapter 8].

ARROW

A British-made record of 1913-14 vintage which had limited distribution in Australia.

ARTIPHON

A German label produced from 1924 by Hermann-Eisner-Schallplattenkonzern of Berlin. The Australian agents were Kelson & Company of Sydney.

AUSTRAL

The principal label produced by World Record (Australia) in Melbourne in 1924-25 although all the masters were imported [see Chapter 3].

APPENDICES

AUSTRAL DUPLEX

An 8in. long-playing disc produced in Melbourne by World Record in mid-1925. All issues on this label were Australian recordings and the earliest locally recorded discs marketed in Australia [see Chapter 3].

AUSTRALIA

Cylinder records, produced in Sydney from 1904 to 1909, among the earliest Australian recordings to be commercially released [see Chapter 2].

BABY SUMMIT

A 6in. children's record made in 1931-32 by Klippel Records [see Chapter 12].

BANNER

A disc produced by the Plaza Music Company, New York, and imported into Australia by Kenneth A. Besley & Co. They sold for either 1/6 or 1/11, depending on which source is correct. Stock of American *Regal* records, made by the same company, were relabelled in America with specially printed *Banner* labels for sale in Australia because *Regal* was already registered in this country by Columbia Graphophone. The discs given *Banner* labels retained the original *Regal* catalogue numbers and artist credits (including names like *Regal Dance Orchestra*).

BEEDA

The trademark registered by Allan & Co., the long established Melbourne music store, on 27 February 1925. Allan's also retailed a cheap portable gramophone under the *Beeda* trademark, so this name was used for other 'own brand' products, not just records. There were two distinct *Beeda* labels. Neither showed any manufacturer's credit, but the first was produced by the Compo Company of Canada in early 1925. This single issue featured a composition by the well-known Melbourne composer Jack O'Hagan on one side, although the recording was made by Canadian musicians. Around mid-1925, Allan's arranged for more *Beeda* records to be made in America by the Plaza Music Company; this series ran to 20 issues.

BEKA/BEKA-GRAND

A disc originally manufactured in Germany as early as 1905 for the export market, but by 1913 they were being manufactured in Britain. Both labels were distributed in Australia.

BEKA-MEISTER

A 12in. record manufactured in Britain by the same company that produced the *Beka-Grand* label. Its catalogue consisted mainly of light classical material.

BEL CANTO

A disc manufactured in Germany for the British company J. G. Murdoch around 1910. It seems to have had some limited distribution in Australia.

BELL

A 6in. children's record manufactured in Britain from 1921 to 1927 by Edison Bell. It was widely distributed in Australia, presumably through the same outlets as *Winner* records.

BELL DISC
The first disc record to be produced by Edison Bell. It was manufactured in Britain from 1908 to 1912, but discontinued with the introduction of the *Winner* label. It sold here for 2/6.

BELLBIRD
A flexible record produced in Melbourne by Unbreakable Record Manufacturers in 1930-31 [see Chapter 9].

BELTONA
A label produced by the British Vocalion Gramophone Company for Murdoch Trading Company of London. Introduced in 1922, it was widely available in Australia until 1927 for 3/6. The local distributor may have been A. Macrow & Sons of Melbourne, as they handled *Beltona* gramophones.

BELTONA DE LUXE
A higher-priced version of *Beltona*, featuring mostly light classical repertoire.

BERLINER
The first disc records produced by the United States Gramophone Company, established in 1894 in Washington DC by Emile Berliner, who applied Edison's sound recording techniques to disc recordings rather than cylinder recordings. Initially these discs were 8in. in diameter, single-sided, and without labels as the contents description was etched directly onto the blank area in the middle of the record and often included a recording date. Although usually described as *Berliner* records, the actual discs show 'E. Berliner's Gramophone' at the top. This company was succeeded in 1895 by the Berliner Gramophone Company. In July 1898 Fred Gaisberg, who also acted as recording 'expert' and piano accompanist, established Berliner's European branch in London.

Berliner's disc records must initially have been produced in very small quantities as discs dated earlier than 1897 are rarely seen. The gramophone and the disc records it played was at first a minor competitor to the more widely available phonograph and its cylinder records. Thus only a tiny number of Berliner records would have been imported into Australia, and they were probably only available in 1898-99. In 1900 Berliner ceased operations and the rights passed to the Victor Talking Machine Company in America and to the Gramophone Company in Britain.

BETA
A label pasted over British-made *Winner* records in about 1921. The *Beta* label says 'British Manufacture', but the kangaroo logo leaves no doubt that it was intended for distribution in Australia.

BON MARCHÉ
A label begun in mid-1927 and produced in two formats. The first (in a 1000 series), manufactured in America by the Plaza Record Company for export to Australia, stated on the label: 'Made in America for Payne's Bon Marché, Bourke Street, Melbourne.' The second (in a 100 series) was made in Britain by the Crystalate Manufacturing Company.

APPENDICES

BON TON RECORD
Pasted over British *Regal* records for sale through a specific but unidentified outlet.

BROADCAST
An 8in. record produced in Australia by Vocalion Foreign between 1928 and 1930 [see Chapter 8].

BROADCAST DE LUXE
A conventional 10in. record (as opposed to the 8in. *Broadcast* record), which was introduced by Vocalion Foreign in 1929 [see Chapter 8].

BROADCAST TWELVE
Despite the 'twelve' in the title, this was a normal 10in. record, but was claimed to play as long as a standard 12in. record (just as the 8in. *Broadcast* was promoted as playing as long as a 10in. record). It was also manufactured in Australia by Vocalion Foreign [see Chapter 8].

BRUNSWICK
American-made record distributed in Australia from 1921 by D. Davis & Co., then from July 1924 pressed in Australia at the Brunswick factory in Sydney. Brunswick (Australia) ceased trading in 1931 [see Chapter 4].

BULLDOG
A British-made label of World War I vintage with some distribution in Australia.

BUTTERFLY
A label pasted over *Popular* records apparently intended for Australian distribution about 1921.

CAMDEN
A label used in 1927 on deleted stocks of both 10in. and 12in. British *Vocalion* records to be retailed by Buckinghams, a Sydney store. The catalogue numbers on the new labels were simply the *Vocalion* numbers reversed.

CAMEO
Labels of several different designs pasted over British *Columbia* and *Regal* records sold in Australia. It seems these were resold by Columbia Graphophone itself, as it had registered this trademark on 23 January 1922. This label had no connection with the American *Cameo* label of the 1920s.

CAPITOL
Initially in 1926 a label pasted over deleted British-made *Parlophone* records sold locally. Despite the spelling, the label featured a drawing of the original Parliament House in Canberra opened in 1927. From 1927 to 1931 a *Capitol* label depicting a Greek temple was also used on Australian-made *Parlophone*, and less commonly on *Columbia* records. There is no connection between this label and the American *Capitol* label which began production in the 1940s.

CHAPPELL
A British-made label produced around 1913 for London music publishers Chappell & Co., probably to promote their compositions. This label seems

to have had some limited distribution in Australia. It should not be confused with the much later *Chappell's* label of the 1940s-1960s, featuring 'mood music' for radio and television programs.

CINCH

A low-price label produced by the Gramophone Company in Britain in 1913-15. It was presumably distributed in Australia through the regular Gramophone Company outlets and sold for 1/1.

CLARITÉ

A record label marked 'Made in USA' credited to the Clarité Record Company, but actually produced by the American Plaza Music Company for export to Australia. The trademark was registered by James Charles Miles on the 7 September 1926 in Sydney. It seems likely that only one batch of records was produced on this label, about 40 issues, which did not survive beyond 1927. The price has been reported as being 1/9 or 1/11.

CLIFFORD

A label produced in Sydney by Clifford Industries 1930-31. It duplicated the couplings available on *Angelus*, with the 5000 series being equivalent to the *Angelus* 3000 series and the 4000 series being equivalent to the *Angelus* 1000 series [see Chapter 12].

CLOVER

A record produced for a short period about 1926 for the Nutmeg Record Corporation of New York and distributed in Australia by the Grand Pree Record Company, Sydney. It was probably priced at 1/9.

COLISEUM

A disc made by Vocalion in Britain for Cooper Brothers, London and available in Australia from 1912 to 1927.

COLONIAL

A disc manufactured in Germany in 1910 for Lockwoods of London. The label indicates that these discs were intended for export to Australia and is marked 'Not For Sale in UK'. This is quite a rare label today, so it must have had limited distribution.

COLUMBIA

Limited quantities of both the American-made *Columbia Disc Record* and the British-made *Columbia Graphophone Record* seem to have been imported into Australia before 1908. The British Columbia Graphophone Company released a trial batch of double-sided discs in 1904, but it was not until 1907 that double-sided *Columbia* records became readily available. These were certainly imported into Australia and subsequently all *Columbia* records were available here. In 1908 the American Columbia Graphophone Company also introduced double-sided records, but very few of these or subsequent American-made Columbia records were imported [see Chapter 5].

CONDOR

A label introduced by World Record (Australia) in late 1925. It was a conventional shellac disc, unlike the cardboard-based *Austral* and *Austral Duplex* [see Chapter 3].

APPENDICES

DACAPO
A German-made record of 1910-14 vintage widely distributed in Australia. The 10in. records sold for 2/6 and the much rarer 12in. discs for 4/-.

DAHLMONT
A trademark registered on 17 September 1925 by the Myer Emporium of Melbourne. Myers also sold a *Dahlmont* brand portable gramophone. The earliest use of the *Dahlmont* trademark is on relabelled British-made *Vocalion* and *Aco* records sold in Myer stores. In 1926 Myers ordered a batch of records with their own trademark label from the Plaza Music Company, with labels declaring 'Sole distributors for Australasia, The Myer Emporium Ltd.', but which do not identify the manufacturer.

DECCA
The first Australian *Decca* label, the M1000 series, was produced in Melbourne by Moulded Products in 1932-33 and had a blue label [see Chapter 8]. It had no connection with the later EMI *Decca* label produced in Sydney from 1936.

DIAMOND
A disc produced in Britain by Pathé Frères between 1915 and 1918 and imported into Australia in limited quantities only.

DIPLOMA
A disc originally manufactured in Germany by J. Blum & Co. in 1911, but later made in Britain until 1915. Some issues are credited to the Diploma Record Company, London, but this was probably a fictitious name.

DOMINO
On 15 August 1926 the *Music Trader* announced that 'Brunswick Furniture Pty. Ltd. of Glenlyon Road, East Brunswick, makers of the Glenola gramophone [no connection with the Brunswick-Balke-Collender company] have recently secured the sole agency for Australia for the Domino record. Manufactured by the Plaza Music Co. of New York, and by electrical recording process, these records are a dull brick color, and retail at 2/9. Mr. V.G. Green, Cromwell Buildings, Bourke Street, has been appointed wholesale agent.' By 1927 *Domino* records were selling for 1/6.

DUOPHONE
A label produced between 1925 and 1926 by Vocalion Gramophone for the Duophone Syndicate in London. There were both 10in. records in a B5000 series and 12in. records in an A1000 series. The Australian distributor was the Gloria Light Company of Australia, located in Sydney. The 10in. records sold for 3/6 and the 12in. for 5/-.

By 1926, a new product had been developed called the *Duophone Unbreakable Record*. According to a press report of the time, an Australian company was formed to market it:

> Mr. Launcelt Gaunt, managing director of the Duophone Co., which is launching unbreakable gramophone records on the market, explains that the records are made of waste paper. The cheapest paper, says Mr. Gaunt, makes the best records, and these are printed as easily and quickly as a newspaper. The whole secret is the finishing process, and

SOUND BEGINNINGS

the secret is closely guarded. Out-of-date records can be recalled and reprinted at the cost of a half-penny. Mr. Gaunt, who is a Victorian, says that a double sided record can be split to make two single records, whose excellence will not be impaired in the process.

Mr. Launcelt Gaunt is the youngest son of the late Judge Gaunt, of Victoria, and a brother of Sir Guy Gaunt, Sir Ernest Gaunt, and Mr. Clive Gaunt. He was educated at Melbourne Grammar School and Melbourne University. For some time he practised as a solicitor in Gippsland, and later at the Bar in Melbourne.

Twenty years ago he went to the East, where he practised in the legal profession, and 10 years later he left for England. Since then he has been engaged in several large financial concerns. Eighteen months ago he became managing director of the Duophone Co. This company has already made preparations for the Australian market, a factory having been erected at Coburg, Vic. So far, however, the Australian Co. has not received a sample of the unbreakable record made from waste paper, and no details of its manufacture are known here.

However, the venture does not seem to have proceeded as no *Duophone* records were manufactured in Australia.

EBONOID

A cylinder record manufactured in Britain. A few made their way to Australia.

EDISON

Edison cylinders and *Diamond Disc* records were manufactured in America by Thomas A. Edison Inc., shipped directly to the local branch in Sydney and sold there and at the Edison Shops and in each of the capital cities. The standard 50000 popular series sold for 6/6, while the various series featuring classical music and art songs sold from 9/- to 12/6 each.

Edison records could only be reproduced on an *Edison* gramophone, so despite the high prices there was a specialised market for them and no competition. Those who could afford to pay for the 'prestige' of purchasing the expensive *Edison* gramophones were also prepared to buy *Edison* records. Consequently, *Edison* records continued to be sold in Australia long after most other imported labels were no longer available. Because Edison records did not compete directly with locally manufactured labels, they were specifically excluded from the tariff increases imposed following the 1927 Tariff Board Inquiry.

Eventually even Edison was forced by declining sales to produce a conventional 'needle-cut' record. But this came too late to save the label and the entire record division had to be closed down in October 1929. The impact on Edison dealers in Australia was reported in the January 1930 issue of the *Australian Phonograph News*:

Great happenings have been taking place with T.A. Edison in America. During the last two years the number of better class record releases has greatly diminished, and stars like Claudia Muzio no longer make their monthly appearances. Later an attempt was made to put out a few chamber music works, for the long playing records were a disappointment owing to their weakness of volume. Some months ago revolutionary changes were predicted. Edison entered the field of needle records and his first important engagement was that of Martinelli, the well-known tenor. Just when the time was approaching for the first Edison needle records to be released in Australia, a drastic change of policy was announced by the American headquarters.

Thomas A. Edison Inc. have suddenly decided to immediately cease the production of all records, both diamond disc and needle, and concentrate on radio manufacture. Admirers of Edison products must have keenly felt the blow, and the realisation that no longer will they be able to buy records for their instruments.

The blow also adversely affected the well-known Edison Shop in Castlereagh Street, Sydney, the directors, Messrs. Hewison and Williams, deciding to wind up their business. Machines were greatly reduced, and 12/- records were sold at one shilling each... [111]

EDISON BELL

Cylinder records produced in Britain from 1898 and distributed in Australia through their own agents. They were available until the 1920s.

EDISON BELL WINNER

A disc produced from 1912 in Britain by Edison Bell. The Australian distributor was originally the Melbourne company A. Macrow & Sons who sold *Winner* records for 2/6. Later the label name was changed to *Edison Bell Winner* and by 1925 the 'sole Australian agents' were Weiss, Biheller & Brooks in Sydney who raised the price to 3/6.

ELECTRON

A label produced by Clifford Industries for Coles stores in 1928/29 [see Chapter 12].

EMBASSY

A label produced by various companies for Coles: firstly an 8000 series was made by Vocalion Foreign in 1929-30, then Clifford Industries produced it, using the same couplings as on their *Angelus* label (with the first digit of the catalogue number changed from 3 to 9). The E100 series was the last *Embassy* label, appearing in 1931 and produced by Brunswick (Australia) using material drawn from their *Panachord* label.

EMERSON

From 1915 the principal label of the Emerson Recording Laboratories of New York. At first this company specialised in smaller-diameter 6in., 7in. and 9in. discs, but introduced 10in. records in 1919. All were sold in Australia. Ownership of the company changed several times but it continued operations in some form until 1927. The price would have varied considerably over such a long period, but it is reported to have been as much as 3/6 in the mid-1920s (although there would have been periodic discounting).

EMPIRE

A cylinder record produced briefly in Melbourne around 1908.

EMPIRE

A British-made disc which appeared in Australia in 1911. The following year a 'new' *Empire* record was produced in Britain by Edison Bell and also distributed in Australia, probably through the same outlets as *Winner*.

SOUND BEGINNINGS

ENCORE
A German-made record of 1912 vintage. It featured two tracks on each side by the simple expedient of making the songs of shorter duration.

ENTERTAINER
A cylinder record produced in Melbourne for a short time about 1908.

ERA
A German-made label also from 1908. It was produced by Beka on both single and double-sided discs and distributed through the New Polyphon Supply Company.

EXCELOPHONE
A disc manufactured in Germany for John G. Murdoch & Co. of London through whom it was exported to Australia about 1910. Several manufacturers were involved over the next three or four years. It was subsequently produced in Britain by the Invicta Record Company but ceased production during World War I. Occasionally *Guardsman* records have an *Excelophone* label pasted over them. They probably sold here for about 2/6.

FAIRY
A 6in. children's disc made in Britain during the early 1920s and widely available in Australia.

FAVORITE
A disc produced in Germany from 1906 to 1913 and exported widely including to Australia.

FEDERAL
A cylinder record manufactured in Sydney during 1903-04 and believed to have been the first commercially distributed Australian recording [see Chapter 2].

FEDERAL
An American-made disc produced by the Federal Record Corporation which ceased production in 1924. The *Federal* records sold in Australia were probably obsolete stock bought by an Adelaide store.

FETHERFLEX
An early flexible record made in 1923-24 in Britain by Featherweight Flexible Records. This was another of Noel Pemberton Billing's failed ventures, but the label was distributed in Australia through World Record (Australia), established by his associates in Melbourne in 1923 [see Chapter 3].

FLAG
Despite its patriotic label waving the Union Jack, *Flag* records were produced in Germany in 1910.

FONOTIPIA
A label established in Milan in 1904 and famous for the wide range and high quality of its operatic repertoire. It was distributed worldwide until ceasing production in 1911. There were unconfirmed rumours that obsolete stock was 'dumped' in Australia at low prices, however the normal price was higher than most equivalent recordings of the period.

APPENDICES

FOSSEY'S
A label used on American-made *Regal* and *Oriole* records in the mid-1920s sold by Fossey's Department Store, then only in Sydney.

GAIETY
A disc produced in Melbourne by the Vocalion Gramophone Company for a few months in 1927 and was sold exclusively by Craig Williamson & Co. [see Chapter 8].

GEM
The *Music Trader* of 15 May 1926 reported: 'It has been announced that arrangements have been completed for the pressing of Gem records in Sydney. Operations will commence during June.' However, no *Gem* label was ever produced or sold in Australia during the 1920s; and the source of this statement remains a mystery.

GENNETT
An American label produced by the Starr Piano Company and imported and distributed by Suttons in Sydney (with branches in Melbourne, Ballarat, Bendigo, Geelong and Adelaide). These imported discs were available from about 1923 until 1926 and sold for 3/6 or 4/-. Vocalion made a brief attempt in 1927 to manufacture *Gennett* locally, but they seem to have made only a single release of 13 issues which sold for 4/-.

GIBSONA
A label pasted over American *Lincoln* records sold by Gibson's in Sydney. According to the label they cost 4/-, but this seems high for remaindered records sold through this type of outlet.

GLOBE
A label of this name was made in Germany by Homophon about 1912 and sold only in Australia.

GLOBE
A label produced by the Grey Gull Record Company of Boston and available in Australia about 1924.

GLOBOPHON
Another German label which appeared in Australia around 1912.

GOLD BELL
A label pasted over British-made *Aco* records in the early 1920s.

GOLDEN TONGUE
A label produced for sale by Craig Williamson stores in Melbourne and Marcus Clark stores in Sydney. In mid-1928 a small number of flexible records was produced by Unbreakable Disc Record in Melbourne under this label in a C100 series. After the failure of that company, Clifford Industries briefly made a conventional shellac disc on *Golden Tongue* which probably sold for 2/-.

GRAMMAVOX
A disc produced in London for five years from 1910 for the Sound Recording Company and exported to Australia.

SOUND BEGINNINGS

GRAMOPHONE
See *His Master's Voice*.

GRAND PREE
A label first seen when pasted over British *Winner* records around 1920. Slightly later some British-made *Actuelle* records were sold with a *Grand Pree* label pasted over the original label. From 1923 the Perpetual Trading Association, using the name of the Grand Pree Record Company, had a *Grand Pree* record produced for them by Pathé Frères Pathéphone in London. These used the same couplings as on Pathé's own *Actuelle* label, but only selected issues were pressed on *Grand Pree* for export to Australia. The *Grand Pree* was advertised as 'England's Masterpiece, The Acme of Perfection'. 10in. records were 1/9 each or £1 per dozen, while 12in. *Celebrity Grand Pree* records were 3/6 each. The company advertised that 'all records are brand new, double-sided, in absolutely perfect order and condition, and are imported solely by us. They are not distributed through agents, hence the difference in the price charged by us and the 4/6 or 5/6 usually paid by the users. This is the only difference; the quality is the best procurable.' In 1928, after the imposition of duty on imported records, *Grand Pree* was briefly manufactured in Australia by Clifford Industries. A new series was started at 18700 but less than 50 issues were produced and sales seem to have been poor.

GREY GULL
A product of the Grey Gull Record Company of Boston. They were sold in Australia from the mid-1920s for 1/6.

GUARDSMAN
A British-made record which began production in 1914, replacing the *Invicta* label. Limited quantities were distributed in Australia.

HERSCHELLS
A single issue produced by Moulded Products in 1932 [see Chapter 8].

HIS MASTER'S VOICE (HMV)
'Nipper', the dog listening to a horn gramophone, is one of the most famous symbols of the record industry. In Australia the company was controlled by the Gramophone Company which became active in the local market in 1900. The first records produced by this company used an 'Angel on a Gramophone Record' trademark on the label and the discs were simply named *Gramophone Record* (for 7in. discs), *Gramophone Concert Record* (for 10in. discs), or *Gramophone Monarch Record* (for 12in. discs). 'Nipper' first appeared on the labels in 1909 and in 1910 the label name was changed to *His Master's Voice* [see Chapter 5].

THE HIT
An export label produced by the German Homophon Company which had registered the trademark on 30 September 1926. It is not known if it was produced exclusively for an Australian outlet or distributor.

HOMOCHORD
Produced by the British Homophone Company, it was a successor to the German label *Homophone* manufactured in Germany prior to 1914 for the

British market. In 1921 the Universal Music Company re-introduced the label to Britain.

HOMOPHONE

The predecessor of *Homochord*, manufactured in Germany from 1906 by the Homophon Company for the British market. It was also exported to Australia and sold here for 2/6 for the 10in. record, and 3/6 for the 12in..

ILCO

A label made by the German Fidelio Musikwerke. It appeared around 1910 and seems to have had some distribution in Australia.

IMPERIAL

A record manufactured by Crystalate Manufacturing in Britain from 1922. The Australasian agents were Alfred A. & H.B. Newman of Sydney. Originally it sold for 2/-, but by 1927 the price had been reduced to 1/6.

INVICTA

A disc which first appeared in late 1912, manufactured by Berolina Schallplatte. From 1914 it was manufactured in Britain by Crystalate and the name was changed to *Guardsman*.

JEWEL

A label credited the Jewel Record Company, New York but actually manufactured by the Plaza Music Company who also produced *Banner*, *Regal* and *Domino*. The distribution was probably handled by the ACE Company and they cost 1/11.

JOHN BULL

Despite its name, this label was manufactured in Germany in 1909 for the Beka Record Company.

JOYPHONE

A label pasted over Australian-made *Brunswick* records. The 'sole agent' was N. Rumeisen, Sydney.

JUMBO

A 'cheap' label aimed at the popular market originally manufactured by the International Talking Machine Company in Germany (who also made *Fonotipia*) from 1908. It was later made in Britain at the Crystalate factory. It is not known who distributed the label in Australia.

KALOPHONE

A record made in Britain during 1913-14 by the Beka Record Company for export to Australia. Beale & Co. (piano manufacturers) were the exclusive agents.

KIDDIE RECORD

A 6in. single-sided children's record with the reverse containing a full-colour picture illustrating the song on the playing side. It was manufactured for only a short time in 1923 by the British company Kodisc.

KIDDYPHONE

A 6in. children's record manufactured in Britain by Crystalate in 1926-27. It had some distribution in Australia, possibly through the same outlets as *Imperial* records.

SOUND BEGINNINGS

KID-KORD
An 8in. children's record produced by British Homophone from 1932. It was sold in special albums of six records for 4/6.

KISMET
A disc manufactured in Sydney by Parlophone for sale in Woolworth's stores [see Chapter 7].

KLINGSOR
A German label made by the Polyphon Musikwerke around 1912.

KODAK
A short-lived label of the early 1920s produced in Britain by the Vocalion Gramophone Company.

LEONORA
The only information on the label is 'Made in Canada' but in fact it was produced by the Compo Company for export to Australia, and the catalogue series duplicates those on Compo labels sold in Canada, including *Apex*, *Starr* and *Starr Gennett*. The National Trustees Executors and Agency Company of Melbourne registered the trademark on 4 August 1925 – an unlikely name for a record distributor. This label was available until 1927 at a cost of 4/-.

LILY OF THE VALLEY
A label produced for sale in McWhirter's general store in Fortitude Valley, a suburb of Brisbane. About 1920 the store bought batches of old British *Columbia* stock and pasted 'McWhirter's Special Records' over the label. Later they had obsolete *Winner* records relabelled with their own *Lily of the Valley* label and in 1925 another batch of remaindered British *Columbia*s. Finally in 1926 they had a special label produced in Germany by Homophon who used couplings already issued on their *Homocord* label with the original catalogue numbers.

LINCOLN
The cheap label of the American Cameo Record Corporation. It was distributed in Australia from 1924 by A.A. Ellisdon & Son in Sydney and by Coronola in Melbourne and sold for 2/6. In 1926, according to the *Music Trader*, an attempt was made to manufacture them in Sydney:

> Good music cannot be measured in terms of money; but the public is entitled to receive the best that can be obtained, at a price in keeping with its legitimate spending power, and compatible with the ability of the manufacturer to supply that need.
>
> The Lincoln Record Company, Ltd., obviously has recognised this fact. What is more, the firm has recognised that such a purpose can be best achieved by manufacturing its records in Australia, for Lincoln records are now to take their place in the ever growing list of Australian manufacturers. More, these makers promise that, by manufacturing their records on the spot, they will give the public the resultant benefit of their decision – a consistently low price for a consistently high-grade product.
>
> Music-loving Americans have long regarded the Lincoln as a leader. They have realised very fully its rich tonal qualities, its smoothness

and durability, and have been quick to appreciate its perfect recording. Add to these considerations its low price, and it is perfectly reasonable to conclude that Australians will not overlook such inducements in their constant quest for the newest and best in records. Already Lincoln records have earned the unstinted approval of thousands of Australians who have used them. Now, their production in Australia will ensure to them, and to the many more who will use them, a complete range of titles, available upon the shortest notice.

One of the greatest producers of records in the world, the American Record Manufacturing Company, makers of Lincoln records in America, has offered to purchase a substantial number of shares in the Australian undertaking – a fact which, in itself, tends to inspire confidence in the future of Lincoln records in this country.

Lincoln records will be made from master forms of every Lincoln production, which will be sent to Australia. Nothing made in America that has any appeal to Australian tastes will be omitted. Lincoln records promise to be first here with the very latest, and judging by the elaborate plans which are being laid to ensure that promise being carried into effect, there seems to be no reason why it should not be translated into material evidence within a very measurable future.[72]

It would appear that the proposal to manufacture Lincoln records here was made by a local syndicate supported by some investment from the American manufacturer, rather than a proposal by the American company to establish an Australian branch. Details are vague, and it seems that the 'elaborate plans' were no more than a proposal. In any case, the plans came to nothing. By late 1927 the price of *Lincoln* records had been reduced to 1/6.

LITTLE GEM

Another 6in. British-made children's record imported into Australia in the early 1920s.

LITTLE MARVEL

A 6in. children's record manufactured in Britain from 1921 to 1928 initially by the Aeolian Company, and later the Vocalion Gramophone Company. It was widely distributed in Australia – presumably by the Aeolian Company's Australian branches – and sold for 6d.

LYRIC

A label pasted over British-made *Winner* records for an unknown Australian outlet.

LYRIC

This label has no connection with the previous entry. It was produced in Sydney during 1931-32 by the Klippel Record Company, continuing the *Angelus* 3000 series and containing some earlier *Angelus* couplings [see Chapter 12].

MCWHIRTER'S

[See Lily of the Valley]

MASTERPIECE

A label pasted over obsolete American *Cameo* records. The label does not give any details, but *Masterpiece* is known to have been used by Franklin's stores in Melbourne and the records were apparently sold through them about 1925.

MELBAPHONE

A label pasted over British *Winner* records for sale by an Australian outlet.

MELLOTONE

A 6in.children's record manufactured in Britain by Crystalate around 1927. Although they were made specifically for export to Australia, the local distributor is not known.

MELODICS

A label pasted over Australian-made *Brunswick* records for sale in the mid-1920s. The vendor is not known. They carried the slogan *For a real musical treat*.

MELOTO

A label which credited the Meloto Company, London, but they were actually produced by the Aeolian Company. They first appeared in Britain in 1922 but were not imported to Australia until a few years later when they were sold through Foy & Gibson department stores. In 1925-26 they were advertised for 2/9, but by 1927 they were being remaindered for 2/6.

MELOTONE

A record produced in 1928 in Sydney by Clifford Industries for sale in Foy & Gibson stores [see Chapter 12].

MIMOSA

A 6in. children's record manufactured from 1921 to 1928 in Britain by Crystalate for the Sound Recording Company. They sold in Australia for 6d.

MUSIPHONE

A label pasted over British-made *Duophone* records for sale by the Melbourne firm Craig Williamson & Co. According to evidence before the 1927 Tariff Board Inquiry by Craig Williamson's Reginald Sanders, these were purchased after the Australian distributor of *Duophone* records went into liquidation.

MUSOLA

A British-made label pressed by Crystalate for the Orchestrelle Company especially for the Australian market.

NICOLE

A record produced from 1903 by Nicole Frères of London. It was unusual in that it consisted of a cardboard base with a celluloid playing surface. The label information was printed directly onto the surface at the centre of the disc. Both 8in. and 10in. records were released; most were single-sided. Single-sided records sold for 1/6 and double-sided for 3/6.

NURSERY RHYME

A children's record produced in Sydney by the Klippel Record Company in 1931 [see Chapter 12].

ODEON

A disc initially produced in 1903 in Germany by the International Talking Machine Company and later by Crystalate in Britain.

APPENDICES

OLIVER
A 6in. children's record manufactured in Britain by Crystalate in the 1920s.

OLYMPIC
A label pasted over British-made *Imperial* records for export to Australia around 1925. It had no connection with the 1921 American *Olympic* label. The Australian distribution apparently involved a large shipment, as there were several hundred issues with various catalogue numbers. Artists' names did not appear on the labels, just generic descriptions such as 'Dance Band' or 'Song'.

OMAH/OMAR
A label pasted over British *Aco*, *Vocalion* and *Winner* labels, as well as the American *Puritan*. Later *Omar* was used on Australian-made *Aco* records and possibly others. Given the number of batches, it would appear that *Omah/Omar* records were sold for a considerable period in the 1920s.

ORIOLE
An American-made record though no manufacturer is credited; produced by Plaza and imported by Arionola in Sydney and distributed briefly about 1926-27 by the ACE Company. At first they sold for 3/-, but the price was reduced to 2/6 within a year.

ORPHEUS
Another Clifford Industries label produced briefly in 1930 for an as yet unidentified outlet.

PALINGS
A disc produced by the Compo Company of Canada for export to Australia during 1925, specifically for this major Sydney music store. The label bears the inscription 'W.H. Paling & Co. Limited, Sydney'.

PANACHORD
A budget-priced label produced by Brunswick (Australia) in February 1931. Most of the masters were from the American *Melotone* records introduced in the United States in 1930. However some Brunswick masters were also released on *Panachord* under pseudonyms, most notably two early recordings by Bing Crosby. [see Chapter 4].

PARAMOUNT
Yet another Clifford Industries label existing only from mid-1928 to early 1929 [see Chapter 12].

PARLOPHONE
A disc initially imported from Britain in 1923. By 1927 an Australian branch of the Parlophone Company had been established in Sydney, and subsequent releases were pressed in Australia [see Chapter 7].

PATHÉ
The company was of French origin, but by 1906 had established a British branch and discs were exported to Australia from there. They were manufactured in a variety of mostly unconventional sizes.

PERFECT
The cheap label of the Pathé Frères Phonograph Corporation of New York. At one stage it was imported by the Grand Pree Record Company of Sydney and sold for 1/9 each, or a dozen for one pound. There was also a short-lived British *Perfect* label about 1927, but only small quantities reached Australia.

PHOENIX
A budget-priced label produced by the British Columbia Graphophone Company in 1913 to compete with the flood of cheap labels then being imported into Britain by many German manufacturers. The label only lasted for two years. A few were distributed in Australia, presumably by the regular Columbia outlets and sold for 1/1.

PHONETO
A disc manufactured in Britain by Crystalate specifically for export to Australia. There seems to have been some connection with *Musola*.

PIGMY GRAMOPHONE
Another children's record manufactured in Britain by Crystalate in the mid-1920s.

PILOT
In 1913 the German-made *Polyphon* record was re-named *Pilot* but production ceased the following year.

THE PILOT
A label pasted over British *Winner* records and available around 1920. About seven years later it was pasted over Edison Bell *Winner* recordings. It seems likely that there was some relationship between the two labels.

PIONEER
A record which first appeared in 1914, pressed in Germany for J Blum & Co. and subsequently manufactured in Britain by the Disc Record Company. *Pioneer* had limited distribution in Australia during its short life.

PLAZA
A label manufactured in Sydney by Clifford Industries in 1929. Some issues appeared in a 3000 series (duplicating *Angelus* catalogue numbers) while others bore a 6000 series catalogue number.

POLYDOR
The export label of the Deutsche Grammophon Gesellschaft in the 1920s and 1930s. The same couplings appeared in Germany on the *Grammophon* label. From 1926 the Australian agents were Austral Import and Export, Melbourne who sold the 10in. popular releases for 4/- and the 12in. and celebrity recordings for 6/6 to 9/- made *Polydor* label in 1927. Some issues used the German catalogue series, although some couplings differ from the German pressings. There was also a uniquely Australian W100 series of 10in. records which contained local recordings and this continued to be produced until 1928, with prices the same as for the imported pressings.

APPENDICES

POLYPHON
A label produced in Leipzig by the Polyphon Musikwerke from 1904 and exported to Australia from 1910. The label was later changed to *Pilot*.

POPULAR
A label pasted over remaindered stock of the American *Lincoln* label and sold in Sydney about 1925.

POSSUM
A record made in Britain in 1917 for sale by Allan & Co. of Melbourne.

PYRAMID
A label mostly used over Canadian *Apex* labels. It seems to date from 1925, although the vendor is not known.

RADIEX
A disc produced by the Grey Gull Record Company of Boston. It was available in Australia in the 1920s.

RAINBOW
Recordings produced from 1920 by the Rodeheaver Record Company of Chicago and containing mostly religious material. It was apparently available locally in the 1920s.

REALTONE
A label pasted over the British *Beltona* label and naming the outlet as Sydney Jackson of the Eastern Markets, Melbourne.

REGAL
A label introduced in Britain in 1914 by Columbia Graphophone. It was immediately distributed in Australia through Columbia outlets. After Columbia began local production in 1926, *Regal* records were also manufactured at the Sydney factory [see Chapter 5]. In 1933 the label became *Regal-Zonophone*.

REGAL-ZONOPHONE
The first EMI label, initiated in 1933 replacing Columbia's *Regal* label and the Gramophone Company's *Zonophone*. It continued the *Regal* G20000 series although some issues were re-pressings of items from the discontinued *Zonophone* catalogue. Some early issues on *Regal-Zonophone* used the previous Regal or Zonophone catalogue numbers [see Chapter 13].

REGENT
A label pasted over British-made *Regal* for an unknown Australian outlet.

REGENT
A second label with no known connection to the previous entry. Clifford Industries made this label in 1928, probably for sale by Selfridges [see Chapter 12].

REGENTONE
A local label pasted over British-made *John Bull* records for an unidentified Australian distributor.

RENA
Recordings produced in Britain from 1908 by Columbia Graphophone for the Rena Manufacturing Company of London to be sold in conjunction

with their German brand of gramophones. Rena was taken over by Columbia in 1909 who continued production of *Rena* records until 1910, when the label was renamed *Columbia-Rena*.

REXOPHONE

A disc made by the Berlin company Homophon GmbH about 1910 for the Sydney firm Jos. Jackson & Macdonald. The 5000 series contained 10in. records and the 1000 series 12in. After 1914 *Rexophone* was manufactured in Britain specifically for the Australian market. The cost of 10in. discs was 2/6 and 12in. discs 3/6.

ROBERTO

A label pasted on British *Columbia-Rena* records. In 1914 when the *Regal* label was introduced and *Columbia-Rena* discontinued, the *Columbia-Rena* deleted stock was apparently relabelled as *Roberto* and 'dumped' in Australia.

RONDOPHONE

A disc manufactured in Germany from about 1910 by the German Homophon company for export to Australia. It was distributed by British Record Pty. Ltd. of Sydney which also had branches in Newcastle, Brisbane and Melbourne. These records, priced at 3/-, were advertised as the 'clearest, loudest and best' and were apparently used to promote the *Rondophone* gramophone.

ROSEBUD

A label pasted on pre-1918 vintage British *Columbia* and *Regal* records. Both 10in. and 12in. stock was relabelled with new H.1000 series numbers and 'dumped' in Australia.

RUBIN

A German label produced by Homophon about 1912.

SAVOY

A label produced in Melbourne by Vocalion Foreign during 1929-30 [see Chapter 8].

SCALA

A disc made in Britain from 1911 by Vocalion Gramophone for the Scala Record Company but sold by Pathé for 2/-.

SCALA IDEAL

Another label produced in Britain for the Scala Record Company, but manufactured by Pathé Frères Pathéphone.

SERENOLA

A label used around 1925 on American *Banner* and *Gennett* records sold by Anthony Horden & Sons, a Sydney department store, who retailed them for 1/6.

SIMOLIAN

A label pasted over *Apex*, *Banner*, *Brunswick*, *Gennett* and *Parlophone* records sold by Mick Simmons stores in Sydney, Newcastle and Brisbane. Mick Simmons seem to have bought up quantities of obsolete labels during the 1920s and resold them on the *Simolian* label for 2/- each, or 6 for 10/6 for 'standard 3/6 or 4/- records re-labelled', according to contemporary advertisements.

APPENDICES

SNOWS
A label used locally on British-made *Parlophone* records.

SPECIALLY IMPORTED
A label pasted over American *Columbia* records of pre-1920 vintage.

STANDARD
A disc produced in Britain by Crystalate Manufacturing during the mid-1920s although no manufacturer was credited on the label.

STAR
A label pasted on British *Aco* records for sale locally.

STARR
A disc made by Clifford Industries in 1929 for sale by Coles Stores [see Chapter 12].

STERLING
A cylinder record produced in Britain by the Russell Hunting Record Company from 1905 to 1909.

STERLING
A disc manufactured by Clifford Industries in 1928, probably for Farmers department stores [see Chapter 12].

SUMMIT
A label introduced by the Sydney-based Klippel Record Company in late 1931 [see Chapter 12].

TEMPO
A label used on remaindered American *Oriole* records and sold in Adelaide around 1925.

TREMONT
A disc produced by the Cameo Record Corporation of New York in 1924-25. The label credits the American Record Manufacturing Company, Cameo's pressing plant in Massachusetts which was only was active in 1924-25. This disc was sold in Australia about 1926, possibly by the same distributor that handled the *Lincoln* label.

THE TWIN
An early form of double-sided disc made in Britain by the Gramophone Company from its *Zonophone* masters. This label was introduced in 1908 and subsumed into the *Zonophone* label in 1911. It was retailed in Australia by Gramophone Company outlets and sold for 2/6.

UNIVERSAL DOUBLE DISC
A disc made in Germany by the Homophon Company from about 1910 solely for export to Australia.

VELVET FACE
A disc produced by Edison Bell in London from 1910 to 1927 and distributed in Australia by Weiss, Biheller & Brooks of Sydney at a price of 4/- or 4/6 for 10in. records and 5/6 or 6/- for 12in. records.

VICTORY
A disc made in Germany by Kalliope Musikwerke for J.Blum & Co., London.

VOCALION

A British label imported into Australia by the Aeolian Company from 1920. All Vocalion products were manufactured locally after the establishment of their pressing plant in Melbourne in 1927. The *Vocalion* XA18000 series was released in 1927-28. A further *Vocalion* 500 series began in July 1930 and continued until the Vocalion operation was wound up in 1931 [see Chapter 8].

VOCALION MIDGET

A 7in. children's record briefly produced by Vocalion (Australasia) in 1931 [see Chapter 8].

VOX

A disc produced by Deutschen Vox AG of Berlin. On 15 November 1926 the *Music Trader* announced that 'The Vox, a German record, is being handled by M. Brash and Co. Pty. Ltd., of Elizabeth Street, Melbourne. The Vox, which is made in 10 and 12 inch sizes, covers a wide range of musical subjects, and is a high-quality product. It has a distinctive red triangular shaped label, in place of the circular form of label adopted by all other record makers.' *Vox* was registered as a trademark on 28 October 1926 by Charles Slade & Co. of Sydney but the application was later withdrawn.

VOX HUMANA

A disc produced in 1926 by Pathé Frères in London for export to Australia, probably on order from the Perpetual Trading Company of Sydney, who also sold the more common *Grand Pree* label. There were only 68 issues on *Vox Humana*, all of which appear to have been produced simultaneously, and they sold for 1/9.

WAFER

A flexible single-sided record similar to *Fetherflex*, marketed by World Record (Australia) about 1925. It used masters already released on *Austral* and according to contemporary advertisements single selections could be ordered on request. The discs were so fragile they would have had little chance of withstanding the wear and tear of the heavy soundboxes of the period. Now extremely rare [see Chapter 3].

WENDY

A 5in. conventional shellac children's record made in Britain around 1924-25 but sold only in Australia by World Record (Australia), acknowledged as 'Wocord, Australia' on the label.

WEYMARK

A label pasted over American *Cameo* records for an Australian outlet.

WINNER

See Edison Bell *Winner*.

WORLD

A record manufactured in Britain using an unconventional constant linear speed process, enabling a longer playing time than usual with records of this period. However, a 'controller' attachment was required to play these discs which could not be played on a normal gramophone. Both 10in. and

APPENDICES

12in. records were marketed in Australia by World Record in 1923-25 [see Chapter 3].

WORTH

A disc made in Sydney by Clifford Industries in 1928-29 for sale in Woolworth's stores [see Chapter 12].

ZONOPHONE

A disc originally produced in Europe by the International Zonophone Company which was acquired in June 1903 by the Gramophone & Typewriter Company. It had no connection with the American *Zon-O-Phone* label. The British *Zonophone* 7in. and 9in. discs were discontinued in 1908 but the 10in., 11in. and 12in. discs, all single-sided, were made until 1911. In May 1911 the *Zonophone* catalogue was amalgamated with that of *Twin Record* (another Gramophone Company subsidiary) and previous *Twin* issues re-appeared as *Zonophone*, but continued the *Twin* catalogue series (which had begun at 1 and already reached about 500). All these labels were available in Australia. In 1912 a *Zonophone* export series was initiated with many issues aimed specifically at the Australian market. After the Gramophone Company's Sydney factory opened in January 1926 *Zonophone* records were pressed there [see Chapter 5].

BIBLIOGRAPHY

Because of the variety of resources used in the compilation of this book the references have been numbered in alphabetical order. This has the advantage of aiding access by assembling the bulk of the references in groups under the company to which they refer. The superscript numbers in the text do not, therefore, appear chronologically.

A. Unpublished Sources
(including government, industry and company documents and internal publications)

1 Alfred A. & H.B. Newman [Importers of Imperial records]. Correspondence with Commonwealth Tariff Board, 1927.
2 Brunswick (Australia) Ltd. Correspondence with Commonwealth Tariff Board, 1931.
3 Barton & Company Ltd. [Shipping, customs & insurance brokers]. Correspondence with Minister for Customs, 1927.
4 Clifford Industries Limited. Extraordinary resolution, 7 August 1931.
5 Columbia Graphophone (Australia) Ltd. Artist royalties, sales, and costs of material prepared... for the manufacture of records..., 1928-31.
6 Columbia Graphophone Co. Ltd. Selected correspondence between Head Office and the Australian branch 1925-27.
7 Columbia Graphophone (Australia) Ltd. Correspondence to Head Office re Parlophone, 5 December 1932.
8 Columbia Graphophone (Australia) Ltd. Monthly production of biscuit material for two years to 30 June 1931.
9 Columbia Graphophone (Australia) Ltd. Profit and loss account and Balance sheet as at 30 June 1927.
10 Columbia Graphophone (Australia) Ltd. Profit and loss accounts and Balance sheets from 30 June 1929 to 31 December 1930.

BIBLIOGRAPHY

11 Columbia Graphophone (Australia) Ltd. Recording accounts 1929-30.
12 Columbia Graphophone (Australia) Ltd. Statement of cost of production and distribution of records for July and August 1927.
13 Columbia Graphophone (Australia) Ltd. Correspondence with Commonwealth Tariff Board, 1927.
14 Columbia Graphophone (Australia) Ltd. Correspondence with Commonwealth Tariff Board, 1931.
15 Craig Williamson Pty. Ltd. Letter to Vocalion Gramophone Co. Ltd. re production of *Gaiety* records, dated 26 October 1927.
16 D. Davis & Co. Ltd. Correspondence with Department of Trade & Customs, 1927.
17 D. Davis & Co. Ltd. Factory cost – 10in. Brunswick records, 1927.
18 D. Davis & Co. Ltd. Record factory manufacturing and trading accounts, 1924-26.
19 D. Davis & Co. Ltd. Statement of assets of record factory as at 31 December 1925.
20 Commonwealth of Australia. Department of Trade and Customs. Imports of gramophone records into the Commonwealth for the year 1926-27.
21 Commonwealth of Australia. Department of Trade and Customs. Minutes, 1927.
22 Gramophone Co. Ltd. Extracts from Board minutes 1924-31.
23 Gramophone Co. Ltd. Selected correspondence between Head Office and the Australian branch 1922-27.
24 Gramophone Co. Ltd. Letter regarding formation of EMI 31 December 1931.
25 Gramophone Co. Ltd. Constitution of the Sydney factory of the Gramophone Company Ltd., 12 August 1925.
26 Gramophone Co. Ltd. & Columbia Graphophone (Australia) Ltd. Cables and correspondence re establishing *Regal-Zonophone* label, 1932-33.
27 Gramophone Co. Ltd. Correspondence with Department of Trade & Customs and Commonwealth Tariff Board, 1927.
28 Gramophone Co. Ltd. Sydney factory: Cost of records January to June 1927.
29 Gramophone Record Workers' Union of New South Wales. Submission to the Commonwealth Government dated 14 January 1930.
30 Speech by the Rt Hon. J.T. Lang, Premier of New South Wales, on the occasion of the opening of the factory of the Gramophone Co. Ltd. at Erskineville (Sydney) on 18 January 1926 & Reply by Mr Manson.
31 Kelson & Co. [Agents for Artiphon records]. Correspondence with Commonwealth Tariff Board, 1927.
32 Moulded Products (Australasia) Pty. Ltd. Complete specification [for] an improved composition for the manufacture of phonograph records and the like, and records made therefrom, 4 May 1932.

33   Parlophone Co. Ltd. Correspondence with Department of Trade & Customs, 1927.
34   Parlophone Co. Ltd. Profit and loss accounts as at 30 June 1927.
35   Parlophone Co. Ltd. Recording expenses from 1 July 1929-30 June 1931.
36   Paul Offenbacher, Director, Carl Lindström Aktiengesellschaft, Berlin. Letter to Alan Wright dated 7 February 1933.
37   Perpetual Trading Association [Importers of Grand Pree records]. Correspondence with Commonwealth Tariff Board, 1927.
38   Perpetual Trading Association [Importers of Grand Pree records]. Invoices & documentation re imports for September-October, 1927.
39   Retail Music Traders Protective Association of NSW. Correspondence with the Tariff Board, 1927.
40   Commonwealth of Australia. Tariff Board. Minute paper [establishing inquiry into] Material prepared in slab, biscuit, or any other form for the manufacture of records, by J.E. Fenton, Minister for Trade & Customs, 10 July 1930.
41   Commonwealth of Australia. Tariff Board. Minutes, 1927.
42   Commonwealth of Australia. Tariff Board. Notes of interview on 17 November 1927 by Charles Henry Gendle, Australian Manager, Vocalion Gramophone Co.
43   Thomas A. Edison Inc. Shipping invoices for imported disc records August 1927.
44   Trevitts Ltd. Correspondence with the Tariff Board, 1927.
45   Transcripts of hearings held by the Tariff Board: 'Evidence on Gramophone Records (Disc Type Only) – Request for Increased Duty' Sydney 18 October 1927 & 21 October 1927 [and] Melbourne 10 November 1927.
46   Transcripts of evidence [of the] Tariff Board public inquiry: 'Gramophones, phonographs and other talking machines, n.e.i. – Request for increased duty', Sydney 19 December 1929.
47   Transcript of evidence [of the] Tariff Board public inquiry: 'Material prepared in slab, biscuit or any other form for the manufacture of records for gramophones, phonographs and other talking machines [and] stamping matrices for use in connection with the manufacture of records for gramophones, phonographs and other talking machines – Question of necessity for proposed increased duty', Sydney 31 August 1931 [and] Melbourne 9 September 1931.
48   Unbreakable Disc Records Ltd. Return of allotment [filed on] 24 October 1927.
49   Unbreakable Disc Records Ltd. Advice of change of registered office address, 8 October 1928.
50   Unbreakable Disc Records Ltd. Advice of change of registered office address, 5 March 1930.
51   Unbreakable Disc Records Ltd. Advice of change of company name [dated] 23 April 1930.

BIBLIOGRAPHY

52   Unbreakable Disc Records Ltd. Liquidator's statement of account [dated] 31 May 1932.
53   Unbreakable Disc Records Ltd. Memorandum of association [dated] 21 June 1927.
54   Unbreakable Disc Records Ltd. Notice of liquidation [dated] 24 September 1930.
55   Unbreakable Disc Records Ltd. Prospectus [dated] 23 June 1927.
56   Unbreakable Disc Records Ltd. Return of allotment [dated] 10 October 1927.
57   Unbreakable Disc Records Ltd. Statutory report [filed on] 14 January 1928.
58   Unbreakable Disc Records Ltd. Memorandum of terms of agreement [filed on] 24 October 1927.
59   Vocalion (Australasia) Ltd. Information circular [dated] 12 January 1931.
60   Vocalion Gramophone Co. Ltd. Correspondence with Commonwealth Tariff Board, 1927.
61   Notes of interview on 17 November 1927 by Charles Henry Gendle, Australian manager, Vocalion Gramophone Company Ltd., 49-59 Coppin Street, Richmond (Vic).
62   Vocalion Gramophone Co. Ltd. Registration documents [filed on] 27 April 1927.
63   Vocalion Gramophone Co. Ltd. Schedule of wholesale and retail selling prices for *Vocalion* and *Aco* phonograph records [as at] 21 July 1927.

Most of the above material was obtained through the courtesy of EMI Archives (London), Australian Archives (Canberra) or through the various State Registrars of Companies.

B. Published sources

64   Abridged Prospectus of Vocalion (Australasia) Ltd., *Smith's Weekly*, 7 June 1930 p.28.
65   'Aeolian Vocalion', *Music Trader* 31 October 1925, p.14.
66   'Amalgamation – Gramophone Company and Columbia', *Sydney Morning Herald* 21 March 1931, p.14.
67   'Angelus records' [advert.] *Music in Australia* 20 August 1929, p.9.
68   'Another industry – Phonograph records to be made here', *Music Trader* 15 September 1926, p.4.
69   Archibald, Douglas, 'The world wanderings of a voice'. London: *Phonogram* Vol. I No. 2, June 1893.
70   'The Australian phonograph', *Music Trader* 5 April 1926, p.3.
71   'Australian made records', *Star* 25 September 1909.
72   'Australian made records', *Music Trader* 15 September 1926, p.7.
73   'Australian phono records – Factory for Melbourne', *Australian Musical News* 1 February 1924, p.31.

SOUND BEGINNINGS

74 'Australian record', *Daily Telegraph* 29 April 1925, p.11.
75 'Australian *talkies*', *Argus* 30 October 1929, p.8.
76 'Australian Vocalion records', *Music Trader* 15 January 1927, p.8.
77 'Australia's first anniversary – Governor of New South Wales pays a tribute to *His Master's Voice*', *Voice* April 1927.
78 'Australia's musical outlook', *Australian Musical News* September 1928, p.26b.
79 '*Back Again* – New revue at Athenaeum Theatre', *Table Talk* 6 August 1925, p.18.
80 'Bert Howell's Orchestra', *Listener In* 16 May 1925, p.9.
81 'Brilliant Parlophone records – Electrical process', *Australian Musical News* October 1927, p.37.
82 'Broadcast record', *Music in Australia* 20 September 1928, p.46.
83 'Broadcasting an ally to selling records', *Music Trader* 15 March 1926, p.20.
84 'Broadcasting gramophone music', *Listener In* 22 August 1925, p.5.
85 'Broadcasting – Restriction on records – Manufacturers taking action', *Sydney Morning Herald* 23 October 1931, p.9.
86 'Brunswick (Australia) Ltd.', *Australian Phonograph News* May 1930.
87 'The Brunswick factory', *Australian Phonograph News* March 1930.
88 Burston, Howard, 'Unbreakable Gramophone Records – An impudent flotation', *Herald* 27 January 1927, p.17.
89 'Cheap records for the phonographs – Swiftly passing craze', *Sydney Morning Herald* 22 October 1927, p.17.
90 'Columbia advertising', *Music in Australia* 20 September 1928, p.46.
91 'Columbia factory opened by Sir Dudley de Chair', *Australasian Phonograph Monthly*, October 1926, p.13.
92 'Columbia Gramophone Co. Ltd. – Australian factory opened by the Governor' (Sir Dudley de Chair), *Australian Musical News* November 1926, p.25.
93 'Columbia-HMV merger', *Australian Phonograph News* April 1931.
94 'The Columbia New Australian Factory', *Talking Machine & Wireless Trade News*, London, September 1925, p.320.
95 'Columbia opens new factory', *Music Trader* 15 November 1926, p.15.
96 'Columbia Graphophone records', *Music Trader* 15 October 1926, p.8.
97 'Columbia transactions', *Music Trader* 15 February 1927, p.23.
98 *Commonwealth of Australia. Tariff Board. Gramophone Records (Disc Type only): Report and recommendation.* Sydney: Government Printer 1927.
99 'Dance Supplement No. 1 now on sale' [Columbia advert.], *Australasian Phonograph Monthly* 20 September 1926.
100 'D. Davis & Co. Ltd. move', *Australian Phonograph News* May 1930.
101 'Davis Co. of Australia suing Brunswick and Warner Bros for big damages', *Variety* 15 October 1930, p.66.

BIBLIOGRAPHY

102 Dawson, Peter, 'Thirty years of record making', *Gramophone* January 1933, p.315.
103 'Mr Peter Dawson – Views on recorded music', *Sydney Morning Herald* 20 July 1933, p.10.
103 Discusses business-getting methods of Australian, *Talking Machine World* 9 May 1925.
105 'Distribution change', *Australian Phonograph News* May 1931, p.4.
106 Dominion expansion of British business, *Talking Machine and Wireless Trade News* September 1925, p.1.
107 'Domino records', *Music Trader* 15 August 1926, p.5.
108 'Don Bradman's record', *Australian Phonograph News* December 1930, p.4.
109 'Electrical recording helps', *Music Trader* 15 July 1926, p.19.
110 'Exchange telegram from Melbourne announces the death of Mrs Pemberton Billing...' *The Times* 1 December 1923, p.9.
111 'Exit Edison', *Australian Phonograph News* January 1930.
112 Fane, Maud, 'My broadcasting experiences', *Listener In* 27 June 1925, p.14.
113 'First orchestral records made in Australia', *Australian Phonograph News* 15 February 1930.
114 'Gladys Moncrieff', *Australasian Phonograph Monthly* 20 July 1925, p.30.
115 'A Gramaphone [sic] factory in Melbourne', *Punch* 24 September 1925, p.44.
116 'The Gram-O-Phone' [advert. for disc record producer] *Bulletin* 15 July 1899, p.28.
117 'Gramophone records – High protection imposed – Purchaser disregarded', *Argus* 10 December 1927, p.40.
118 'The Graphophone and the fun you can have with it' [advert. for cylinder reproducer] *Bulletin* 15 April 1899, p.1.
119 'Graphophone's Australian factory opened by the Governor', *Sydney Morning Herald* 15 October 1926.
120 'Hail Columbia! – New industry for Australasia', *Australian Musical News* November 1926, p.24.
121 '*His Master's Voice*: anniversary of Sydney factory', *Music Trader* 15 February 1927, p.9.
122 '*His Master's Voice* factory for Australia' *Sound Wave*. London: August 1925 p.580.
123 'How can we keep our children at home?' [advert.] *Musical Australia* January 1921, p.28.
124 'Imported atrocities', *Listener In* 9 July 1932, p.15.
125 'Interesting souvenir record', *Music Trader* 15 January 1927, p.8.
126 'Is the phonograph about done?', *Australian Phonograph News* December 1930, p.3.

127 'It has been estimated that there are about one million phonographs... in Australia' [news item] *Music Trader* 31 October 1925, p.5.
128 James, William G., 'Our place in music – The achievement of Australia', *Australian Musical News* October 1927, p.9.
129 'Klippel Record Co. Ltd.', *Australian Phonograph News* October 1931.
130 'This machine talks, sings...' [advert. for disc record reproducer] *Bulletin* 9 September 1899, p.29.
131 'Magic disc – Sydney's new song', Sydney *Sun* 16 March 1927, p.15.
132 'Making records in Australia', *Daily Guardian* 10 July 1926.
133 'Mr W. Manson retires', *Australian Phonograph News* May 1931, p.23.
134 'Marconi sound reproducer for talkies', *Film Weekly* 10 October 1929.
135 'Melbourne's new industry – factory for pressing records', *Music Trader* 15 December 1926, p.6.
136 Metcalf, Herbert E., 'Radio in the music store', *Radio in Australia & New Zealand* 29 September 1926, p.36.
137 'Music and life', *Graphic of Australia* 2 February 1924, p.10.
138 'Musical culture', *Music Trader* 15 January 1926, p.25.
139 'A new Australian industry', *Music Trader* 31 October 1925, p.14.
140 'New German record', *Music Trader* 15 November 1926, p.7.
141 'New industry – Australian-made records', *Daily Telegraph* 11 March 1926, p.9.
142 'New phonograph records of waste paper', Sydney *Sun* 2 July 1926, p.2.
143 'New Zealand Notes', *Australian Phonograph News* May 1931, p.22.
144 'Official opening of the new Columbia instrument and record factory for Australasia', *Sydney Morning Herald* 31 October 1926.
145 'One disc orchestra records – Claims for new device', *Australian Musical News* August 1923, p.32.
146 'The only unbreakable gramophone record in the world – Wocord' [advert. by World Record Australia Pty. Ltd.] *Sun News Pictorial*, 1 August 1925, p.11 – and in a slightly revised form, *Punch* 24 September 1925.
147 Orton, Walter B., 'Revival in music trade – Can it be effected?' *Australian Musical News* October 1927, p.17.
148 'Panachord records', *Australian Phonograph News*, April 1931.
149 'Papal Legate makes a record', *Music in Australia* 20 September 1928, p.41.
150 'Mr N. Pemberton Billing' [Obituary] *The Times* 13 November 1948, p.6.
151 'Percy Grainger and jazz', *Graphic of Australia* 17 June 1926, p.9.
152 'Personality – Can it be built into gramophone records?', *Wireless Weekly*, 20 October 1933, p.13.
153 'Phonograph records – Made in Australia by Australian artists' [advert.] *Argus* 2 February 1907, p.24.

BIBLIOGRAPHY

154 'Phonograph records – Broadcasting to be restricted', *Sydney Morning Herald* 22 October 1931, p.10.
155 'The Phonograph', *Illawarra Mercury* 9 May 1891, pp.2-3.
156 'The Phonograph', *Telegraphic Electrical Society Journal* February-April 1878, p.356.
157 'Phonograph records', *Sydney Morning Herald* 26 May 1928, p.21.
158 'Phonograph – The only one for sale in the colony' [advert.] *Sydney Morning Herald* 27 February 1892, p.2.
159 'Phonograph record company', *Sydney Morning Herald* 29 May 1930, p.5.
160 'Phonograph v. wireless – Should there be rivalry?' *Australasian Phonograph Monthly* 20 July 1925, p.27.
161 'Phonographs: ten million records a year – New industry', *Sydney Morning Herald* 12 January 1927, p.19.
162 Pindaret, Peter, 'The records of a plain man', *Triad* 1 April 1926, p.54.
163 'Plea for jazz', *Listener In* 19 November 1932, p.16.
164 'Polydor records', *Music Trader* 15 October 1926, p.8.
165 'A popular hit', *Music Trader* 15 January 1926, p.24.
166 'Popular music', *Australian Music and Dramatic News* 1 November 1913, p.144.
167 'Present favourite jazz songs', *Graphic of Australia* 16 August 1923.
168 'Pressing of records', *Music Trader* 15 May 1926, p.10.
169 'The price cutting evil', *Music Trader* 15 April 1926, p.3.
170 'Prominent Melbourne entrepreneur', *Everyone's* 4 May 1925, p.3.
171 'Radio and the music trade', *Music Trader* 31 October 1925, p.19.
172 'Radio and the phonograph', *Australasian Phonograph Monthly* 20 September 1925, p.53.
173 Ramsey, Alan, 'CD monopoly goes into a spin', *Sydney Morning Herald* 11 October 1997, p.43.
174 'The real kookaburra', *Australian Phonograph News* May 1931, p.4.
175 'Record that should be broken', *Listener In* 18 June 1932, p.15.
176 'Recording of music – Sir Henry Wood's praise', *Music Trader* 15 November 1926, p.13.
177 'Recording the voices of the Aborigines of the Northern Territory of Australia', *Phonogram* November 1913, p.7.
178 'Records – Ban removed from B stations', *Wireless Weekly* 7 July 1927.
179 'Records – High protection imposed', *Argus* 10 December 1927, p.40.
180 'Records pressed locally', *Music Trader* 15 July 1926, p.9.
181 'Records! – Radio's invaluable ally', *Listener In* 25 August 1934, p.11.
182 'Returning wave', *Australian Phonograph News* May 1931, p.3.
183 'Rhapsody in blue', *Music Trader* 30 November 1925, p.23.

184 Right, Lincoln. 'Politics calls tune for compact discs', *Canberra Times* 15 July 1998, p.9.
185 'School of arts' [advert.]. Demonstration of Edison's phonograph, *Sydney Morning Herald* 7 June 1879, p.2.
186 'Science in Melbourne', *Telegraphic Electrical Society Journal* April-August 1879, p.51.
187 'Send your voice home!' [advert.], *Listener In* 26 September 1928, p.57.
188 'Should radio be used for advertising?', *Listener In* 6 June 1925, p.7.
189 'So this is Australia!', *Australian Phonograph News* December 1930, p.23.
190 'Spring motor gramophone – Latest type' [advert. for disc record reproducer], *Bulletin* 15 April 1899, p.28.
191 Tait, Viola, *A Family of Brothers*. Melbourne: Heinemann 1971, p.21.
192 'Tariff on gramophones', *Age* 3 October 1929, p.11.
193 'Tariff on records', *Australasian Phonograph Monthly & Music Trade Review* January 1928, p.25.
194 'Tariff Board: Alleged dumping of records – Protection sought', *Sydney Morning Herald* 19 October 1927, p.16.
195 '3OL broadcasting sketch', *Music Trader* 15 February 1927, p.7.
196 'Tomorrow a new record appears!' [advert.], *Sun-News Pictorial*, 1 May 1928, p.13.
197 'Touch this switch' [advert. for phono-radio], *Listener In* 29 January 1930, p.7.
198 'Town Hall, Wollongong' [notice of early phonograph exhibit], *Illawarra Mercury* 5 May 1891, p.3.
199 'Trade notes', *Australian Phonograph News* October-December 1930.
200 'In defence of jazz', *Graphic of Australia* 28 February 1924, p.10.
201 'Ubiquitous music – Jazz and the University', *Music Trader* 15 October 1926, p.9.
202 'Unemployment – Seeking the cause', *Sydney Morning Herald* 27 March 1928, p.11.
203 'Unique test – At radio exhibition', *Daily Telegraph* 4 March 1927, p.3.
204 Vice-Regal visit to Gramophone works [photograph] *Sydney Morning Herald* 2 February 1927, p.8.
205 'The Vocalion debacle', *Australian Phonograph News* October 1931.
206 'Vocalion flotation', *Argus* 5 May 1928, p.28.
207 [Vocalion] 'Gramophone company', *Sydney Morning Herald* 22 March 1928, p.11.
208 'Vocalion (Australasia) Ltd.', *Sydney Morning Herald* 30 May 1930, p.13.
209 'Vocalion company sold', *Argus* 9 May 1930, p.4.
210 [Vocalion] 'An unexplicit prospectus', *Sydney Morning Herald* 7 June 1930, p.17.
211 'Vocalion company', *Argus* 27 March 1928, p.15.

212 [Vocalion] 'Company wound up', *Argus* 25 August 1931, p.4.
213 Waters, Thorold, 'Hysteria about our musical taste', *Australian Musical News* October 1927, p.1.
214 Waters, Thorold, 'Where the plain man finds a tune', *Listener In*, 15 October 1932, p.13.
215 Webber, Hamilton, 'The place of jazz in music', *Graphic of Australia*, 28 May 1925, p.13.
216 Westbrook, C D, 'How I became an Edison jobber', *Edison Phonograph Monthly* September 1907, p.11.
217 'Will provide for Australia – Disc factory for Sydney', *Australian Musical News* June 1925, p.11.
218 'Mr William Manson', *Australasian Phonograph Monthly* 20 December 1925, p.13.
219 'Winding up of company', *Sydney Morning Herald* 10 October 1931, p.6.
220 'Wireless notes for amateurs', *Herald* 27 January 1927, p.22.
221 'Wocord Ltd. recording studio' [photograph] *Listener In* 6 June 1925, p.7.
222 'The wonderful graph-o-phone', *Argus* 9 July 1898, p.16.
223 'World Records' [advert.] *Australian Musical News* 1 May 1924, p.14.
224 Dreyfus, Dr Kay, 'Biography of May Brahe', *Australian Record & Music Revue* No.15, p.12.
225 Edge, Ruth, 'Mr Bohanna goes *Down Under*', *Australian Record & Music Review* Nos.7, 10, 17 & 21, 1990-94.
226 Long, Chris, 'Australia's earliest known recordings: Thomas Rome's Collection'. IASA *Australian Branch Newsletter* No.19 1985, p.5.
227 'Profile of the Australian record industry'. Sydney: ARIA – Australian Record Industry Association Ltd., 1990.
228 Tucker, Mike, 'The Federal and Australia cylinder records: a history', *Australian Record & Music Review* No.5, p.3.

C. Further Reading

Anderson, Bruce, *Story of the New Zealand record industry*. Wellington: self-published 1984.

Andrews, Frank, *World Records*. Spalding [England]: self-published 1992.

Barry, Keith, 'The Gramophone and Australia's phenomenal musical Progress', *Record Guide* July 1954, p.4.

Burgis, Peter, 'Alan Wright – Parlophone pioneer', *Australian Record & Music Review* No.26, p.9.

Dreyfus, Dr Kay, 'Biography of May Brahe', *Australian Record & Music Revue* No.15, p.12.

Edge, Ruth, 'Mr Bohanna goes *Down Under*', *Australian Record & Music Review* Nos.7, 10, 17 & 21, 1990-94.

EMI, *Studios 301, 1926-1986: the first 60 years*. Sydney: EMI 1986.

Laird, Ross, 'Beeda'. *Australasian Sound Archive* No.2, 1986, p.17.

Laird, Ross, 'An introductory survey of Australian 78rpm record labels', *Australasian Sound Archive* No.3, 1987, p.1.

Laird, Ross, '78rpm pressed in the US for export to Australia', New York: *Record Research*, Nos.247/8 September 1991 & 249/5 May 1992.

Laird, Ross., 'Macquarie records', *Australian Record & Music Review* No.12, 1992, p.5.

Laird, Ross, 'A discography of Wocord recordings'. Canberra: *International Discographer* No.1 1992, p.55.

Laird, Ross, 'The historical dimension to discographical research: researching the early Australian record industry'. Paper delivered at the Conference of the International Association of Sound Archives (IASA) Canberra, 1992.

Laird, Ross & Mitchell, Jack, 'Prestophone 78rpm releases', *Australian Record & Music Review* No.29 1996, p.6.

Long, Chris, 'Australia's earliest known recordings: Thomas Rome's Collection'. IASA *Australian Branch Newsletter* No.19 1985, p.5.

Long, Chris, 'World Record in Australia'. Canberra: *International Discographer* No.1, 1992, p.39.

Petts, Leonard, 'Notes on the formation of the Gramophone Co. Ltd. (Australian Branch) and His Master's Voice (NZ) Ltd.', *Australian Record & Music Review* No.24 1995, p.13.

225 'Profile of the Australian Record Industry'. Sydney: ARIA – Australian Record Industry Association Ltd., 1990.

226 Tucker, Mike. 'The Federal and Australia cylinder records: a history', *Australian Record & Music Review* No.5, p.3.

NOTE: There are also many articles on every aspect of the Australian record industry as well as Australian performers and composers in the excellent magazine *Australian Record &Music Review* published and edited by Mike Sutcliffe. Anyone interested in research on the Australian record industry can subscribe to this publication. Subscription inquiries should be directed to the Editor at 15 Lowanna Avenue, Baulkham Hills, NSW 2153, Australia.

D. Discographical References

Laird, Ross, 'A discography of popular music recorded in Australia or by Australians overseas, 1924-1950'. 5th (revised) ed. Canberra: *Discographic Researchers* 1997.

Laird, Ross, 'A discography of classical & Western art song recordings made in Australia and by Australians overseas, 1896-1950'. Canberra: *Discographic Researchers* 1998.

Mitchell, Jack, 'Australian jazz on record, 1925-80'. Canberra: Australian Government Publishing Service 1988.

NOTE: The discographies published by *Discographic Researchers* can only be obtained from the author at GPO Box 22, Canberra ACT 2601, Australia.

INDEX

A.A. Ellisdon & Son Ltd. 336
A. Macrow & Sons 326, 331
Abeshouse, Ernest 27
'Abolition of Duplication of Industrial Control' 166
Aboriginal & Torres Strait Islander recordings 15-16
ACE Company 335, 339
acetates – *see* instantaneous recordings
Aco 23, 187, 190, 191, 192, 267, 323, 329, 333, 339, 343
Actuelle – *See* Pathé Actuelle
Adams, A. Emmett 25
'Advance Australia Fair' 93
Advertiser Broadcasting Network 315
Aeolian Co. Ltd. 187, 188, 219, 323, 337, 338, 344
Aeolian Co. (Aust.) Ltd. 189, 191, 267, 275
Aeolian Vocalion 187, 323
Aerona 230, 323-324

Aeroplane 224, 324
Afriat, Herbert 242, 252, 255
Aircast Players 211
Airmaster Dynamic Phono-Radio 286
Albert & Sons 116
Alfred A. & H.B. Newman 238, 239, 242, 258, 335
Allan & Co. 13, 22, 25, 116, 325, 341
Allsop, Ray 165
Alston, Richard 317
Amadio, John 24, 187
Amalgamated Wireless (Australasia) – *see* A.W.A.
Amberol 324
American Gramophone Co. 89
American Radio Corp. 309
American Record Corporation 87, 196, 298
American Record Manufacturing Co. 337, 343
Amfonola 324
Anderson, Oswald 289, 293, 294

Angelus 300-301, 302, 303, 324, 328, 331, 337, 340
Anthony Horden & Sons Ltd. 242, 342
Apex 324, 336, 341, 342
'Appeal against entertainment tax' 165
Arcadia 194, 202, 324
Archibald, Prof Douglas 3-9; visits Edison 3.
ARIA (Australian Record Industry Association) 316
Arionola Co. 339
Arnold, George 36
Arrow 324
Artiphon 239, 324
Associated Radio Co. 63
'Astor-isms' 194
'Aussie Rose' 175
Austral 63, 64, 65, 66, 67, 68, 69, 70, 324, 328, 344
Austral, Florence 24
Austral Duplex 65, 66-70, 325, 328
Austral Import & Export Co. 340
Australia (cylinder records) 19, 325

Australia Military Band 19
Australia Phono Record Co. 18-19
Australian Broadcasting Commission 293
Australian Commonwealth Band 188
Australian identity 24-25
Australian Made Preference League 151, 153
Australian Moulding Corporation 209
Australian Newcastle Steel Works Band 188
Australian Radio Transcriptions Pty. Ltd. 315
Australian Record Co. 315
Australian recordings 26-29; first Australian disc recordings 56, 66-67; lack of 22; produced for Australian market 24; production in Australia 22, 27, 49; Columbia's recording activities 156-162; Moulded Products Decca's recording activities 211-213; Parlophone's recording activities 177-180; Vocalion's recording activities 191, 193-196.
Australian Sound Gazette 226
Australian Talkies Newsreel 206
Autori, Fernando 180
AWA (Amalgamated Wireless Australiasia) Ltd. 142, 309, 310, 311, 315
Baby Summit 304, 325
Back Again 67

Backhaus, Wilhelm 123, 136
Baldwin Spencer, Sir Walter 15
Band of H.M. Grenadier Guards 156
'Banish the Budget Blues' 172
'Banjo Song' 37
Banner 237, 247, 262, 263, 264, 325, 335, 342
B.A.P. – *see* British Australian Programmes Pty. Ltd.
Barton, Charles R. 242, 243
Barton & Co. Ltd. 242, 243
Beale, O. Cyril 222
Beale & Co. 22, 27, 335
Beecham, Sir Thomas 284
Beeda 230, 231, 325
Beka 325, 332
Beka-Grand 325
Beka-Meister 325
Beka Record Co. 335
Bel Canto 325
Bell 325
Bell, Alexander Graham 3
Bell Disc 326
Bellbird 226-227, 326
'Bells of St Mary's' 25
Beltona 265, 326, 341
Beltona De Luxe 326
Benjamin, W.J. 303, 305
Bennett, Harriet 158
Bentley, George 18
Berliner 326
Berliner, Emile 326
Berliner Gramophone Co. 326
Berolina Schallplatte AG 335
Besly, Kenneth A. 242, 262

Best & Gee Pty. Ltd. 175, 177, 180
Beta 326
Big Four 57, 66
Binnie, Mr 18
'Bless This House' 25
Blue Amberol (cylinder records) 324
'Blue Skies' 255
Board, Peter 153
Bohanna, Peter H. 89-92
Bon Marché 230, 231, 326
Bon Ton Record 327
Booty, Stuart 26-29
Bosworth, Arthur F. 51
Bourne, Una 24
Box, D.H. Clyde 203
'Boys of the Dardanelles' 93
Bradman, Don 144, 170
Brahe, May 24-25
Brash & Co. 344
'Brighton Pier' 19
British Australian Programmes Pty. Ltd. 315
British Homophone Ltd. 336
British Preferential Tariffs 23
British Record Prop. Ltd. 22, 342
British Sterling Co. 93
British Zonophone Co. Ltd. 93
Broad, E.F. 138
Broadcast 191-192, 193, 194, 202, 268, 327
Broadcast De Luxe 194, 327
Broadcast Services 315
Broadcast Twelve 194, 327
Broadcasters (Sydney) Ltd. 114

INDEX

Brownlow, Wallace 18
Bruce, Mr 133
Bruce, Stanley 166
Brunswick 73-87, 95, 99, 105, 138, 188, 219, 243, 248, 253, 257, 267, 269, 275, 297, 311, 327, 335, 338, 342; first distributed in Australia (1921) 73; first disc records to be manufactured in Australia (1924) 75, 77; factory extended (1925) 77; Australian corporate entity registered (1930) 81; company wound-up (1931) 85-87.
Brunswick (Australia) Ltd. 81-87, 174, 327, 331, 339
Brunswick-Balke-Collender Co. 48, 73, 76, 79, 81, 82, 85, 86, 147, 329
Brunswick Furniture Pty. Ltd. 329
Brunswick Radio Corporation 82
Buckinghams Stores 327
Bulldog 327
Bulmas, Signora Aida 27
Butt, Dame Clara 25, 26
Butterfly 327
Butters, Sir John 200
Camden 327
Cameo 237, 327, 337, 344
Cameo Record Corporation 298, 336, 343
Capitol 327
'Captain Cook Discovers Australia' 142
Carl Lindström AG 175
Carlyon's (night club) 36, 67

'Carolina in the Morning' 37
Carrington, Lord 6
'Carry On' 211
Caruso, Enrico 104, 136
Cazabon, Albert 168
Cecil, Lionel 24
Chaliapine, Fedor 104
Chappell 327-328
Chappell & Co. 327
Charles Slade & Co. 344
Chas. E. Blanks Pty. Ltd. 315
Cheaters 206
Cherkassky, Shura 52
Chevalier, Albert 17
Chichester, Frank 160
choral symphony 42
Cinch 328
'City of the Plains' 19
Clarité 231, 328
Clark, Alfred 115, 137, 309
Clarke, Arthur 158
Clifford 301-302, 328
Clifford Industries Ltd. 80, 83, 164, 174, 224, 297-305, 324, 328, 331, 333, 334, 338, 339, 340, 341, 343, 345; registered (1928) 297; source of masters 298; labels produced 298-302; financial difficulties 302; company wound-up 302; sale of assets 302.
Clover 328
Clutsam, George H. 25
Cocks, Sir Arthur 146
Cohen, H.F. 163
Cohen, H.V. 80-81
Cohen, Harriet 81
Coin-operated phonograph machines 8

Cole, John 146
Coles Stores 84, 171, 194, 299, 301, 331, 343
Coliseum 328
Collier, Frederick 24, 187
Collinson, John 188
'Colonel Campbell and Mister Lang' 172
Colonial 328
Columbia 149, 158, 160, 162, 164, 166, 168, 170, 171, 174, 179, 181, 253, 257, 265, 267, 288, 292, 308, 327, 328, 336, 342, 343
Columbia Graphophone Co. 143
Columbia Graphophone Co. Ltd. 145, 146, 147, 198, 324, 327, 328, 340, 341; incorporated (1917) 143; purchases American firm (1925) 143, 145; acquires Parlophone label (1925) 175.
Columbia Graphophone Co. (Aust.) Ltd. 45-46, 48, 49, 93, 123-127, 129, 131, 132-133, 138, 141, 142, 149-174, 177-178, 181, 188, 219, 236, 242, 243, 249, 269, 275, 285, 288, 308, 315, 325; plans to establish Australian record factory (1925) 146-147; acquires Homebush site (1925) 148-149; recording studios active (1926) 149-150; factory officially opened (1926) 150-157; scope of local recording activities 157-162; private recordings 164-165; production of discs using sound-on-disc system 165-166, 169;

359

effect of Depression on sales 171; introduction of 'long-playing' record (1931) 172; Columbia Graphophone Co. joins merger to form E.M.I. (1931) 173-174, 309-311.
Columbia (International) Ltd. 145, 175
Columbia Phonograph Co. 145
Columbia Phonograph Co. General 143
Columbia-Rena 342
'Comfort Ye My People' 26
compact discs 275; imports 317-318.
Compo Co. 324, 325, 336, 339
Condor 57, 62, 70, 328
constant linear speed process 55, 59
Controlaphone Ltd. 58
Cooper Brothers Ltd. 328
'Coppelia Waltz' 168
Copyright Act 241
Copyright Amendment Bills 317
Cordell, C.C. 203
Coronola Ltd. 336
Country Broadcasting Services Pty. Ltd. 315
Craig Williamson Pty. Ltd. 190, 224, 242, 264, 298, 333, 338
Crane, Colin 206
Crawford, Thomas W. 238
Crosby, Bing 339
Crossley, Ada 21
Crown Record Co. 298
Crystalate Manufacturing Co. Ltd. 238, 239, 258, 298, 323, 326, 335, 338, 339, 340, 343

Customs Tariff Act (1928) 273
Cylinder records 19-21; local manufacture 18-19; obsolescence 17; scarcity 13.
D. Davis & Co. 73-82, 85, 232, 233, 236, 242, 248, 264, 327
Dacapo 329
Dahlmont 231, 329
Dandy, Reginald 158
Dani, Carlo 18
Davidson, J.H.M. 16
Davis, David 73, 80, 85, 297, 303
Davis, Herbert 73, 76, 80, 81, 85, 105, 242, 248, 251, 252, 254, 255, 264, 297, 303
Davis, Jack 73, 78, 80, 81, 85, 297, 303
Dawson, Peter 21, 24, 29, 46-47
Dawson, Tom 19
Deane, C.R. 303
'Dearest' 41
Debussy, Claude 37
Decca 210-213, 329
Decca Record Co. Ltd. 210
Dech, Gil 144
Dech (Gil) & His Syncopators 144
De Chair, Sir Dudley 134, 137, 150
De Gunst, Molly 142
De Villaverde, E.C. 82
Deutsche Grammophon Gesellschaft 190, 340
Deutschen Vox AG 344
Diamond 329
Diploma 329
Diploma Record Co. 329
Disc Record Co. 340

Disc records 17
Dobrinski, Mischa 27
Dodds, Johnny 79
Domino 237, 247, 329, 335
'Donna e Mobile' 37
Donner, William A. 160, 168, 169, 172, 174, 181, 183, 184, 288, 308, 309
'Don't Bring Lulu' 42
'Down Here' 25
'Down Went McGinty to the Bottom of the Sea' 42
Doyle, Stuart 165
'Dreams of Mine' 164
Du Maurier Productions Pty. Ltd. 315
Duncan, Robert 220
Dunlop Rubber Co. 213
Duophone 266, 329-330, 338
Duophone Syndicate Ltd. 329
Ebonoid 330
Edison, Thomas A. 1-6, 9, 11-12, 21, 284; message to people of Australia 6.
Eileen Alannah 11
Edison cylinder records 18, 21, 330
Edison Diamond Disc records 21, 42, 275, 330-331
Edison-Bell Consolidated Phonograph Co. 16, 257, 275, 325, 326, 331, 343
Edison Bell Winner 331, 340
Edison Shop 331
Edments Stores 194, 324
electrical recording process 44-46, 124, 190, 191; installed in Columbia studio (1926)

INDEX

150; results in availability of cheap imports 230, 233; utilized by Parlophone (1927) 177.
Electron 298, 299, 331
Elen, Gus 92
Elkins' (Jimmie) Orchestra 66, 150
Ellington, Duke 79
Elman, Mischa 136
Emanuel, Joseph S. 200
Embassy 84, 194, 202, 299, 301, 331
Emerson 331
Emerson Phonograph Co. 58
Emerson Recording Laboratories 331
E.M.I. (Electrical & Musical Industries) Ltd. 141-142, 145, 173-174, 184, 210, 275, 309-312, 313.
EMI Custom Service 165
Empire (cylinder records) 19, 331
Empire (disc records) 331
Encore 332
'England to Australia Flight' 160
Entertainer (cylinder records) 19, 332
Era 332
Eucharistic Congress (1928) Sydney 179-180
Eutrope, Clarence 242
'Ever or Never' 168
'Every Day Is Rainbow Day' 144
Excelophone 22, 332
Fairy 332
Fane, Maud 66, 67
'Farewell Message Spoken From the Cockpit of the Southern Cross' 160

Farmer's Stores 300, 343
'Father Fixes the Wireless' 164
Favorite 332
Fay, Austin 206
Featherweight Flexible Records Co. 58, 332
Featuradio Sound Productions Pty. Ltd. 295, 315
Federal (cylinder records) 18-19, 332
Federal (disc records) 332
Federal Phonograph Record & Supply Co. 18
Federal Record Corporation 332
Federal Transcriptions & Television Pty. Ltd. 315
Federation 8
Felix the Cat 176
Fellers 206
Fetherflex 58, 61, 332, 344
Fidel-a-Tone Sound Productions 315
Fidelio Musikwerke AG 335
Finlayson, Robert Norman 220
Fitts, Ernest 18
5AD 293
Flag 332
Flexible Record Co. Ltd. 166, 174, 226-227, 314
Fonotipia 332, 335
Ford, Edward 18
Forde, Florrie 21, 24
Fossey's 333
Fossey's Department Store 333
4QG 294
Fowler, W.M. 242, 251
Foy & Gibson Stores 299, 338
Franklin, Arthur H. 242

Franklin's Pty. Ltd. 242, 337
Gaiety 190, 333
Gaisberg, Fred 326
Galli-Curci, Amelita 136
Garland, C.L. 5, 9
Gaunt, Launcelt 329, 330
Gem 333
Gendle, Charles Henry 71, 189, 192, 196, 203, 236, 238, 243, 267
Gennett 190, 265, 333, 342
Gennett Records – *see* Starr Piano Co.
'Georgette' 40
Gershwin, George 40
'Get Your Hair Cut' 42
Gibson's Bazaar 260, 333
Gibsona 333
Gladstone, William 5
Glass, Dudley 66, 67
Glenola (gramophone) 329
Globe 333
Globophon 333
Gloria Light Co. 329
Gold Bell 333
Golden Tongue 224, 298, 333
Goldfinch, William 223
Goldhill, Jack L. 242
'Goodbye Melbourne Town' 19
Goodman, Isador 142
Goody, Herbert 61, 225, 226
Government Prices Surveillance Authority Inquiry (1990) 316
Grace Brothers Ltd. 301
Gracelon 301
Grainger, Percy 21; on jazz 35-36.
Grammavox 333

Grammophon 340
Gramophone increased sales 32-33; introduction into Australia 17.
Gramophone (disc records) 334
Gramophone & Typewriter Ltd. 89, 92, 93, 345
Gramophone Co. Ltd. 48, 49, 75, 89-142, 146, 147, 153, 173, 174, 198, 215, 219, 236, 238, 242, 243, 249, 267, 273, 275, 311, 326, 328, 334, 343, 345; Australian branch established (1900) 89-91; Hoffnung's appointed 'sole distributors' (1904) 91-92; Australian branch re-established (1923) 97; record factory proposed (1923) 97; factory confirmed (1925) 101; William Manson appointed general manager (1925) 102; factory officially opened (1926) 108; additional capacity required (1926) 118; advisability of doing local recording discussed 128-129, 131-133; new factory site acquired (1927) 139; Gramophone Co. joins merger to form E.M.I. (1931) 141-142, 309-311.
gramophone record industry in Australia 48-49
gramophone records and musical taste 42-44; improved quality 44-47.
Gramo-phonium Co. Ltd. 97

Grand Pree 230, 247, 253, 254, 255, 256, 257, 298, 299, 323, 334, 344
Grand Pree Record Co. 242, 252, 323, 328, 334, 340
Green, V.G. 329
Grey Gull 237, 247, 334
Grey Gull Record Co. 298, 333, 334, 341
'Guard's Patrol' 168
Guardsman 332, 334, 335
Guest, Sid 206
Haddon, Alfred 15
Hamilton, Sir Robert 8
'Harbour Bridge' 142
Harmonizers 66
Harris, Marion 79
Hawker, Donald G.C. 146
Hazel, Rupert 157, 164
Henderson, Edwin C. 18-19
Henlere, Herschel 175
Henley, Sir John 154
Henry, John 142
Herford, Percy 19
Hermann-Eisner-Schallplattenkonzern AG 324
Herschells 213, 334
Higgins, Arthur 206
High Treason 71
Hinkler, Bert 160
'Hinkler's Message to Australia' 160
His Master's Voice 49, 93-142, 174, 188, 248, 253, 257, 265, 269, 288, 292, 308, 334
'History and Song of the Lyre Bird' 211
Hit, The 230, 334
Hodgson, Lieutenant Commander 138

Hoffnung & Co. Ltd. 75, 76, 90, 93, 94, 95, 98, 99, 115, 117, 120, 121, 122, 124, 125, 128, 133, 138, 311; appointed 'sole distributors' for Gramophone Co. (1904) 91-92; contract expires (1924) 96; offered shares in new company (1923) 97.
home recordings 15
Homochord 334-335, 336
Homophon GmbH 333, 334, 335, 336, 342, 343
Homophone 334, 335
Homophone Co. 22
'Horsey Keep Your Tail Up' 41
'How De Do Dee' 42
'How It's Done' 170
Howden, Maxwell 64
Hughes, W.M. 166
'Hungarian March' 168
Hyams, E.J. 97, 99, 115, 121
Hylton (Jack) & His Orchestra 129, 211
'I Passed By Your Window' 25
'I Wish I Knew' 37
Ilco 335
'I'm Going Back Again to Yarrawonga' 24
Imperial 239, 258, 335, 339
Imported disc records 229-231, 234, 249, 261-262, 275; breakdown by country of origin (1926/27) 319.
'In a Little Spanish Town' 255
'Incidents of My Flight' 160

INDEX

'Industrial Arbitration in Australia' 166
Industries Preservation Act 235
Instantaneous recordings 294, 314
International General Electric Co. Ltd. 142
International Sound Recordings 315
International Talking Machine Co. 335, 338
International Zonophone Co. 92, 345
Invicta 334, 335
Invicta Record Co. 332
'Issue of the Election' 166
'Issues Before the People' 166
'It Ain't Gonna Rain No More' 41
J. Blum & Co. 329, 340, 343
Jack Davey Productions Pty. Ltd. 315
Jack O'Hagan Music Pty. Ltd. 211
Jackson, Sydney 341
jazz 35-36, 40
Jewel 335
Jewel Record Co. 335
John Bull 335, 341
John G. Murdoch & Co. 22, 325, 332
'Johnnie, Our Aeroplane Girl' 160
Johnson, Amy 160
Johnson, Gertrude 24
Johnstone, Russ 24
Jolson, Al 79
Jones, Isham 38
Jos. Jackson & Macdonald 22, 342
Joyphone 335

Jumbo 335
Kaili, David 179
Kalliope Musikwerke AG 343
Kalophone Grand 22, 335
Kelson, Mr 239
Kelson & Co. 239, 324
Kempton, C.L. 201
Kenneth A. Besley & Co. 325
Kiddie Record 335
Kiddyphone 335
Kid-Kord 336
Kingsford-Smith, Charles 160
Kingsley, Walter 124, 149
Kirk, Andy 79
Kismet 180, 336
Klingsor 336
Klippel, A. 303
Klippel, David Davis – *see* Davis, David
Klippel, S. 303
Klippel Record Co. Ltd. 298, 303-305, 325, 337, 338, 343
Knapp, Alexander 58-60
Kodak 336
Kodisc Ltd. 335
Kreisler, Fritz 38, 49, 136
lacquer discs – *see* instantaneous recordings
'Land of Hope and Glory' 156
Lane, Dr W.H. 3
Lang, J.T. 108-112, 113
'Largo' 104
Latham, S.L. 16
Lauder, Harry 92
Legionnaire Sound Productions Pty. Ltd. 315
Leonard, Art 170, 172
Leonora 230, 336
Liddy, James 158

Lily of the Valley 230, 336
Lincoln 247, 275, 333, 336-337, 341, 343
Little Gem 337
Little Jessie James 37-38
Littlejohns, Ray 213
Little Marvel 337
Lloyd, Major 135
Lockley, A.E. 99, 101, 104, 105, 106, 115, 118, 120, 135, 139
Lockwoods Ltd. 328
'Lo, the Gentle Lark' 104
long-playing recordings 172, 205
Lucas, Nick 79, 80
Ludlow, Godfrey 24
Lumsdaine, Jack 24, 66, 144, 160, 175
Lyre Bird, The 213
Lyric (1920s) 337
Lyric (1930s) 303-304, 337
McCance, Norman 206
MacDonagh Sisters 206
McEachern, Malcolm 24, 187
Macfarlane, Sandy 80
MacMahon, Charles 5
MacMahon, James 5, 8
Macquarie Broadcasting Services Pty. Ltd. 315
McWhirter's 336, 337
McWhirter's Special Records 336
'Ma Curly-Headed Baby' 25
Madame Pompadour 158
'Manly Pier' 19
Manson, Mabel 105
Manson, William 104, 105, 112, 113, 115, 118, 119, 124, 125, 127, 129, 131, 133, 137, 147, 153, 215, 242, 243;

appointed general manager of Australian branch of Gramophone Co. (1925) 102; leaves Australia (1930) 140.
Maori records 169-170, 177
Marconiphone Ltd. 308
Marcus Clark Ltd. 298, 333
Marini, Signor 27
Marks, Sir George Croydon 45, 146
Marks, R.A. 153
Martinelli, Giovanni 331
Massey, Hon. W.F. 103
Massounoff, Ivan 206
Masterpiece 337-338
Maurice, Len 161, 163
Mehden, Carl 36
Melba, Dame Nellie 21, 135, 136, 138
Melbaphone 338
Melbourne International Exhibition (1880) 3
Mellotone 338
Melodics 338
Melola Salon 301
Meloto 338
Meloto Co. 338
Melotone (1920s) 83, 298, 299, 338
Melotone (1930s) 339
Melville, Jean 24
Metcalf, H.E. 281
Miles, James Charles 328
Miller, Renn 194, 208
Mills, Beryl 158
Mills, Charles 28
Mills, June 206
'Mimi' 40
Mimosa 338
'Miss Australia Speaks to Australians' 158

'Mister Depression (Will Soon Be Dead and Gone)' 172
Mitchell, Frederick George 61, 215, 216, 217, 221, 223, 225
Mittell, B. 309
Moisewitsch, Benno 52
Molloy & Keany 301
Monarch records 90
Moncrieff, Gladys 24, 187
Moore, Fred 66
Morgan, Alfred Joseph 81
Morrison's (Cec) Orchestra 165
Moses, Charles 227
Moulded Products (A'asia) Pty. Ltd. 209-213, 295, 314, 329, 334
Moulded Products Pty. Ltd. 209
Mound City Blue Blowers 79
Muir, James 95, 119, 125, 127, 131, 133
Mummery, Browning 24
Murdoch Training Co. 326
Murphy, James 81, 84, 87, 242, 253
Music Box, The 242
Musical criticism 23, 31, 33-35, 42-44
Musiphone 338
Musola 338, 340
Muzio, Claudia 330
'My Home' 164
'My Sweet Australian Wattle Girl' 175
'My Task' 26
Myer Emporium 231, 242, 266, 329
N. Rumeisen Ltd. 335
Nathan, Morris H. 242

National Phonograph Co. 20
National Trustees Executors & Agency Co. 336
Naval Brigade Band 18, 19
Nelson, Leonard 19
New Polyphon Supply Co. 332
New York Recording Laboratories 298
Newman, Horace 231, 242, 258
Nicholls, Dr Brooke 207, 208
Nicholls, Percy 27
Nichols (Red) & His Five Pennies 79
Nicole 338
Nicole Frères Ltd. 338
Norman L. Burnell & Co. 242
Nursery Rhyme Record 304, 338
Nutmeg Record Corporation 328
'O! Sydney, I Love You' 161-162, 164
Odeon 184, 338
off-air recording 28-29
Offenbacher, Paul 182
Official Congress Record 180
'Oh Mo'nah' 290
O'Hagan, Jack 24, 66, 193, 211, 325
'Old Fashioned Locket' 170
Oldershaw's Edison Electric Parlour 13
Oliver 339
Oliver, King 79
Oliver J. Nilson & Co. 62-63
Olympic 339

INDEX

Omah/Omar 339
Orchard, Arundel 155, 168
Orchestrelle Co. 338
Oriole 237, 333, 339, 343
Orpheus 302, 339
'Our Bungalow of Dreams' 170
'Our Don Bradman' 170, 172
'Out of the Shadows' 226
Owen, W.B. 90
Page, Earl 166
Palais de Danse (St Kilda) 36, 67
Paling's 230, 339 (*see also* W.H. Paling Ltd.)
Panachord 83-84, 87, 209, 331, 339
Panatrope (gramophone) 83, 138
Paramount 298, 299, 339
Parker, H.A. 149, 155, 156, 236
Parker, Sydney A. 242
Parlophone 141, 174, 175, 177, 179, 180, 181, 182, 185, 288, 308, 327, 339, 342, 343
Parlophone Co. Ltd. 48, 174, 175-185, 236, 242, 254, 269, 336, 339; established (1923) 175; export series for Australia initiated (1926) 175-176; Australian branch established (1926) 177; local recording activities 177-180; proposal to discontinue label 181-182; subsumed into newly-formed E.M.I. (1931) 184.
Pathé 339
Pathé Actuelle 23, 255, 323, 334
Pathé Frères Pathéphone Ltd. 203, 323, 329, 334, 342, 344
Pathé Frères Phonograph Co. 73, 340
Payne's Bon Marché 326
Pearse, Eric 161, 163
Pemberton Billing, Noel 28, 53-72, 216, 221, 225, 295, 332; activities in Britain 56-58; arrival in Australia (1923) 58; constant linear speed patents 55; death of wife (1923) 58; early life 55-56; establishes radio station (1925) 62; invites Charles Gendle to visit Australia (1924) 71; leaves Australia (1926) 71; obituary (1948) 71-72; unbreakable record patents 58.
Percy, W.S. 24
Perfect 266, 340
Perpetual Trading Association 299, 334, 344
personal recordings – *see* private recordings
Peterkin, W.A. 18
Philips, J.A. 203
Phar Lap 172
Philadelphia Orchestra 289
Phoenix 340
Phoneto 340
Phonograph 12, 17; development 3; early exhibits 2-12; first Australian report 1-2; invention 1; motor-driven 13; use as recording instrument 13.
Phonograph &
Gramophone Society of New South Wales 26
Pigmy Gramophone (children's record) 340
Pilot 340, 341
Pindaret, Peter 43
Pinnock, Clarence 242
Pinnock Sewing Machine Co. Ltd. 242
Pioneer 340
Pirani, Max 24, 187
Plaza 301, 340
Plaza Music Co. 250, 324, 325, 326, 328, 329, 335
Plummer, Frank 13
Polydor 190, 265, 275, 340
Polyphon 340, 341
Polyphon Musikwerke AG 336, 341
Popular 327, 341
Popular music publishing 40-41; denigration of 33-42.
Portus, George 27
Possum 22, 341
Power, Stella 24
Power, Sydney P. 146, 155, 169, 242
price cutting 229
Primrose 67
Prior, Will 168
private recordings 69, 164-165, 193-194
Process Recording 164
Prowse, Alice 27
Puritan 339
Pyramid 341
Quintrell, Fred 168
Quirk, J.W. 203
Radiex 341
radio broadcasts 62-66, 71, 277-295; effect on record sales 277-295;

SOUND BEGINNINGS

recording of 28-29; recordings made for 295, 313-315; records used on 287-294; studio orchestras 286-287.
Radio Corporation of America 142
Radio House Broadcasting Station 290
Radio Theatre Guild 315
radio transcription services 315
radio transcriptions 313-315
ragtime 23, 36
Rainbow 341
Ralton's Havana Band 66, 67
Raycophone (sound projection system) 165
Realtone 341
Record Holdings Ltd. 225
Record production – company figures: Brunswick 320; Gramophone Co. 320; Columbia 320.
record sales – company sales figures: Columbia 320-322; Gramophone Co. 320; Parlophone 321; effect of Depression 171, 181, 287, 307-308; effect of radio broadcasts 277-295.
record stampers – statistics: Columbia (1929-31) 322-323
Records Ltd. 224
'Red Moon' 41
Regal (British) 23, 24, 141, 162, 327, 341, 342
Regal (American) 324, 325, 333, 335
Regal (Australia) 162, 164, 171-172, 181, 209, 308, 311, 312, 341

Regal-Zonophone 142, 311-312, 341
Regan, Alec 172
Regent (1910s) 341
Regent (1920s) 298, 300, 341
Regentone 341
Reidy, Kitty 24, 188
Rena 341-342
Rena Manufacturing Co. 341
Rene, Roy 179
Retail Music Traders Protective Association 242, 246, 253
Rexophone 22, 342
'Rhapsody in Blue' 40
Ritchie, John 140, 288, 309
Roberto 342
Roberts, W.H. 26
'Rocked in the Cradle of the Deep' 19
Rodeheaver Record Co. 341
Rogaly, Leo 156, 165
Rogers, Mrs 26
Rogerson, Mr T. 11
Rome collection 15
Rondophone 22, 23, 342
Rose Marie 158
Rosebud 342
Rosenthal, Maurice 196, 200, 201, 203, 207, 242, 299
Rosenthal & Salon 242, 251
Rothwell, Thomas 225, 226
Royal Australasian Ornithologists Union 213
Royal Commission on Copyrights 293

Royalties paid to Australian artists: Columbia (1928-30) 321
Rubin 342
Rubini, Jan 39
'Rupert Hazell Dreams He Is The Sheik' 164
Russell Hunting Record Co. 343
Russo, Ubaldo 27
Ryan, Mr P. 11
Sabine, John A. 285
Salkeld & Wallace Ltd. 324
Salonola (gramophone) 33
Samuels, Alfred L. 213
Sanders, Reginald E. 190, 242, 264, 338
Savery's Pianos 222
Saville, Frances 21
Savoy 194, 202, 342
Savoy Orpheans 129
Scala 342
Scala Ideal 342
Scala Record Co. 342
Scotney, Evelyn 21, 187
Scott, Malcolm 223
Scott Henderson & Co. 299
Scullin, James Henry 206
Selfridges Stores 300, 341
Serena, Clara 24, 188
Serenola 342
Sheard, Mr 94
sheet music sales 50-52
Sheldon, Horace 168
Sheldon, Sir Mark 112, 113
Sheppard, Haliburton A. 200
Shields, Ella 24
Shmith, Jessie 179
'Shoo Fly, Don't Bother Me' 42

366

INDEX

Simmons, Mick 251, 342
Simolian 251, 342
Simpson's (Sydney) Wentworth Cafe Orchestra 124, 149
6WF 294
Smith, Clay 67
Smith, Fanny 15
Smith, William 220, 223
Snazelle, G.H. 92
Snows 343
So This Is Australia 206
'Somewhere South of Shanghai' 24
sound-on-disc process 165-166, 205-207, 226
Sound Recording Co. 333, 338
Sound Recording Studios Pty. Ltd. 315
Sousa's military band 17
'Southern Cross Trans-Pacific Flight' 160
Southey, Reg. V. 142, 150, 161, 163
'Southward Ho with Mawson' 226
Spaull, Vera 158
Specially Imported (record label) 343
Standard 343
Star 343
Starr (Canada) 336
Starr (Australia) 301, 343
Starr Gennett 336
Starr Piano Co. 190, 298, 333
Sterling (cylinder records) 343
Sterling (disc records) 298, 300, 343
Sterling, Louis 143, 145, 184, 309
Stevens, Horace 24, 187
Stevenson, C.V. 290

Stewart, Nellie 5
Stiffy & Mo 179
Stigant, Arthur 158
Stoneham, Reg 24
'Story of My Flight' 160
Stralia, Elsa 24
Strong, Nellie 158
Student Prince, The 158
Summit 303-304, 343
Suttons 333
'Sweet Hawaiian Sands' 164
Sydney Conservatorium of Music 33, 155
Sydney Exhibition (1879) 3
Sydney Harbour Bridge 172
Symphonic jazz 37-39
Tainter, Charles Sumner 3
Tait, Charles 13
Tait, Harry 92
Tariff Board 87
Tariff Board Inquiry (1927) 73, 177, 229-275, 316, 330, 338; background paper 237-238; inquiry formally established 238; submissions 238-268; summary and recommendations 268-273; subsequent legislation 273.
Tariff Board Inquiry (1931) 161, 181, 308
Tellier's (Ray) San Francisco Orchestra 66, 67
Tempo 343
Tennyson, Lord Hallam 16
Theodore, E.G. 166
This Is Australia 205
Thomas, Albert V. 242, 266

Thomas A. Edison Inc. 275, 324, 330, 331
'Thru the Night' 41
'3OL – A Radio Fan's Dream' 157-158
3PB 62-66, 71, 295
3UZ 62-63
Thwaite's Edison Phonograph Co. 13
Trader, The 211
Trans-Radio Advertising & Program Service 315
Tremont 237, 343
Trevitt, Cyril D. 242
Trevitt's Ltd. 242
Twin, The 92, 343, 345
2BE 28
2BL 294
2CH 293
2FC 294; Studio Dance Band 161.
2GB 293
2UW 289, 293
Unbreakable Disc Records Ltd. 72, 215-225, 297, 324, 333; flotation (1927) 215-222; production begins (1928) 223-224; production ceases (1928) 224; liquidator appointed (1930) 225; wound-up (1932) 225.
Unbreakable Record Manufacturers Ltd. 226, 326
Union Theatres 165
United Radio Distributors 184
United States Gramophone Co. 326
Universal Double-Disc 22, 343
Universal Music Co. 335
'Valencia' 125, 127

367

SOUND BEGINNINGS

Velvet Face 343
Verbrugghen, Henri 33, 77
Vicars, Sir John 154
Victor 312
Victor Talking Machine Co. 100, 101, 115, 116, 326
Victorian Broadcasting Network 315
Victory 343
Vinogradoff, Paul 27
Virtuoso String Quartette 103
Vitavox 26-29
VOA Sound Productions 315
Vocalion 23, 24, 39, 171, 187, 188, 190, 191, 193, 201, 202, 209, 237, 239, 253, 260, 265, 267, 323, 327, 329, 339, 344
Vocalion (Australasia) Ltd. 174, 197-209, 226, 313, 314, 344; prospectus (1930) 197-199; incorporated (1930) 199-200; sound-on-disc recordings 205-207; financial difficulties 207; bankruptcy (1931) 209; deregistered (1934) 209.
Vocalion Distributing Pty. Ltd. 207, 208
Vocalion Foreign Ltd. 191, 199, 200, 213, 236, 324, 327, 342; flotation (1928) 192-193; company registered (1928) 193; recording activities 191, 194; financial difficulties 196; sale of company (1930) 196.
Vocalion Gramophone Co. Ltd. 71, 166, 188, 191, 193, 198, 243, 269, 326, 328, 329, 333, 336, 337, 342
Vocalion Midget 201, 344
Vox 344
Vox Humana 230, 253, 344
Wafer 61, 65, 70, 344
Walker, James Alford St Clair 81
Warner Bros. Pictures 82, 84
Wattle Path Palais 67
Webber, Hamilton 37-38
Webster, Frank 158
Weiss, Biheller & Brooks 331, 343
Wendy 61, 344
Westbrook, C.D. 20
Westinghouse International Co. 142
Weymark 344
'What Ho, She Bumps' 42
Whelan, Albert 24, 188
'Where Did You Get That Hat?' 42
Whitburn, Will 18
White, Lee 66, 67
Whiteman, Paul 38-40
W.H. Eutrope & Sons Pty. Ltd. 242
W.H. Paling & Co. 226, 231, 339
Williams, Billy 21, 177
Williams, Clarence 79
Williams, Daryl 317
Williams, Harold 24, 156
Williams, Trevor 75, 101
Williamson-Melba Opera Company 52
Wilson, Francis 242, 246
Winner 23, 257, 325, 326, 331, 334, 336, 337, 338, 339, 340, 344
wireless – *see* radio
Wise, Mr 130
Wocord Australia 61-62, 344
Wodonga 37
Wood, Sir Henry 46
Woolworths Stores 180, 301, 303, 336, 345
Workers Compensation Act 235
World 63, 64, 65, 344-345
World Record (Australia) Pty. Ltd. 28, 49, 53-71, 215, 223, 225, 295, 324, 325, 328, 332, 344, 345; registered (1923) 60; manufacturing begins (1924) 61; releases first Australian disc records (1925) 66-68; initiates Condor label (1925) 70; ceases production 71.
World Record Co. Ltd. 53, 56-58
Worth 301, 345
Worth, William V. 200
Wright, Philip Alan 177, 178, 179, 181, 182, 184, 185, 242
Yerkes S.S. Flotilla Sextette 66, 67
'Yes, We Have No Bananas' 41, 255
York, Duke & Duchess 137, 177
Zelman, Alberto 187
Zon-O-Phone 345
Zonophone 49, 92, 93, 122, 124, 127, 140, 141, 142, 308, 311, 312, 341, 343, 345